Consummation

Consummation

The Promise of Arnold A. van Ruler's Eschatology

~

ARNOLD A. VAN RULER

Edited by Ernst M. Conradie
Translated by Douglas G. Lawrie
With an Introduction by Dirk van Keulen

RESOURCE *Publications* · Eugene, Oregon

CONSUMMATION
The Promise of Arnold van Ruler's Eschatology

Copyright © 2025 Ernst M. Conradie. All rights reserved. Except for brief quotations in critical publications or reviews, no part of this book may be reproduced in any manner without prior written permission from the publisher. Write: Permissions, Wipf and Stock Publishers, 199 W. 8th Ave., Suite 3, Eugene, OR 97401.

Resource Publications
An Imprint of Wipf and Stock Publishers
199 W. 8th Ave., Suite 3
Eugene, OR 97401

www.wipfandstock.com

PAPERBACK ISBN: 979-8-3852-5817-8
HARDCOVER ISBN: 979-8-3852-5818-5
EBOOK ISBN: 979-8-3852-5819-2

Contents

Editor's Preface vii

Translator's Preface xi

Glossary of Dutch Terms xiv

Abbreviations xviii

Introduction 1

God's Law 20

Kingdom of God and Church 30

The Millennium 50

The Meaning of the Mosaic Law 57

The Kingdom of God and History 71

Law and Gospel 88

I Believe in Eternal Life 108

Relativizing Death and Life 122

Questions of Life and Death 125

Being Saved or Being Lost 129

Living in the Kingdom: Christ's Birth and Politics 134

Life after Death 138

The Parousia of Christ 143

Eschatological Notices 148

Limits to Eschatologizing 172

The Christian Future Expectation 195

Biblical Future Expectations in Earthly Perspective 199

All Things New? 227

Van Ruler's Eschatology and Ecotheology: An Afterword 231

Index of Names 241

Editor's Preface
Ernst M. Conradie

THE WORKS OF A number of Dutch theologians are available in English translation. These include some of the major publications by Abraham Kuyper, the series of Studies in Dogmatics by Gerrit Berkouwer, some books by Hendrikus Berkhof, and, more recently, the *Reformed Dogmatics* and *Reformed Ethics* of Herman Bavinck. However, English translations of the works of Kornelis Miskotte, Oepke Noordmans and Arnold van Ruler, arguably the three most innovative Dutch theologians of the (mid) twentieth century, are rather scarce.

As far as Van Ruler is concerned, there are some early booklets, including an exposition of 1 Corinthians entitled *The Greatest of These is Love* (Eerdmans, 1958), *God's Son and God's World* (Eerdmans, 1960), and *Zechariah Speaks Today* (Lutterworth, 1962). There is also a translation of Van Ruler's *Die christliche Kirche und das Alte Testament* (originally published in German) by Geoffrey Bromiley entitled *The Christian Church and the Old Testament* (Eerdmans, 1971) and then an important collection of essays translated and edited by John Bolt under the title *Calvinist Trinitarianism and Theocentric Politics: Essays Toward a Public Theology* (The Edwin Mellen Press, 1989). More recently, a translation of Van Ruler's *Ik geloof* was edited by Garth Hodnett under the title *I Believe* (Xlibris, 2015). The publication of a volume of Van Ruler's essays on God, creation, providence, humanity, sin and earthly life entitled *This Earthly Life Matters* (Pickwick, 2023) adds to the availability of such English translations of Van Ruler's oeuvre. This translation was based on selected essays from Volume 3 of Van Ruler's *Verzameld Werk*.

Eleven volumes of Van Ruler's *Verzameld werk* ("Collected Works") have been edited by Dirk van Keulen and published by Boekencentrum / KokBoekencentrum thus far as indicated below:[1]

- Verzameld Werk, Deel I: De Aard van de Theologie (2007), 550 pages
- Verzameld Werk, Deel II: Openbaring en Heilige Schrift (2008), 518 pages
- Verzameld Werk, Deel III: God, Schepping, Mens, Zonde (2009), 524 pages
- Verzameld Werk, Deel IV-A: Christus, de Geest en het Heil (2011), 794 pages
- Verzameld Werk, Deel IV-B: Christus, de Geest en het Heil (2011), 825 pages
- Verzameld Werk, Deel V-A: Kerk, Liturgie, Prediking, Sacramenten (2020), 771 pages
- Verzameld Werk, Deel V-B: Kerkorde, Kerkrecht, Ambt (2018), 994 pages
- Verzameld Werk, Deel V-C: Belijdenis en Leertucht – Kerk, Wereld, Diaconaat – Volkskerk – Zending en Apostolaat – Eschatologie (2023), 981 pages
- Verzameld Werk, Deel VI-A: De Theocratie (2016), 973 pages
- Verzameld Werk, Deel VI-B: Cultuur, Samenleving, Politiek, Onderwijs (2016), 988 pages
- Verzameld Werk, Deel VII-A: Reformatie en Oecumene (2024), 984 pages

The Dutch volume of Van Ruler's *Verzameld werk, Deel V-C* includes six clusters of texts, namely on confession, doctrine and doctrinal discipline; church and world; diaconate; national church [volkskerk]; mission and apostolate and then eschatology. The aim of the Dutch series is to collect Van Ruler's writings and to make available some previously unpublished material, including some radio talks and lecture notes. The emphasis is on archival completeness with ample cross-references to Van Ruler's oeuvre and to other Dutch and German publications available to Van Ruler.

1. See www.aavanruler.nl.

By contrast, the aim of this volume of essays is to enable English readers to acquaint themselves with one of the core aspects of Van Ruler's oeuvre, namely his eschatology. The Dutch version of Volume 5C includes 19 copiously annotated essays. All but one of these essays (an essay on prayer healing) are included here. The 18 essays are placed in chronological order. Remarkably, they can be more or less grouped together under three rubrics, namely Van Ruler's views on the law in its relation to the kingdom of God. This was also the topic of his doctoral dissertation, *De vervulling van de wet* ("The fulfillment of the law," 1947) and his inaugural lecture at the University of Utrecht, also in 1947. The second rubric covers essays on eschata, i.e. on the parousia of Christ, the millennium, the resurrection of the dead and eternal life. The third rubric covers some of Van Ruler's later essays on approaches to eschatology.

The translation of Van Ruler's essays was done by Douglas Lawrie, while the translation of Dirk van Keulen's editorial introduction, and his annotations to Van Ruler's essays was done by Ernst Conradie – with extensive cross-checking. The editorial introduction was shortened by omitting background provided to the essays in the Dutch edition that are not included here. Dirk van Keulen's annotations to Van Ruler's essays are detailed, as befits a critical scholarly edition of Van Ruler's oeuvre. Some of these have been omitted, for example where there are small variations between the original manuscript and published versions of the text (that disappear in translation). Other annotations are truncated, for example by referring to a particular endnote in the Dutch edition where cross-references to literature only available in Dutch may be found. Biographic details on Dutch persons that may be relevant only to Dutch readers are kept to a minimum. With a few exceptions, these annotations have not been revised. Additions and revisions have been clearly indicated as "Translator's note" or "Editor's note".

In a few of the essays Van Ruler himself added some references or a bibliography in footnotes. These are mainly to Dutch, German and some English sources. Likewise, Dirk van Keulen's annotations are mainly to Dutch and German but occasionally also to French and Danish sources that Van Ruler would have had access to. These are maintained as such, even where English translations are available. Longish citations from such sources have typically not been included. For shorter quotations from such sources, English translations are used where available and referenced as such, alongside the Dutch or German references. Other quotations from Dutch and German sources form part of the translation. The reference system of the Dutch editions of Van Ruler's *Verzameld Werk* has been maintained. For Dutch and German titles upper case is used as in the Dutch and German originals.

As was the case with *This Earthly Life Matters*, this collection of essays is again partly framed in terms of Van Ruler's significance for contemporary Christian ecotheology. To this end an editor's afterword is included that offers some comments on aspects of Van Ruler's eschatology that may be attractive or unattractive given current debates in ecotheology.

We are most grateful to Dirk van Keulen for his helpful advice on thorny aspects of the translation of Van Ruler's essays and also for checking the translation of his editorial introduction.

30 April 2025

Translator's Preface
Douglas G. Lawrie

Having translated a collection of shorter pieces by Van Ruler before, I could draw on greater familiarity with his style and idiosyncrasies this time. Though the current translation still leans towards the literal and generally avoids clarifying additions and simplifying paraphrases, it includes more interventions in the interest of clarity.

Long, unwieldy sentences—one runs to 401 words in Dutch, another to 345 words—have been broken up. This sometimes necessitated recasting the sentences. There are more translator's notes and minor insertions, the latter being indicated by square brackets. Some awkward sentences have been recast where Van Ruler's meaning seemed abundantly clear. But where his meaning was open to doubt, no attempt was made to clarify in the translation.

The resulting text still does not invariably read smoothly. Van Ruler was not what books on composition call "a careful writer". His wife, Ms Van Ruler-Hamelink, indicated in a marginal note that she had to read a particular sentence several times before could make sense of it. The translator had this experience regularly. Van Ruler was apparently unaware that some of his sentences, as they stand, are vague or ambiguous. When he uses common Dutch words that have a host of meanings, the context does not always indicate which of these he has in mind. His choice and placement of words can often be questioned.

This creates difficulties for readers. When Van Ruler writes, "The kingdom of God is not Godself (Ruusbroec)," it requires knowledge of Ruusbroec to know that the latter *did* equate the kingdom with God and that Van Ruler is disagreeing. The statement that "the abundance of the fulfilment" that has "been given to us in Christ" makes it "self-evident that we should expect the future" is puzzling unless one keeps in mind that "future" ("in the strict sense") has a particular meaning for Van Ruler. This he explains in another piece. "The eschaton casts a person fully back into the present." That this statement appears with minor variations several times indicates that Van Ruler regarded it as significant. But what is the significance? What or who exactly does the casting back and where was the person if not in the present? "[T]hey have for long and quite naturally shared in a deeply concerned way in the crisis in the conception of science that has shocked our culture over the last decades"? Here the basic meaning survives the semantic bumps.

When the translated text seems awkward, it is not always Van Ruler's fault. No doubt the translator's ignorance and ineptitude played a role. Some insertions were necessary to clarify the pronominal deixis because the English pronouns, unlike the corresponding Dutch ones, are not gendered. The editorial decision to replace (with rare exceptions) Van Ruler's exclusively male forms with inclusive ones led to stylistic atrocities for which Van Ruler cannot be blamed. Above all, readers should keep in mind that most of the pieces were initially written for oral presentation. No doubt he filled some gaps during the presentation; non-verbal cues and conversational implicature might have supplied further clarification.

Perhaps the orientation to oral presentation also explains some of the idiosyncrasies in the text. Sometimes Van Ruler writes with breathless enthusiasm, employing exclamation marks and hyperboles liberally. Sometimes his tone is solemn, even declamatory; sometimes it is light to the point of flippancy. It is seldom the sober academic tone of most Dutch theologians who were his contemporaries. His frequent use of somewhat old fashioned "churchy" language may be aimed at audiences that included non-theologians. Those who wish to follow Van Ruler's train of thought may benefit from imagining each text as a performance. For, though Van Ruler demands careful readers, he also rewards them for their trouble.

The following general strategies have been adopted in the translation:

When Van Ruler quotes the Bible, he usually follows the wording of the old Statenvertaling (1637). As before, the translation retains something of this by using the Revised Standard Version for biblical quotations.

Italics in the English generally indicate that Van Ruler emphasized the words by means of accents. More rarely, they represent words in italics in the original or emphases effected by means of modal words or word order in the original that could not be rendered in English in the same way.

Where Van Ruler uses languages other than Dutch, his wording has generally been retained in the main text, English translations being provided in the footnotes. Longer quotations in Dutch and German have been translated in the main text. The wording of standard English translations has been used when these are available.

Where the Dutch word is given in square brackets after the English it indicates either that the word has a special connotation in Dutch or in Van Ruler's vocabulary that is lacking in the English, or that the Dutch allows for other translations as well. Most of these Dutch words are listed in the glossary that follows.

Glossary of Dutch Terms

THE LIST BELOW OFFERS explanations of some Dutch words and phrases that may puzzle readers. Some Dutch words have no exact English equivalents, refer to specifically Dutch matters or are ambiguous in Dutch. Van Ruler also draws on the academic discourses of his time and on authors who influenced him, particularly Hegel, Kierkegaard and Heidegger. For instance, his use of "existence" is derived from the prevalent existentialism of his time. This would not necessarily be obvious to modern readers.

"Accent": Rendered as "accent" even where "emphasis" would also seem to fit. In using "accent" rather than "klem" or "nadruk", Van Ruler is apparently following Kierkegaard. If so, the "accent" on something modifies the thing as diacritical marks modify the pronunciation of words.

"Bevinding, (bevindelijk)": Rendered as "spiritual (or religious) experience", followed by the Dutch in square brackets. It was a *terminus technicus* in a stream within Dutch pietism. It refers specifically to the experience of God's presence.

"Daad en lot(gevalle)": Van Ruler uses this phrase and similar ones several times to indicate the two major components of human experience: what we do and what happens to us. Though the distinction makes sense, the meaning may not always be immediately clear to readers.

"Enorm" (adjective and adverb): Rendered as "enormous(ly)", which is the literal meaning. In colloquial Dutch, however, it is used loosely as an intensifier, meaning no more than "great" or "very".

"Gaat om": Commonly used in Dutch to indicate what it is about, what is at stake or what is important (in the context). Van Ruler often uses "gaat om" together with "draait om" to differentiate between the goal and the necessary condition for reaching it. But he also uses it much more loosely, sometimes to indicate "what is relevant here". The various uses can cause confusion because it may create the impression that Van Ruler is contradicting himself.

"Geest": Rendered as "mind" or "spirit", depending on the context, followed by the Dutch in square brackets. When Van Ruler apparently uses the word in the Hegelian sense, it is capitalized.

"Gerechtigheid": Usually rendered as "righteousness", though "justice" would often be equally possible. Van Ruler was apparently influenced by a trend in his time that saw the words הקדצ and δικαιοσυνη as a reference to an overarching "right order" that goes beyond justice in the limited sense, an order in which everything is in its proper place.

"Gereformeerd(e) / Hervormd(e)": Both are rendered as "Reformed". In some contexts, they can be used interchangeably. Sometimes, however, they refer to two denominational branches and their subdivisions within Dutch Protestantism. In such cases the Dutch is placed in square brackets after "Reformed."

"Gestalte (gestaltelik)": This can be translated as "figure" (the human figure), "shape" or "form". Van Ruler often uses it to refer to the concrete manifestation of something abstract. It is rendered in various ways, followed by the Dutch in square brackets.

"Heiden (heidendom)": Rendered as "pagan" or "heathen", but "heidendom" as "heathendom."

"Heil": Van Ruler uses the word in many senses, all current in Dutch. It is usually rendered as "salvation" with the Dutch in square brackets), but one should distinguish between "het heil in Christus" (salvation as saving) and the eschatological "heil" (state of ultimate wellbeing and wholeness). For a discussion, see Conradie's essay in this volume.

"Humaniteit": Rendered as "humanness", followed by the Dutch in square brackets. The alternatives "humanity" and "humaneness" would sometimes be misleading.

"Kerstening": Rendered as "Christianizing". In Van Ruler's view, Christian missionary work should not strive only for a change of religion; it should also bring about a change in actions, attitudes and perceptions of life.

"Levensgevoel": Rendered as "experience of life", followed by the Dutch in square brackets, but the word, not common in Dutch, is complex. When Van Ruler speaks of "het christelike levensgevoel", he means, roughly, "the view of, orientation to and experience of life engendered by the Christian faith."

"Lichaamlijkheid": Rendered as "bodiliness" rather than "corporeality". The latter is a distinctly learned word in English; the Dutch word is not.

"Moment": Rendered as "moment" even when "aspect" and component" would also seem possible. Van Ruler apparently takes this usage from Hegel.

"Ondergang": The literal translation "going under" (as noun) seldom fits into an English sentence. It can mean "decline" or "destruction", but when Van Ruler speaks of the "ondergang" of the world, he means more than "decline" and less than total "destruction". Then it has been rendered as "ruin", with the Dutch in square brackets.

"Plaatjes": Van Ruler sometimes says that what systematic theologians do is to play with, sort through, compare or table "plaatjes". His meaning is relatively clear. Theologians arrange the data of revelation in various ways to create different "images" of how it all fits together. They choose the better ones and reject the worse ones. Translating the words is another matter, since the word has several meanings in Dutch. It has been rendered as "pictures", with the Dutch in square brackets. "Photographs" or "outlines" would also be possible. He seems to use "kaarten" in the same way. It is rendered as "charts", but Van Ruler might have had in mind his practice of storing references and quotations on a set of cards in an elaborate filing system.

"Recht": The Dutch word is as protean as the English "right". Van Ruler seems to use even the single phrase "Gods recht" in several ways. Translation decisions had to be taken ad hoc, but the Dutch is given in square brackets to allow readers to decide for themselves.

"Schuld (schuldig)": The Dutch means both "guilt (guilty)" and "debt (indebted)". The former is generally used in the translation, with the

Dutch in square brackets, but some of Van Ruler's formulations work far better with the latter. Van Ruler's Anselmian view is that guilt is primarily a form of indebtedness.

"Trekpunt": Apparently a word that Van Ruler created. It seems to refer to the fixed point from which a pulling force is exerted (in erecting a wire fence, for instance). It has been rendered as "pulling point", a term that does not exist in English.

"Verbrijzeling": Rendered as "crushing" – "pulverizing" was also possible. It was a term used in pietist (bevindelijk) circles to indicate a stage in spiritual development in which the person's self is "crushed" under the weight of guilt before it can arise again.

"Verzoening": The Dutch means both "atonement" and "reconciliation". The former is generally used in the translation, but sometimes Van Ruler may have the latter in mind. In a christological context the meaning would generally be "atonement," in a pneumatological context "reconciliation."

"Volken": Rendered as "peoples." The Dutch distinction between "volk" (ethnic and cultural) and "natie" (mainly political) is hard to reproduce.

"Wederkomst": Rendered as "parousia" to avoid debates about the merits and problems of other terms such as "second coming" and "return."

"Wezen": Where "essence" would not be appropriate, it is rendered as "(very) being", followed by the Dutch in square brackets.

"Zijn": Where this is the equivalent of the Latin "esse", it is rendered as "Being."

"Zin": The Dutch word is as protean as the English "sense", the normal translation. Where it is juxtaposed to "betekenis" and where the context suggests it, it is rendered as "significance," followed by the Dutch in square brackets.

Abbreviations

GD 4	Herman Bavinck, *Gereformeerde Dogmatiek*, Deel 4 (Kampen: JH Kok, 1930).4
ThW I	Arnold A. Van Ruler, *Theologisch Werk Deel I* (Nijkerk: Callenbach, 1969).
ThW II	Arnold A. Van Ruler, *Theologisch Werk Deel II* (Nijkerk: Callenbach, 1971).
ThW IV	Arnold A. Van Ruler, *Theologisch Werk Deel IV* (Nijkerk: Callenbach, 1972).
ThW VI	Arnold A. Van Ruler, *Theologisch Werk Deel VI* (Nijkerk: Callenbach, 1973).
ThWNT	Gerhard Kittel und Gerhard Friedrich (Hg.), *Theologisches Wörterbuch zum Neuen Testament, Band 1-11*, Stuttgart 1933-1978.
VvdW	Arnold A. van Ruler, *De Vervulling van de Wet: Een Dogmatische Studie over de Verhouding van Openbaring en Existentie* (Nijkerk: Callenbach, 1947).
VW	Arnold A. Van Ruler, *Verzameld Werk*.
VW 1	Arnold A. Van Ruler, *Verzameld Werk, Deel I: De Aard van de Theologie*, edited by Dirk van Keulen (Zoetermeer: Boekencentrum, 2007).
VW 2	Arnold A. Van Ruler, *Verzameld Werk, Deel II: Openbaring en Heilige Schrift*, edited by Dirk van Keulen (Zoetermeer: Boekencentrum, 2008).

VW 3	Arnold A. Van Ruler, *Verzameld Werk Deel III: God, Schepping, Mens, Zonde,* edited by Dirk van Keulen. (Zoetermeer: Boekencentrum, 2009).
VW 4A	Arnold A. Van Ruler, *Verzameld Werk, Deel IV-A: Christus, de Geest en het Heil,* edited by Dirk van Keulen (Zoetermeer: Boekencentrum, 2011).
VW 4B	Arnold A. Van Ruler, *Verzameld Werk, Deel IV-B: Christus, de Geest en het Heil,* edited by Dirk van Keulen (Zoetermeer: Boekencentrum, 2011).
VW 5C	Arnold A. Van Ruler, *Verzameld Werk Deel V-C: Belijdenis en Leertucht – Kerk, Wereld, Diaconaat – Volkskerk – Zending en Apostolaat – Eschatologie,* edited by Dirk van Keulen (Utrecht: Kokboekencentrum, 2023).
VW 6A	Arnold A. Van Ruler, *Verzameld Werk Deel VI-A: De Theocratie,* edited by Dirk van Keulen (Utrecht: Kokboekencentrum, 2016).

Introduction

Dirk van Keulen

ORIGINALLY, IT WAS ENVISAGED that the Dutch edition of Van Ruler's *Verzameld werk* ("Collected Works") would comprise seven volumes, divided according to themes. According to this layout, Volume 5 was to cover "The church, the sacraments and the last things." However, it became clear that Van Ruler thought and wrote so much on these topics that it was necessary to divide this volume into three parts:

- Volume 5A: Church, liturgy, preaching and sacraments
- Volume 5B: Church law, church polity, church offices
- Volume 5C: Confession and doctrinal discipline; Church, world and diaconate; national church [volkskerk], mission and apostolate; and eschatology.

Volume 5C covers six clusters of texts:

- Confession, doctrine and doctrinal discipline;
- Church and world;
- Diaconate;
- National church [volkskerk];
- Mission and apostolate;
- Eschatology.

[This translation covers only the final cluster on eschatology and includes eighteen of the essays that appeared in the Dutch edition of Volume 5C of Van Ruler's *Collected Works*.[1]]

1. See Arnold A. van Ruler, *Verzameld werk Deel5C: Belijdenis en leertucht—Kerk,*

In what follows I will introduce the essays in this cluster and where possible will refer to the reception of these essays.

The cluster on eschatology[2] comprises nineteen essays. Eight of these were first published in the Dutch edition of Volume 5C of the Collected Works. These nineteen texts are presented in chronological order. I now introduce them in four sections.

1. LAW AND KINGDOM OF GOD

Five of the first six essays may be brought together under the theme of the law and the kingdom of God. This is a central theme in Van Ruler's oeuvre—as is evident from an interview with Van Ruler, dated 7 June 1969. George Puchinger,[3] the interviewer, asked Van Ruler about his relationship to the theology of Karl Barth. Van Ruler responded in some detail, saying, among other things, the following:

> I would not want, in any way whatsoever, to pose against his [Barth's] christological theology a pneumatological one. When I reflect on the true structure of theology, I arrive at three disparate perspectives: The Trinity, the kingdom, and predestination. The later comment by Barth that everything in his *Church*

---

wereld, diaconaat—Volkskerk—Zending en apostolaat—Eschatologie. Edited and introduced by Dirk van Keulen (Utrecht: Kokboekencentrum, 2023), 772–965. This translation covers only the parts of Van Keulen's introduction that deal with the cluster on eschatology.

2. On an aspect of Van Ruler's eschatology in English, see John Vander Reest's doctoral thesis *The Presence of the Future in the Theology of A.A. van Ruler* (Melbourne College of Divinity 2012); also Ernst M. Conradie *Saving the Earth?*, 217–276 (Berlin: LIT Verlag, 2013). See also the detailed analysis of Van Ruler's eschatology in a number of Dutch texts, including W.H. Velema, *Confrontatie met Van Ruler: Denken vanuit het einde* (Kampen: Kok, 1962); P. van Hoof, *Intermezzo: Kontinuïteit en diskontinuïteit in de theologie van A.A. van Ruler* (Amsterdam: Bolland, 1974); B. Plaisier, *Instrumentaal tussenspel. Van Rulers ecclesiologie onder het gezichtspunt van het apostolaat* (Master thesis Rijksuniversiteit Utrecht, 1977), 3–28 (Amsterdam, 1974); J.J. Rebel, *Pastoraat in pneumatologisch perspectief: Een theologische verantwoording vanuit het denken van A.A. van Ruler* (Kampen: Kok, 1981), 37–48, 64–96; J.M. van 't Kruis, *De Geest als missionaire beweging: Een onderzoek naar de functie en toereikendheid van gereformeerde theologie in de huidige missiologische discussie* (Zoetermeer: Boekencentrum, 1997), 93–114; Herma van der Veen, *Het Koninkrijk Gods en het menselijk handelen: Een vergelijking tussen Arnold A. van Ruler en Reinhold Niebuhr* (Master thesis, Universiteit Utrecht, 2008).

3. George Puchinger (1921–1999), Dutch historian and director of the "Historisch Documentatiecentrum voor het Nederlands Protestantisme 1800-heden" (1971–1986).

> *Dogmatics* should be rewritten, namely in a less christological and a more pneumatological way, would not satisfy me.[4]

For Van Ruler, the kingdom of God is therefore one of three "disparate perspectives" that guides his theological reflections. Indeed, the kingdom of God plays a central role in his work. This is, for example, evident from his doctoral dissertation, *De vervulling van de wet* ("The fulfilment of the law")[5] for which he graduated cum laude in Groningen on 1 July 1947. His promotor was Th.L. Haitjema and his paranymphs were J.R. Wolfensberger (a minister from Amsterdam) and J. Loos (a minister from Hilversum).

The first part of the dissertation—entitled "Background" by Van Ruler—includes an introduction and four chapters. He commences with a chapter on the kingdom of God and continues with one on "Consummation and Fulfillment."[6] This is followed by two chapters on the kingdom of God and the category of fufilment from a christological[7] and then, far more extensively, from a pneumatological perspective.[8] The title clarifies that the actual theme is the fulfilment of the law. For Van Ruler, there is a close connection between the kingdom of God and the law. The law is the law of the kingdom.

How did Van Ruler arrive at this theme for his doctoral research? In his handwritten bibliography he writes:

> The history of the topic of my dissertation is a lengthy one. At first I would have graduated under Prof Dr. W.J. Aalders.[9] He wanted me to work on Ernst Troeltsch on the basis of number

---

4. See G. Puchinger, *Hervormd-gereformeerd, één of gescheiden?* (Delft: Meinema, 1969), 356.

5. See A.A. van Ruler, *De vervulling van de wet: Een dogmatische studie over de verhouding van openbaring en existentie* (Nijkerk, 1947). The inclusion of this doctoral thesis in the series of his *Verzameld werk* is not envisaged at the time of writing. I [DvK] regard this as sad. This dense study on the fulfilment of the law is certainly no easy read, but is the hinge on which Van Ruler's whole oeuvre turns. [No English translation of it is available either—ed.]

6. Van Ruler, *De vervulling van de wet*, 29–47; 48–71.

7. Van Ruler, *De vervulling van de wet*, 72–117.

8. Van Ruler, *De vervulling van de wet*, 118–262.

9. Willem Jan Aalders (1870–1945), Reformed minister and professor at the Rijksuniversiteit Groningen (1915–1940) where he taught dogmatics, church history, church law, ethics and philosophy of religion. He was one of Van Ruler's teachers when he studied in Groningen.

70.[10] In Kubaard I studied Troeltsch's writings for a few years. Thereafter it became physically impossible for me to busy myself with such a compromise position. I still maintained the absolute tone of Barthian theology and still had to gain personal clarity on a theocratic theology with which I was wrestling. This was significantly amplified by the situation in a congregation in a town in Friesland and the coming into power of nationalsocialism—that posed the problem of church and state acutely, within a cultural situation that interested me in any case. I therefore discussed the matter with Prof Aalders and changed to the theme of church and state in the thought of Kuyper (and Hoedemaker).[11] In the meantime, Prof. Aalders passed away and I tended to restrict the topic to ecclesiology. In consultation with Prof Aalders, I had gone over to Prof. Hajtema as promotor when the material became ever more dogmatic.[12] I considered ecclesiology quite broadly. When working on the aspect of the church and the kingdom of God and the subsection of that, the category of fulfilment, I came upon the issue of the fulfilment of

---

10. In Van Ruler's handwritten bibliography number 70 refers to "Ernst Troeltsch en het historisme" (Ernst Troeltsch and historicism"). Van Ruler added a note: "thesis of ±225 pages for Prof. Dr W.J. Aalders. Probably written in 1932/3. Used for 171. In three booklets. This and the previous thesis were non-prescribed writings while I studied for the doctoral exams." See Van Ruler, "Handgeschreven bibliografie." s.v. [I,]70. The "previous thesis" refers to number 69: "Hegel en Kierkegaard in de geschiedenisphilosophie." This was a thesis of 96 pages for Prof. Dr W.J. Aalders. Probably written in 1932/3. Both these theses are missing in the Van Ruler archive. Number 171 is an article entitled "Historische cultuurvorming" ("Historical formation of culture") that offered an analysis of Ernst Troeltsch's philosophy of history.

11. Elsewhere in his handwritten bibliography Van Ruler notes that conflict arose between Aalders and himself following the publication of Van Ruler's book *Kuypers idee eener christelijke cultuur* (Nijkerk: Callenbach, 1940): "This book was written in Kubaard in the summer of 1939. The intention was to write an article for *Vox Theologica* (as far as I can recall, upon the request of the editors) but this article got out of hand and grew into a book. Prof. Dr. W.J. Aalders, my assigned promotor, was greatly offended about this manipulation, i.e. that I published a book *before* my thesis. That was fully resolved through correspondence and conversation." See his *Handgeschreven bibliografie*, s.v. [I,]127.

12. Haitjema would later write that "One of the singular merits of his [Van Ruler's—DvK] dissertation is that he earnestly strove to bring to the fore the "Trinitarian articulation" of eschatology. Haitjema is nevertheless also critical: "I would, however, have preferred it if Van Ruler had been somewhat less audacious in assigning a dominant emphasis to the "patrocentric perspective". So much so that he clung to the category of the eschaton, i.e. the kingdom of God, with such tenacity that he scarcely left himself any room to describe the eschaton in different ways from a christological and a pneumatological perspective respectively. See Th.L. Haitjema, "De trinitarische ontvouwing van de eschatologie," *Kerk en Theologie* 8 (1957), 83f.

the law. My promotor then advised me to restrict myself to that aspect. That was attractive to me as the issue of the Old Testament had long become urgent to me. Of course, this provided an entirely new frame. Much of the material that I had already worked on had to be discarded. I could use a few chapters: large parts of Chapters I, II and III are old, as are very small parts of chapter VII, §2 and 3. The rest was written in one go between October 1946 and February 1947.[13]

This text speaks for itself and is illuminating. One may nevertheless raise the question: How is it possible that Van Ruler could have written more than half of his dissertation in only five months? He was at that stage also a minister and deeply involved in drafting a new church order. No wonder that he was overworked and had to take some rest after his doctoral defence.

Another interesting aspect of Van Ruler's account of the genesis of his dissertation is the observation that the issue of the Old Testament had long become urgent for him. Some years before he gained his doctorate, this already became evident in two essays written in 1941 and 1943 on "The value of the Old Testament" that he published in his book *Religie en Politiek* ("Religion and Politics," 1945). In these he first proposed that the Old Testament is the actual Bible and that the New Testament is nothing more than a glossary of foreign terms words at the back for further explanation.[14] His interest in the Old Testament reached much further back though. Haitjema, who would later become Van Ruler's promotor, also had him in his cathechism class when he was a minister in Apeldoorn. After Van Ruler died on 15 December 1970, Haitjema wrote the following in an "In Memoriam":

> A few years later, he became one of the pupils in my catechism class for younger boys. I could see already then that he was not only intellectually gifted, but also that his interest in biblical instruction was extraordinary. Especially the "dense" subject matter in the historical books of the Old Testament as part of the Holy Scripture of the Christian church attracted him. Spontaneously and completely on his own initiative, he sometimes wrote lengthy essays on biblical figures in the Old Testament. In a few of these one may perhaps find a prophecy of his later theologoumenon, which is not always appreciated in the circles

---

13. See Van Ruler, *Handgeschreven bibliografie*, s.v. [I,] 217.

14. For cross-references to literature in Dutch, see Van Ruler's *Verzameld werk 5C*, 89, note 424.

of modern scientific researchers in the terrain of biblical studies, namely that the texts of the Old Covenant are the authentic Scripture, while the New Testament is nothing but an explanatory register to the revelatory message of the Old Testament.[15]

Van Ruler's interest in the Old Testament therefore dates back to his youth. Early interest in the Old Testament and in the theme of the law and the kingdom of God is also evident in the first of the essays on eschatology included here. As I pointed out earlier in this introduction [in a section not included here—EMC], Van Ruler was involved in the Dutch Christian Student Union (NCSV) during his student years. [...] The lecture "God's Law" was presented by the young student Van Ruler at the Hardenbroek castle in Driebergen-Rijsenburg on 17 October 1931. That was where the rural center of the NCSV was located between 1917 and 1932. The audience came from the Delft and Rotterdam sections of the NCSV. "God's Law" is, as far as I know, the first text that he wrote on the theme of the law and the kingdom of God.

Ten years later, after a period in Kubaard, Van Ruler worked as minister in the Reformed congregation in Hilversum. Then the Second World War broke out. This did not prevent meetings of the convent of active and retired ministers in Hilversum. On 3 June 1941, Van Ruler delivered a lecture before this convent entitled "Kingdom of God and Church".[16] This indicated once more his interest in the theme of the kingdom of God. The lecture was published in the journal *Onder Eigen Vaandel* later that year.[17] Four years later, Van Ruler also included it in his book *Religie en Politiek*.[18] As far as I know, there was no response to this lecture.

By the middle of 1947, the Faculty of Divinity at the Rijksuniversiteit Utrecht would often be in Van Ruler's thoughts. He was nominated as professor for the Nederlandse Hervormde Kerk at this faculty on 3 June 1947—a few weeks before his doctoral defence (1 July 1947). A few weeks before that, on the Monday evening of 12 May 1947, he delivered a lecture entitled "The Meaning of the Mosaic Law." According to a report

---

15. See Th.L. Haitjema, "In memoriam prof. dr. A.A. van Ruler', *Hervormd Weekblad De Gereformeerde Kerk* 82 (1970–1971), 106.

16. See Van Ruler, *Handgeschreven bibliografie*, s.v. [I,]155.

17. A.A. van Ruler, "Koninkrijk Gods en kerk," *Onder Eigen Vaandel* 16 (1941), 268–86.

18. A.A. van Ruler, "Koninkrijk Gods en kerk" in *Religie en Politiek* (Nijkerk: Callenbach, 1945), 52–68.

in the magazine *Sol Iustitiae*,[19] he delivered this lecture to a packed audience in the so-called small auditorium (in the Academiegebouw on the Domplein). Would the venue be packed because Van Ruler's name was mentioned as a possibility for the nomination of a professor?

At the start of the lecture, which was, as the title indicates, closely related to his dissertation, Van Ruler distinguished between four meanings of the Mosaic law: (1) the kerygmatic, (2) the existential, (3) the functional, and (4) the material. All four are discussed in more detail in what follows. This lecture was first published in the journal *Nederlands Theologisch Tijdschrift*, and was also included in the first volume of Van Ruler's *Theologisch Werk* and also in the volume *Van Schepping tot Koninkrijk*.

Graafland reacted in an explicitly positive way to this lecture. Referring in general to "De betekenis van de mozaïsche wet" ("The Meaning of the Mosaic Law" as well as to Van Ruler's essay "Theocratie en tolerantie" ("Theocracy and Tolerance"), he wrote: "We are convinced that, when we listen to the Old Testament commandments more attentively and seriously, it will lead to an enormous upliftment of human existence. Put differently, were we to think and live more theocratically, it would be more beneficial and would, regarding the chances of human survival, attest to more realism, than that which is imposed on us in the many laws that come about through democratic processes. In the latter, even if they appear very sociable, people still do what they please and strive towards that—at the cost of others, if necessary, all because the actual norm is located with humanity itself, which is delivered up to its own distorted desires and demonic possibilities."[20]

Five months to the day after his appointment as professor—on Monday 3 November 1947 at 14h00—Van Ruler gave his inaugural lecture in the Aula of the Academiegebouw on the Domplein. The title was *Het Koninkrijk Gods en de Geschiedenis* ("The Kingdom of God and History") and was published as a brochure by G.F. Callenbach in Nijkerk.[21] In his oration Van Ruler weaved together core elements of his theological

---

19. See "Verslag van de lezing door Ds. A.A. van Ruler," in *Sol Iustitiae: Orgaan der Utrechtse universitaire gemeenschap*, 2/31 (24 May 1947), 2.

20. C. Graafland, *Het vaste verbond: Israël en het Oude Testament bij Calvijn en het gereformeerd protestantisme* (Amsterdam: Bolland, 1978), 66f.

21. A.A. van Ruler, *Het koninkrijk Gods en de geschiedenis* (Nijkerk: Callenback, 1947). This oration was later included by Ms van Ruler in *Verwachting en voltooiing: Een bundel theologische opstellen en voordrachten* (Nijkerk: Callenbach, 1978), 29–42.

vision at that stage in relation to the three subjects that he at that time would have to teach: biblical theology, Dutch church history and internal and external mission. Five years later this was changed to dogmatics, Christian ethics, history of the Dutch Reformed (Hervormd) Church and church law. His interest in Troeltsch (on which he had earlier planned to write a dissertation) still came through clearly—*and* he was distancing himself from Barth.²² By now he had been doing that for some years. His vision on theocracy, which he described in his books *Religie en Politiek* (1945), *Visie en Vaart* ("Vision and Voyage", 1947) and *Droom en Gestalte* ("Dream and Figure",1947), was clearly at odds with Barth's theology.

The same applies to his dissertation. Above I have mentioned that Van Ruler's discussion on the kingdom of God and fulfilment from a pneumatological perspective is more extensive than the one from a christological persective. This is to be interpreted as implicit criticism of Barth. That Van Ruler explicitly distanced himself from Barth in his inaugural lecture may be related to the fact that he was still seen as a "Barthian" in some circles. This may be be illustrated with reference to a contribution by A.J. Verbrugh (1916–2003), who was at that stage a lecturer in physical chemistry and nuclear physics at the Hogere Technische School in Dordrecht. He belonged to the Vrijgemaakt Gereformeerde Kerk and later became known as a politician. In the weekly magazine *De Reformatie* he wrote the following on 23 June 1947:

> I read in *De Reformatie* that the newly appointed Prof Van Ruler is a Barthian. This is an accurate portrayal of the man. I had an unpleasant altercation with Rev Van Ruler once because I said to him that I have heard from various sources that he is a disciple of Barth. Rev. Van Ruler was upset about "the Reformed habit of attaching labels to everyone without inquiring what the person was aiming at." He declared, among other things, his view that this is actually sadly symbolic of the decadence of this age that someone like Barth could gain such prominence. He acknowledged that he had been influenced by Barth for a while but insisted that he (AAvR) now stood well clear of him (KB). I can't quite figure out Rev. Van Ruler's way of expression and his view on the meaning of the state in God's plan for the world (I did exchange some thoughts with him in this regard), but it was not immediately obvious to me that his attitude was Barthian. At most I thought that this is the attitude of a man who made use of non-Reformed language so that a listener has

---

22. For a more detailed discussion, see the essay included in this volume.

to be on the alert. Provisionally, I assumed that Rev. Van Ruler is "Van Rulerian" and considerably influenced by Hoedemaker. As an outsider I thought that his appointment by the Hervormde synod was not related to his Barthian sympathies but instead to his "high church" views. I acknowledge that Barth is sometimes cited in Van Ruler's dissertation, but I lack the specialized interest to study this text (possibly because I lack the specialized knowledge). If the editorial board could clarify whether and why Rev. Van Ruler is Barthian, it could be useful. Rev. Van Ruler does have some followers who claim to be Reformed but wouldn't want to have anything to do with Barth. The editorial board could help to inform them in this way.

Klaas Schilder, the leader of the Vrijgemaakte Gereformeerde Kerk, answered the question by Verburgh:

> Prof. van Ruler is indeed a Barthian. He was that already when he was still a student and was "used" by Prof Haitjema to provide a refutation (which, however, glossed over the grounds that I had rejected) of the arguments I had used against Prof Haitjema. Moreover, the weekly newspaper of the Hervormden Raad voor Kerk en Publiciteit recalled that it was Barth himself who said of the student Van Ruler: "keep an eye on him" (which was meant as a compliment). That Dr Van Ruler moved away from Barth in his views on theocracy is well-known to us. But then Barth himself also moved away from Barth. What is decisive is the core insights and the core motifs.[23]

Van Ruler knew this text because a cutting was pasted into one of his scrap-books.[24] Such comments may have brought him to distance himself from Barth more explicitly in his inaugural lecture. In his handwritten bibliography Van Ruler notes: "What I actually wanted to say appears—highly compressed—on the last page."[25] He could not complain about a lack of attention. A report on Van Ruler's lecture appeared in various national and regional newspapers on 3 or 4 November 1947.

---

23. See Schilder's weekly column "Stemmen uit onze kerken," ("Voices from our churches") in *De Reformatie* 22/39 (5 July 1947), 313. In his autobiography, *Jong zijn en oud worden* (Amsterdam, 2002), Verburgh wrote about Van Ruler in a more positive tone.

24. See the Van Ruler archive, inventory number VII, Box 1, Scrap-book 1, number 50.

25. See Van Ruler's comment in *Handgeschreven bibliografie*, s.v. [I], 225. See also the last page of the essay included in this volume.

Five months later the theme of the law and God's kingdom crops up once more in Van Ruler's oeuvre. This time the text bore the title of "Wet en evangelie" ("Law and Gospel"). This Lutheran-sounding theme was no coincidence. Van Ruler gave this as a lecture, in which he draws upon his dissertation quite often, to the Evangelical Lutheran Society for Ministers in Amsterdam on 8 April 1948. This lecture was published for the first time in the Dutch edition of the *Verzameld werk*.

Finally, there is another brief essay on this theme, entitled "Leven in het koninkrijk: Christus' geboorte en de politiek" ("Living in the Kingdom: Christ's Birth and Politics."). It was first published in December 1957 in the Christmas edition of the weekly paper *De Hervormde Kerk*. Twelve years later (1969) it was published for the second time in the Christmas edition of the magazine *De Vrije Natie*. And again, three years after that, Ms Van Ruler included this in the collection *Blij zijn als kinderen* (1972).[26]

2. THE MILLENNIUM

Among Van Ruler's older texts on eschatology that focused on law and the kingdom of God there is single text that is quite distinct. It is entitled "'Het duizendjarige rijk" ("The millennium"). It was published for the first time in the Dutch edition of the *Verzameld werk* (Volume 5C).

The theme of the millennium, that goes back to Revelations 20, has a long history. Throughout the centuries, this chapter in the Bible has been read and interpreted in Christian churches. Moreover, in dogmatics it was customary to attend to it when dealing with the doctrine of the last things.[27] It is also possible to identify moments in history when the theme of the millennium demanded specific attention. That was the case, for instance, in the period before the year 1000. But also in times of tension, war and violence there has been more reflection than is usual—also in

---

26. See A.A. van Ruler, "Leven in het koninkrijk: Christus' geboorte en de politiek," in *De Hervormde Kerk: Weekblad voor hervormd Nederland* 13/50 (21 December 1957), 4; also published in *De Vrije Natie: Orgaan van de Protestantse Unie* 18/4 (December 1969), 1–2; and in *Blij zijn als kinderen: Een boek voor volwassenen* (Kampen: Kok, 1972), 127–30.

27. See, for example, H. Bavinck, *Gereformeerde Dogmatiek, Deel 4* (Kampen: Kok, 1930[4]), 634–72.

Editor's note: This volume is translated by John Vriend and edited by John Bolt as Herman Bavinck, *Reformed Dogmatics, Volume IV: Holy Spirit, Church, and New Creation* (Grand Rapids: Baker Academic, 2008), 644–690.

the Netherlands[28]—on the millennium and the closely related theme of the Antichrist. The First World War was one such catalyst.

One illustration of this is that in 1916 the South African theologian M.J. van der Westhuizen obtained a doctorate from the Vrije Universiteit Amsterdam with an exegetical study on the Antichrist.[29] Three years later, V. Hepp, a professor at the same institution, published a study entitled *De antichrist* ("The Antichrist").[30] In 1919 the well-known evangelist Johannes de Heer published *De antichrist in zijne drievuldige openbaring* ("The Antichrist in its threefold revelation").[31] And another few years later M.H.A. van der Valk wrote a study with the telling title *De naderende Antichrist in het licht van de Wereldcrisis* ("The coming Antichrist in the light of the world crisis").[32]

Likewise, the theme of the millennium attracted attention during these years. J. Waterink, at that time a Reformed [Gereformeeerde] minister in Zutphen wrote a brochure entitled *Het chiliasme* ("Chiliasm").[33] A.M. Berkhoff, at that stage still still a Christian Reformed minister, published a lengthy boek on the millennium in 1929.[34] During the years 1931 and 1932, K. Dijk, a Reformed [Gereformeerde] theologian, published a long series of editorials in the weekly paper *De Heraut* under the title "Het Millennium" ("The millennium"). The reason for this was that "in recent years, there was a revival in propaganda for the chiliastic notion of a 'reign of thousand years' during which Christ would reign over a captive Satan." A year later, Dijk collected these articles in an equally lengthy book *Het rijk der duizend Jaren* ("The reign of a thousand years").[35] In that same year, H. Veldkamp, at that stage a Reformed (Gereformeerd)

---

28. See, for example, Rie Hilje Kielman, *In het laatste der dagen: Eindtijdverwachting in Nederland op de drempel van de moderne tijd* (Delft: Eburon, 2017).

29. M.J. van der Westhuizen, *De antichrist in het Nieuwe Testament: Exegetiese studie* (Amsterdam: Van Bottenburg, 1916).

30. V. Hepp, *De antichrist* (Kampen: Kok, 1919).

31. Joh. de Heer, *De antichrist in zijne drievuldige openbaring* (Rotterdam: De Heer, 1919).

32. M.H.A. van der Valk, *De naderende Antichrist in het licht van de Wereldcrisis* (Kampen, 1931).

33. J. Waterink, *Het chiliasme ("Duizendjarig rijk")* (Zutphen: Van den Brink, 1918).

34. A.M. Berkhoff, *De Christusregeering of het in Openbaring XX in aansluiting bij de gansche profetie der Heilige Schrift beloofde duizendjarige rijk* (Kampen: Kok, 1929).

35. K. Dijk, *Het rijk der duizend jaren: Beschouwingen in het verleden en heden over het duizendjarig rijk* (Kampen: Kok 1933).

minister in Sneek, preached a sermon on the same theme.[36] And in 1934, Johannes de Heer published, following his earlier study on the Antichrist, a book entitled *Het duizendjarig vrederijk* ("The thousand year kingdom of peace").[37]

It is therefore not surprising that the theme of the millennium was a focus of attention during the Second World War. In any case, it was discussed in the convent of ministers in Hilversum to which Van Ruler belonged at the time. His essay "Het duizendjarige rijk" ("The Millennium") was written for that convent. In his handwritten bibliography he noted the following about this text: "Collection of comments for discussion in the Hilversum convent."[38] He did not remember when exactly that discussion took place. Because the note appears in between other texts in the year 1942 one may assume that these comments may be dated to around that same year.

From his opening comment in the heading to the text, [...] it becomes clear that several meetings were dedicated to this theme. From the introduction to this essay it is also clear that Van Ruler adopted a position that differed from that of some of his conversation partners. He refers to a "isolated position." Because Van Ruler's thoughts about this theme cannot be found anywhere else in his writings, the essay on "The Millennium" deserves a place within his *Verzameld werk*.

3. LIFE AND DEATH

The six essays around the middle of this volume focus on questions of life and death.

The first is entitled "Ik geloof een eeuwig leven" ("I Believe in Eternal Life"). This was originally a lecture at a conference organized by the Centraal Bond voor Inwendige Zending (an association for internal mission) taking place at De Horst in Driebergen, 19–22 July 1948. The theme of the conference was "… Bad days …" The organizers thought of "sickness,

---

36. H. Veldkamp, *Wat de kerk van het duizendjarig rijk belijdt* (Franeker: Wever, 1933).

37. Joh. de Heer, *Het duizendjarig vrederijk* (Zeist: Zoeklicht-boekhandel, 1934).

38. See Van Ruler's *Handgeschreven bibliografie*, s.v. [I], 167.

old age, the problems, trouble and struggle associated with that."³⁹ They asked a series of speakers to illuminate aspects of this theme.⁴⁰

- S.P. Dee, a hospital chaplain in Rotterdam spoke about the problem of suffering in general. He averred that, because "sin is the deepest source of all suffering, … liberation is only possible through conversion to Jesus Christ."

- Sister P. Thijssen, the head of the nursing staff in Amsterdam, and S. Hoekstra, a general practitioner in Maarssen, "gave an account of how one can establish contact with the sick and suffering as nurse and house doctor. Gaining trust and and tactful understanding are important factors in that regard. The particular function of the nurse and the significance of the ordinary, old-fashioned house doctor as a person trusted by the individual and the family were expressed clearly."

- A. Hijmans, a hospital chaplain in Amsterdam, argued that pastoral visits to the sick should be proclamation, often precisely through an ordinary conversation. As a pastor, one should bring only the gospel to patients, while avoiding positioning oneself between Christ and the patient and especially putting forward any suggestion that sickness or suffering as such could be a source for faith."

- Joh. van der Spek, a psychiatrist, sketched "the place of the elderly in our society from a psychological perspective. The history of humanity proves that such people, including great thinkers, statesmen and so forth, are indispensable."

- J. Everts, a social reformer and manager, argued that the church "has an important task […] on the terrain of social care as well." He also expanded on "the whole problem of the attitude and task of social workers in this social care."

- Finally, Van Ruler spoke on the article of faith, "I believe in eternal life", on 22 July 1948: "In his address, the speaker made it clear that we have to rid ourselves completely of the unbiblical, pagan ways of thinking that still reigns in the church around questions of life and

---

39. See M. Groenenberg, "Ten geleide: Hoe dit boekje ontstond?" in *Leven, ziekte, sterven* (Amsterdam: Ten Have, 1949), 5f.

40. This information and the citations that follow are derived from the conference report under the title, "Centraal Bond voor Inwendige Zending en Chr. Philantropische Inrichtingen," in *Diakonia* 15/7 (July 1948), 109.

death. This brings about the liberation from the dark pressure and burden that we are divine or should become divine. He stressed, as did Rev Hijmans and Dr Hoekstra, the unity of the human person, also in connection with the reality of the resurrection in comparison with the so-called doctrine of the immortality of the soul and the division between soul (spirit) and body—which does not have a biblical-Christian structure but is derived from heathendom and philosophy, but nevertheless still have many followers."

The lectures by Hoekstra, Hijmans en Van Ruler were published by Uitgeverij W. ten Have N.V. in Amsterdam on behalf of "De Lichtdrager" ("the bearer of light"), a Dutch religious association. The booklet was entitled *Leven, ziekte, sterven* ("Life, sickness, dying"). Ms Van Ruler included Van Ruler's essay "Ik geloof een eeuwig leven" in his (posthumously published) *Theologisch Werk 6*.[41]

This essay is followed by a brief text on "De relativering van dood en leven" ("Relativizing of Death and Life"). This appeared earlier as a meditation in the journal *Kerk en Theologie* in 1954.[42]

Thereafter follows a set of notes entitled "Vragen van leven en dood" ("Questions of Life and Death") that had not previously been published. Van Ruler used these notes twice for preparing a lecture. The first was delivered at a "congregation evening" in Kralingen on 16 February 1955, the second in Beukbergen on 27 Febuary 1958. Beukbergen refers to what is now a training center of the service group Geestelijke Verzorging (spiritual care) for the military services at Huis ter Heide. It is not clear what kind of audience attended. Van Ruler commenced his lecture with the remark, "After one's fortieth year, one contemplates, with body and soul, that there will come a moment when one dies." In relation to this remark (which is also found once elsewhere in his oeuvre), I need to mention a letter by Van Ruler (dated 1 February 1969) to a Ms Rijpkema that is kept in the Van Ruler archive. The letter is worth citing in full:

Dear Miss Rijpkema

Thank you for your letter of 28 January. I would like to tell you something of my own experience. Around my fortieth year, the

---

41. See A.A. van Ruler, "Ik geloof een eeuwig leven," in *Leven, ziekte, sterven: Drie lezingen door Sj. Hoekstra, A. Hijmans en A.A. van Ruler* (Amsterdam: Ten Have, 1949), 51–69, also *ThW VI*, 182–92.

42. See A.A. van Ruler, "De relativering van dood en leven," *Kerk en Theologie* 5 (1954), 65–67.

thought of death became virulent for me. It was already there when I was quite young. This is partly related to the milieu of an orthodox-Reformed [Hervormde] congregation in which I grew up and partly because of my strong philosophical inclination. But before my fortieth year it was more of a theoretical issue from a spectator's point of view. In that period, one lives more towards life. From my fortieth year onwards, the question of death started affecting me personally. Then I started living from life. Seven years ago, I reached rock-bottom: I was powerless and despondent. Bit by bit I crawled some way up the wall. Meanwhile I also had to work through a heart attack. Through all this, I never really panicked. But the shadows of inner despair continued to creep along the walls of my heart. In this situation, one can go one of two ways. First, one may go the way of resignation: this is how life is; finite; true meaning [zin] is not to be found in it. Secondly, one may go the way of faith: an absolute meaning [zin] in life would be a disaster, for we would then be necessary; we are, however, not necessary because 1) the Creator willed us in sovereign freedom, 2) it pleased the Creator that we are there, and 3) because the good Creator in goodness granted us too the pleasure of being there. Then what matters is not that we find meaning [zin] in life rationally, but that we take a liking to it conatively, just as the Creator took a liking to it. That is what I mean when I say that love brings to light the meaning [zin] of life. To use Dostoyevsky's words: we need to love life more than the meaning [zin] of life. So love is: taking a liking to life. Usually I add: there is something that is still higher than love, namely joy. In that lies healing from despair.

You were busy reading a few of my books. In this connection I wish to alert you that a volume entitled "I believe" has just been published.[43] I discuss the twelve articles in it.

With my highest regards
Yours faithfully,

A.A. van Ruler[44]

Van Ruler's lecture thus begins with a remark situated against the background of his own life.

43. This text is included in Volume 5C of Van Ruler's *Verzameld werk* as "Ik geloof: De twaalf artikelen van het geloof in morgenwijdingen," 311–420.
  Editor's note: For an English translation of this text, see A.A. van Ruler, *I Believe*, translated by Garth Hodnett (Bloomington: Xlibris, 2019).
44. This letter is preserved in the Van Ruler archive. Inventory number VI.A, map Rijpkema. The person addressed here is probably Rixtia Bauck Rijpkema (1927–2002).

The essay entitled "Behouden worden of verloren gaan" ("Being Saved or Being Lost") that follows upon this is also published in Van Ruler's *Verzameld werk* for the first time. This is based on a set of notes for a lecture that Van Ruler delivered on Wednesday 2 October 1957 at Voorburg. The audience for whom this was intended is not known. No information in the Van Ruler archive is available in this regard. Given the content of this text, it may well have been prepared for a congregation.

The text "Het leven na de dood" ("Life after Death") dates back to 1958. Van Ruler wrote this text (also not published previously) for a lecture to a circle of Roman Catholic and Protestant thinkers on the estate Dijnselburg te Zeist on Friday 3 January 1958. This manuscript is kept in the Van Ruler archive together with a list of names and addresses of members of this "Circle of Catholics and Protestants". The list includes Van Ruler's name and 23 others. All the Protestants on this list were members of the Nederlandse Hervormde Kerk. There are no members from other Protestant denominations.

It is also striking that, while most of these members were trained theologians, there were also some non-theologians (from the fields of chemistry, philosophy, criminal law, jurisprudence, classical culture and literary studies). Van Ruler probably attended this meeting for the first time on 3 January 1958 when he gave this lecture. I deduce this from the *captatio benevolentiae* with which he commenced: "I am slightly embarrassed to be asked to speak at my first appearance [in this gathering]: makes an immodest impression—do not know exactly what is intended by the topic—do not know how things are done here and what is expected."[45] That did not prevent him from articulating his own view on what is called the "intermediary state" in dogmatics.

4. LATER TEXTS ON ESCHATOLOGY

This volume concludes with six texts on eschatology dating from the 1960s. The first is entitled "De wederkomst van Christus" ("The Parousia of Christ") and consists of previously unpublished notes that Van Ruler used when addressing a "congregation evening" in Delfshaven. The notes comprise the following ten statements:

- Of the last things (the hour of our death—heaven—the last days—the kingdom of glory) we have no clear and complete knowledge.

---

45. See the essay on "Life after Death" in this volume.

- Therefore, these cannot be thought or imagined either.
- But we do speak about them on the basis of Holy Scripture.
- The parousia of Christ goes together with the resurrection of the flesh.
- The parousia of Christ and the resurrection of the flesh also go together with the last judgement.
- The God who is our judge was also our Savior.
- At the same time, the Son returns the kingdom to the Father.
- The core of everything we are to receive we have already received.
- Therefore the parousia of Christ is in a certain sense already there in the present.
- *But*: it is for now in the coils of death.

To each statement are appended some thoughts in point form, that provides a good indication of what Van Ruler offered the audience.

The next essay is entitled "Eschatologische notities" ("Eschatological Notices". Originally this was a lecture that Van Ruler delivered under the title "Bible and Natural Science on the Future" for the fifth congress of the Christelijke Vereniging van Natuur- en Geneeskundigen (Christian Society for Natural and Medical Scientists) in Oosterbeek on 28 October 1961. A few months later the lecture was published in *Geloof en Wetenschap* ("Faith and Science"), the journal of this association.[46] Koos van Doorne (1908–1984), who was arts editor and later the head of art redaction for the daily newspaper *Trouw* responded in this paper:

> It is a crystal clear argument that overcomes cultural pessimism, whether pious or not pious, and in which the author emphasises the eternal significance of culture.

Such an article provides material for twenty sermons. What is surprising is the vision on the role of Europe in history. Van Ruler does not believe in the decline of the West: according to him nothing suggests that. On the contrary: the role of the white race is becoming more important by the hour. If Europe is rejected by God as a leading force, "That we shall then

---

46. A.A. van Ruler, "Bijbel en natuurwetenschap over de toekomst." *Geloof en Wetenschap* 60 (1962), 33–53.

note in due course. But in any case, we should not reject ourselves. For *then* we are in any case rejected by God."[47]

This is a liberating argument that provides transparency, that encourages people to work as hard as they can because they are dealing with God's earth. God promised that God will renew the earth and woe to the one who despises the earth. God, after all, knows not only election but also rejection.[48]

In 1969 Van Ruler decided to publish this essay again in the first volume of his *Theologisch Werk*. However, he changed the title from "Bijbel en natuurwetenschap over de toekomst" ("Bible and natural science on the future") to "Eschatologische notities" ("Eschatological Notices"). Since Van Ruler himself was responsible for the first volume of *Theologisch Werk*, the latter title is given precedence in this volume.

"Grenzen van de eschatologisering" ("Limits to Eschatologizing") is an article written for the journal *Vox Theologica*[49] in which Van Ruler reflects on the theological tendency at that time, influenced especially by Ernst Bloch[50] and Jürgen Moltmann,[51] to employ eschatology as a the methodological point of departure. As the title indicates, Van Ruler was critical of this development. A striking moment in this essay is his reference to a "long-standing conversation" that he has had with Moltmann. Van Ruler and Moltmann had a good personal relationship. That does not imply that they agreed with each other on everything.[52] This article was republished in Volume 4 of Van Ruler's *Theologisch Werk*.[53]

---

47. See Van Ruler's essay on "Eschatological Notices" in this volume.

48. See J. van Doorne, "Nieuwe tijdschriftuur." *Trouw*, 14 April 1962, 15.

49. See A.A. van Ruler, "Grenzen van de eschatologisering." *Vox Theologica* 37 (1967), 167–85.

50. See E. Bloch, *Das Prinzip Hoffnung* (Frankfurt am Main, 1959).

51. See J. Moltmann, *Theologie der Hoffnung: Untersuchungen zur Begründung und zu den Konsequenzen einer christlichen Eschatologie* (München, 1964).

52. On the relationship between Van Ruler en Moltmann, see Dirk van Keulen, "Inleiding," in *Verzameld werk 5A*, 29–34, 73, 78–81; also his "'Wie zwei Hände auf einem Bauch'? Arnold van Ruler und Jürgen Moltmann," in George Harinck and Hans-Georg Ulrichs (eds.), *Naaste verwanten/Nahe Verwandte: Het gereformeerde protestantisme in Nederland en Duitsland in de twintigste eeuw. Kenmerken, betrekkingen, verschillen, wisselwerkingen / Der reformierte Protestantismus in den Niederlanden und in Deutschland im 20. Jahrhundert. Signaturen, Beziehungen, Differenzen, Wechselwirkungen* (Amersfoort: Vuurbaak, 2020), 273–95.

53. A.A. van Ruler, "Grenzen van de eschatologisering," in *ThW IV*, 102–18.

"Christelijke toekomstverwachting: ("The Christian Future Expectation)" was originally a morning devotion for AVRO-radio on 20 July 1967. This brief text was previously published in *Blij zijn als kinderen*.[54]

The essay "Bijbelse toekomstverwachting en aards perspectief" ("Biblical Future Expectations in Earthly Perspective") is far more extensive. The text was used by Van Ruler twice for a lecture for continued theological education for ministers in Hydepark—on 8 October and 12 November 1968. The lecture was published three years later in the second volume of Van Ruler's *Theologisch Werk* that was published in 1971 and thus after Van Ruler's death.

It was difficult to decide on the base text for this volume. There are many differences between the hand-written original and the version published in *Theologisch Werk*. Because it cannot be determined with certainty which of the changes and additions go back to Van Ruler himself,[55] the text of the hand-written original was preferred for the critical edition [the version that is used here]. [Where appropriate] the differences between the two versions are indicated in the annotations.

This volume concludes with an essay "Alle dingen nieuw?" ("All Things New?"). It was published in the journal *Woord en Dienst* on 23 December 1968. Afterwards it was also included in the volumes *Blij zijn als kinderen* and *Van schepping tot koninkrijk*.[56]

---

54. A.A. van Ruler, "Christelijke toekomstverwachting," in *Blij zijn als kinderen: Een boek voor volwassenen* (Kampen: Kok, 1972), 77–79.

55. Van Ruler's posthumous *Theologisch Werk II* does not include a preface where such information may have been provided. It only includes an "In Memoriam" for Van Ruler.

56 .A.A. van Ruler, "Alle dingen nieuw?" in *Woord en Dienst* 17/25 (23 December 1968), 349, also published in *Blij zijn als kinderen: Een boek voor volwassenen* (Kampen, 1972), 147–149; and in *Van schepping tot koninkrijk: Teksten (1947–1970) uit het theologische oeuvre van A.A. van Ruler*, introduced and edited by Gijsbert van den Brink and Dirk van Keulen (Barneveld: Nederlands Dagblad, 2008), 299–302.

God's Law[1]

[1931]

My topic is a curious figure in our modern world.

Let us begin this evening by realizing that fact. That would be of decisive importance for the entire framework and tone of our discussions.

God's law[2]—a curious figure in our modern society, where agrarian and economic and political laws jostle for space, or at least dominate the entire space completely. When, for one moment, we enter into the realities of diplomacy, commerce and agriculture, all of these earthly and human, all too human—then God's law has become a specter.

God's law—a curious figure in our personal lives. We do know about our struggle and our prayers and our responsibility. These are things that lie close at hand, every day. We need only look at one another for a moment and to speak to one another seriously for a moment to know that we are all struggling and praying and responsible human beings. But the more realistically we experience these things, the more God's law becomes a sphinx to us.

For the simple piety, that is on familiar terms with God and that lives by the law that descended from heaven, is no longer ours.

God's law is a curious figure in our modern lives: a specter and a sphinx.

---

1. The inventory number of the Dutch text, "God's Wet" is I,54A. This was a lecture offered for the Delft and Rotterdam sections of the Dutch Christian Student Society (NCSV) on 17 October 1931 at the castle Hardenbroek in Driebergen-Rijsenburg where the rural centre of the NCSV was located. The original consisted of 22 handwritten pages. It was first published in Volume 5C of Van Ruler's *Verzameld werk* (2023), 772–79.

2. Translator's note: This translation follows Van Ruler's inconsistent use of upper case for "law" when referring to God's Law.

And this I mean seriously; it is not merely a rhetorical flourish. For it is indeed a fact that God's law has become a strange figure to us.

So we could very well have started this conference[3] tomorrow morning. Simply skipping this evening. Then, tomorrow and on the next days, we could have spoken about things that we *know* and that lie close to our hearts. About our struggle, And about our prayers. And about our responsibility.

That would not be entirely foolish. We would ever again have to end up with these well-known aspects of our lives. And we also always have to make them our point of departure. We would not be permitted to concern ourselves with illusions. Remain true to the earth.[4] Don't imagine that we can rise above that. Don't imagine that we can have, from personal experience, knowledge of more things than of our struggle and our prayers and our responsibility. Do not imagine that the curious figure can become a member of the household.

So we could very well have started this conference tomorrow morning. Simply skipping this evening.

Still, this evening we have to concern ourselves with this curious figure: God's law.

One thing, however, has now become clear: whatever else it may be, this cannot be a dogmatic exposition in which we speak about God's law as one more "topic" that one can choose to deal with at a conference. In itself, God's law is nothing—a specter and a sphinx. And a dogmatic exposition about it could be a clever intellectual game, but would miss the seriousness of life entirely and would therefore be devoid of value.

This evening can have meaning only if we conduct an investigation into the life known to us in the light of God's presence. In this case: when we ask how God's law sheds its light on our struggle and our prayers and our responsibility.

Therefore, this evening and throughout this conference and as NCSV, we take as our point of departure the presupposition that our lives in struggle and prayer and responsibility do not unfold just as it seems, but that they are, in some or other way, governed by God's law.

That is a presupposition to which we subject our reflection on the other topics. That is the novelty, the "Christian," if you wish, that lends

---

3. No further information on this conference is available.

4. This is probably a reference to Friedrich Nietzsche's *Also sprach Zarathustra* (Zarathustra's Vorrede 3). Van Ruler would have used Friedrich Nietzsche, *Aldus sprak Zarathoestra: Een boek voor allen en voor niemand* (Amsterdam s.a.), 27.

a unique quality to our discussions and to our lives. But in this way too, precisely in this way—as presupposition of everything else—our topic remains a curious figure—God's law never becomes a part of our lives that we can know just as we know other fragments and that we can deal with: we remain true to the earth. But in the light that God's law sheds on our naked lives.

Thus I have no firm ground under my feet this evening: not in my specific topic—which does not lend itself to that—nor in other topics—which I may not approach. All that is left to me is this: to reflect on the presupposition of our discussion as presupposition. That is, nothing but this: *to provide an introduction to this conference.*

First I wish to make three formal comments about God's law in which I attempt to determine, each time positively and negatively, its meaning for our lived reality as we know it and will discuss during the course of this conference.

God's law as presupposition of our lives: that means in the first place that we are dealing with God.

That, of course, is a simple truth. But a truth that we ever again have to become aware of. And that is, in all its simplicity, neither self-evident nor in itself clear.

It is not self-evident that we are dealing with God. When we observe our lives and our world soberly and honestly, we do not see much of God. Laplace was correct when he said that he had searched through the entire world and had found God nowhere.[5] And modern philosophy is correct when it believes that it can, in principle, understand the human being without God. For it is not self-evident that we are dealing with God.

We do indeed struggle about God. To that the struggle of our lives bears witness. But who guarantees us that we are not struggling with a phantom?

And we do indeed pray to God. But who guarantees us that our prayers are not to the unknown God[6] who may or, equally easily, may not exist? It is a simple truth that we are dealing with God. But not a self-evident truth.

---

5. Pierre-Simon Laplace (1749–1827), French mathematician and astronomer. Van Ruler refers to a widely cited incident (the exact source is unclear), where Napoleon asked Laplace around 1802 why there is no reference to God in his five-volume *Celestial Mechanics*. Laplace allegedly responded that he had found no need of that hypothesis.

6. See Acts 17:23.

When we dare, nevertheless, to see God's law as presupposition to our lives, then we dare to say that we are dealing with God.

That is, that there is something more than our lives. That there is more than our society. And more than our world. That there is God. That we are not alone. That we stand before God. In our whole lives.

And with this I come to the second aspect of the simple truth that we are dealing with God. It is also not in itself clear.

For what would it mean that we stand before God's face in our lived reality? For now, I wish to say only this: God's law is the meaning of our lives. That we are not alone but are standing before God; that our life's journey takes place before the face of God—that, and only that, can give meaning to our lives.

And God's law is the seriousness of our lives. It subjects our lives to God's criticism, to God's judgement. The end of our life's journey is the day of Judgement. And that makes our lives such a serious matter.

That, too, is the positive side to my first formal comment about God's law in its meaning for our lives: it is the meaning and seriousness of our lives. It sets us, just as we are in the multi-faceted reality of life, before the face of God. We are not alone. But stand before God.

Thus—and this is the negative side—in God's law we are not dealing with a system of ethical norms or, to put it less grandly, with a list of precepts and commandments. Neither Moses, nor the Sermon on the Mount, nor our conscience places God's law in our hands in such a way that we could know that we should do this and that to live according to God's law. That is not what it is about in God's law. On the contrary. A system of moral norms, a list of precepts and commandments, is precisely the opposite of God's law. Because: "for ethics God is a means to an end, also when the end is described as the kingdom of God!" (O. Reinhold).[7] God's law constantly places humanity before the face of God. Ethics elevates humanity above the momentary into the future in which the ideal has been realized, that is to say, into the supra-temporal. Ethics draws humans away from Godself and isolates them abstractly.

And therefore: God's law as presupposition of our lives—that means, in the first place that we are dealing with God, with Godself, and not with a system of ethical norms.

---

7. Otto Reinhold (1890–1971), German Lutheran pastor, member of the Confessing Church, imprisoned in 1941. The source of this quotation is Otto Reinhold, "Anmerkungen zur christlichen Ethik, 1. Teil," in *Zwischen den Zeiten: Eine Zweimonatsschrift* 8 (1930), 73. Van Ruler added the exclamation mark.

That automatically leads me to my second formal comment. God's law as presupposition of our lives: that means, in the second place that we are dealing with God because Godself took the initiative and tackled us in the reality of our lives.

God's law constantly places humans before God's face.

We do not merely struggle about God—we say that we have reached God, that we stand before God in our entire lives.

We do not merely pray to God—we say that God hears us and that we are in conversation with God, that we are close to God in our entire lives.

We are not dealing with a system of ethical norms, with an ideal that has to be realized—we say that we are dealing with Godself, in whom all ideals are realities.

We say all this. And we have to say it this evening. Even if tomorrow and the next day we speak only about our struggle and our prayers and our responsibility. This evening we are speaking of much greater things.

That, however, does not mean that we have found God, but that God has found us in God's law. That is, it not we who have started a conversation with God, but that God has opened a conversation with us in God's law.

That, again, is the positive side to my second comment. This great certainty, that God took the initiative, that God has laid hands on us, that God has tackled us. That God is the Lord who has made us God's servants.

And the negative side resides in this, that we are not dealing with the fabrications of our puny thoughts, with the God of the philosophers, but with the God of revelation.

Not with the God of the philosophers. Philosophy, our puny thoughts, our cutting and joining, always takes the path from below to above, from humanity to God. And at the end of this path stand our representations of God, the images we create of the origin of our lives.

But we are not dealing with that if God's law is the presupposition of our lives. Then we are dealing with Godself, who has taken the path from above to below, has descended to us. God has reached us instead of our having reached God.

It is not with the God of the philosophers that we are dealing but with the God of revelation, the God who is Lord of our lives through God's law

God's law is the Law of the God of revelation. And therefore: God's law as presupposition of our lives means, in the third place, that we are dealing with the living-God-in-God's-revelation as the saving God.

With this we reach an extremely important idea.

This idea: that the duality of Law and gospel is no definitive duality.

Law and gospel—both belong within the single revelation of God. The Law too. Therefore it is not the case that the Law is an entity that we know from within ourselves and that only the gospel is that which has to come to us from the outside—in divine revelation—but it is the case that God's self-revelation comprises both Law and gospel.

And therefore they belong together. Therefore, too, they both have the same intent. They are one in the God who saves us. In God's law, God intends our salvation [heil]. God is not only the Lord of our lives. God is also the Savior. Just as it stands in our mission statement: as Lord and as Savior. The God of Sinai is not a different God from the God of Bethlehem. The ten commandments are—correctly seen—ten promises, in which God promises us God's salvation [heil].

We are dealing with a saving God. Also when God reveals to us God's law, thereby placing us in the light of God's presence. Then, too, God is the saving God who works our rescue, our salvation [heil],[8] who personally accomplishes God's will, God's law.

In dogmatics the law is discussed in two ways. On the one hand, as tutor [leading us] to Christ, on the other hand, as rule for the Christian life of gratitude. The center remains: salvation [heil] in Christ. The center of the Law is the gospel. The Law issues in the gospel. And the Law takes it departure from the gospel. The duality of Law and gospel can thus never be a definitive one. They are both encapsulated in God's self-revelation to us. And both intend our salvation [heil]. In the Law (and with that also: in the gospel) we are dealing with the living-God-in-God's-Revelation as the saving God.

This positive side to my third formal comment has to be expounded in more detail.

But first I oppose it to the negative side. If it is true that God's law *with* God's gospel is comprehended in God's one revelation and that

---

8. Editor's note: The term "heil" is translated here as "salvation"—which is the more typical translation. The Dutch "heil" is etymologically linked to "wholeness" and "healing." For Van Ruler, "verlossing" (salvation, redemption) is clearly not an aim in itself. One may argue that "heil" as wholeness or well-being (see also the Latin *salus*) is the aim of God's work of salvation although Van Ruler does not use the term heil consistently.

[God's law], with the gospel, intends our salvation [heil] and thus ever again finds its center in the gospel, in the salvation [heil] in Christ—then we are dealing with the saving God and not with a legalistic Christianity. Also not when we ask after the meaning of God's law for our lives.

We can live within a legalistic Christianity in two ways.

On the one hand, we can understand Christianity from the outset as law. Then it has brought specific principles into the world, which bring specific demands in their train. And then faith is from a to z taking account of and applying these principles and demands.

On the other hand, we can also live within a legalistic Christianity by adding to an ossified, dogmatic faith an equally ossified legalistic life of gratitude. Then we cling to the atonement of our sins through Christ as to a fixed dogma and demand, as a matter of gratitude, the keeping of various commandments. "This I have done for you; what are you doing for Me?"

In both cases we have to speak of a legalistic Christianity. And both conceptions of Christianity stand condemned by our previous insight, that the law finds its center in the gospel, that we are thus dealing with a saving God.

We should therefore also take care with the term "demands of Christianity". For the God of revelation is a living God, who does not leave it at demands, but works, is active, is in the process of saving us.

So we are dealing with Godself, with the living God, with the saving God—and not with ethics, also not with philosophy, and also not with a legalistic Christianity.

The duality of Law and gospel is not definitive—with that my formal comments pass into material ones. Because now we can say something about the content of God's law.

The content of God's law is the salvation [heil] in Christ.

This we now wish to expound in more detail in three comments.

The content of God's law is the salvation [heil] in Christ. And as such it is the presupposition of our lives.

That means, in the first place, that in our lives we can no longer escape from the cross. The cross of Christ is the summary of the gospel. Erected through God's saving act in Christ, it stands as the sign in which we attain bliss. The cross is the place where humanity has been brought back to God and placed before the face of God. That is the gospel. But that is at the same time the Law.

It is the promise that we receive. It is also the demand to which we are subjected.

The cross as content of the gospel does not remain standing at a great distance from us, but imposes itself in our lives as Law, as imitation of Christ.

Therefore we cannot escape from the cross in our lives.

And to be cross-bearer, that is: to be broken, no longer to grasp at the absolutes or just to lay hands on it: no longer just to enter into world peace along with pacifism, and no longer just to attain the ideal state along with socialism, and no longer just to be satisfied along with conservatism, and no longer to build your life into a harmonious whole. In the cross our will is broken. That is our salvation. Because the distress of human beings, and their sin, resides in their imposing themselves, in their maintaining themselves. The saving God, with whom we are dealing in the Law and gospel, strikes us at exactly this point.

The content of God's law is the salvation [heil] in Christ. And as such it is the presupposition of our lives.

That means, in the second place, that we can no longer escape from our neighbor in our lives. This too is promise *and* demand, gospel *and* Law. Also promise, also gospel. Because to acknowledge our neighbor is not in the first place our duty, but, before anything else: our salvation.

The neighbor in the sense of the gospel is not simply this or that person with whom we come into contact by chance, and the neighbor— that is also not all people. The neighbor—that is the person in whom God encounters us, in whom God has descended to us in such a way that God is now right next to us. Of course, we meet this person by chance. But that is not what is essential. What is essential is that we may recognize that God has placed this person in our way.

And that is why the neighbor means, before anything else, our salvation. God has now become more than we might well have wished. In any case: we are now standing right in front of the person. In the neighbor God has tackled us. God is the living God, who took the initiative and placed the neighbor opposite us.

And that is obviously also Law. The promise, the grace, constantly acts in the guise of the demand so that we may take it seriously. Whoever wishes to understand what God's law really is clings to the neighbor. To talk about it is useless; only actively acknowledging the neighbor can help us.

The content of God's law is the salvation [heil] in Christ. And as such it is the presupposition of our lives.

That means in the third place that we can no longer escape reality in our lives.

That God in Christ has descended into our lived reality, that fact binds us, as Law and as gospel, to this lived reality itself.

Human beings are, outside of God's law and God's gospel, wanderers and philosophers. As wanderers they constantly strive to transcend the boundaries of their lives and, negating the immediate reality within which they stand, to dwell in the world of their endless longing. As philosophers they wish to transform the world in which they stand into ideas and thoughts in order to penetrate and grasp it in this way.

God, however, has judged the wanderer and the philosopher in the incarnation of the Word. God has not entered into the world of fantasy nor into the world of the idea, but into the world of concrete reality: God became human.[9]

That is the gospel, because we are now saved from our angst over the reality of the world. That is Law, because we are now constantly subjected to discipline whenever we once more wish to flee, as wanderers and philosophers, from our existence.

And our lived reality—that we all know. And what it implies to be bound to it—that we all know.

So is proves to be a simple truth indeed that we have to deal with God, with Godself, in our lives.

The cross, the neighbor, reality—with these God's law, in its fixed relationship to God's gospel, is described according to its content.

Allow me now to conclude by trying, in a few words, to draw a link between this evening's topic and what we shall be discussing tomorrow and the day after.

We have actually already arrived at the familiar things of our lives, at our struggle and our prayers and our responsibility. The incarnation of the Word bound us to these things as *the* realities of our existence.

What, then, is the light that God's law sheds on our naked lives?

Of our struggle we shall now have to speak as the deed of our lives, in which we constantly recognize the cross and the neighbor and reality. The struggle has become deed! It has become victory! For when God's law is the presupposition of our struggle—then we struggle before the

---

9. See John 1:14.

face of the living, the saving God, in whom we are more than conquerors.[10] And of our prayers we shall now have to speak as of the subjection and the worship in which we give God God's due as Lord and Savior of our lives. For when God's law is the presupposition of our prayers—then our prayers have become an answer to God's Word in law and gospel that teaches us to bow.

The deed of our lives and our prayers—these two belong together. In both of these God's law is fulfilled.

And now we shall have to speak of our responsibility as our bondedness. When God's law, in its strict relationship to God's gospel, is the presupposition of our lives, then responsibility is transformed into bondedness. Then we are bound to God and the neighbor. That is the sense of the familiar words of the catechism that it is impossible for those who have been incorporated into Christ in sincere faith not to bear the fruit of gratitude.[11]

That is the light that God's law sheds on our lives. And with that the topics of tomorrow and the next day have been introduced. What else have I really done but argue that the things that will be addressed in them can be tackled only in faith?

God's Law calls for faith that acts through love!

---

10. See Romans 8:37.
11. See Answer 64 of the *Heidelberg Catechism*.

Kingdom of God and Church[1]
[1941]

THE QUESTION ABOUT THE relationship between the kingdom of God and the church is of crucial importance for the ecumenical issue in the broadest sense.

Is the ecclesial accent inherent in the ecumenical idea? Can we speak of a full-fledged re-unification of the churches if Christians find one another in attitude, shared Christian reflection and activity, and shared communion? What space should be reserved for dogma, liturgy, ecclesial polity and church formation in the ecumenical quest?

Once one comes to realize that a sociological motivation of the ecumenical idea, in which "ecumenical" can be translated as "international," is most definitely inadequate, these questions immediately arise.

And once one has further realized that any parallelizing of kingdom of God and the church as two comparable entities, whether coordinated or antithetical, is most definitely in opposition to the basic relationship in biblical thought, one can no longer avoid the ecclesial accent in the ecumenical quest. After all, one can then no longer escape from the fragmentation of the churches and pass over to the parallel concept of the kingdom. Therefore, I regard it as the negative aim of this essay to show that any parallelizing of the two entities as two territories is untenable. And I am of the opinion that one can desire ecumenicity *only* if one has

---

1. The inventory number of the Dutch text, "Koninkrijk Gods en Kerk" is I,155. This was originally a lecture for a convent of active and retired ministers in Hilversum on 3 June 1941. The original lecture is lost. It was first published in the journal *Onder Eigen Vaandel* 16 (1941), 268–86 and was included in Volume 5C of Van Ruler's *Verzameld werk* (2023), 780–98. The footnotes numbered in square brackets in this essay were included by Van Ruler himself in *Onder Eigen Vaandel* and are maintained in the style of the original. Other notes are by Dirk van Keulen, the editor of Van Ruler's *Verzameld werk* or, where indicated, by the editor or translator.

the fragmentation of the churches vividly in one's view and then constantly directs all attention to it.

And, in the third place, one should realize that precisely the idea of the kingdom brings about a considerable reduction in the conception of the church: from the *ecclesia triumphans* to the *ecclesia militans*;[2] within the *ecclesia militans* a reduction of the *ecclesia invisibilis* to the *ecclesia visibilis*;[3] within the *ecclesia visibilis* a reduction both of the *Gemeinschaft* idea and the *Anstalt* idea,[4] both of the church as organism and of the church as institute, to the idea of the sign, and with that, highly soberly, the wonder of the highly visible and highly earthly and highly palpable church is incorporated into the series of wonders of Jesus as signs of the kingdom. Then one can, in the first place, not isolate or absolutize the idea of community as opposed to the institutional character of the church to such an extent that that one can be satisfied with the re-uniting of Christians while neglecting the fragmentation of the church organizations. And then one cannot, in the second place, establish such a gradation in the series sacrament—dogma—liturgy—offices that one would value, for instance, the shared communion so highly that, in the process, the question of the re-uniting of the offices would disappear from view as mere human bungling.[5] In the isolating of the idea of community as the true essence of the visible church, the danger of sliding into sociology constantly lurks. In the absolutizing of the sacraments as the essence of the institutional, visible church the no less significant danger of sliding into nature mysticism constantly lurks. And the beneficial effect of the idea of the kingdom on the idea of the church is precisely that it demotes both the communal gathering and the sacrament to mere signs, though they be signs given by God in Christ. And within the field of signs the offices also stand, and with that ecclesial polity, and with that also the liturgy, and finally the dogma. There is obviously gradation in this. But not a gradation from the divine to the human, not even a gradation from the essential to the accidental, but rather a gradation from the central to the peripheral (the gradation being more of an ordering), and then in such a way that the periphery still belongs to the field of the signs as such. For

---

2. *Ecclesia triumphans*: Church triumphant; *ecclesia militans*: church militant.

3. *Ecclesia invisibilis*: Invisible church; *ecclesia visibilis*: visible church.

4. The source of Van Ruler's distinction between *Anstalt* (organization) and *Gemeinschaft* (community) is unknown.

5. Translator's note: In the Dutch the paragraph up to here is a single sentence of 345 words. Breaking it up required some minor changes.

instance, the statement that the offices have been given by Christ cannot be abandoned.

And it is obvious that these matters within the ecumenical quest are significantly more urgent in the national context than in the international context. The issue of the offices, for instance, disturbs the catholicity of the church significantly less when it concerns [the relationship between] the Nederlands Hervormde Kerk[6] and the Anglican Church in England than when it concerns [the relationship between] Nederlands Hervormde Kerk and the Gereformeerde Kerken, the Gereformeerde Kerken in Hersteld Verband and the Christelijke Gereformeerde Kerk.[7] In the latter relationship, we simply may not trivialize this issue. We would then, in our striving for ecumenicity, be combatting only the consequences of the evil and not the evil itself in its origin.

※

I believe that with these observations it has been adequately shown what the link is between our topic and the urgent question concerning the reunification of the churches. But I believe we would do well, before we examine our topic in more detail, to expand our field of vision somewhat by pointing to a few more links.

The relationship between the kingdom of God and the church is of crucial importance not only for the relationship between church and churches, but also for the relationship between church and world. This theme too I take in the broadest sense of the word. I am thinking, for instance, of the relationship of church and state, of church and school, of church and society. Once more, the fundamental question here is: Is it not merely possible but is it the normal course of events that the kingdom of God has yet another form [gestalte] on this earth, apart from its form [gestalte] in the church? How far does the radius of the church's action in the life of the world extend? And which forces of the kingdom are revealed within this radius of action? And are there still other forces of the kingdom that are not included within this radius of action but are nevertheless revealed? And how, then, do the specific form of the kingdom in the world and the form of the church relate to each other? Does

---

6. Editor's note: Van Ruler was a member of this church.

7. Editor's note: Van Ruler is naming distinct denominations, all falling within the Reformed tradition, that existed in the Netherlands at that time. His audience would have been very familiar with these denominations and the complex history behind that.

the kingdom proceed from the church? Does the kingdom encompass the church? Does the kingdom stand next to the church, without any immediate relationship? Does the kingdom stand in opposition to the church? According to how we answer these questions, we would have to conceive, for instance, the relationship between church and state. Does the church have a word *to* the state or do Christians have a word *for* the state? Should the state see the church in its completely unique character as divine-human body of Christ or is it sufficient that the state grant the church ample freedom, perhaps together with "other" moral bodies? Is, theologically speaking, the state there for the sake of the church or is the church there for the sake of the state? In the practical tussle between church and state, is it better that the church should draw within its sphere as much as possible (the youth, the school, etc.), or is it better that the state should conceive its task as going beyond the political? Is the duality of church and state an opposition or a division of labor? The answers to all these questions are in practice determined by the view we have of the relationship between the kingdom of God and the church.

And grouped around all this, there are still other questions that fall under the heading: the idea of a Christian culture. Is there alongside and around the dogma of the church a separate intellectual form of the kingdom in a Christian science? And is there alongside and around the liturgy a separate aesthetic form of the kingdom in Christian art? What sense would it have to found a Christian Scout movement? What is a Christian secondary school?[8]

So one can go on. Finally, one comes to the great theme of ethics, Christian life, the doctrine of sanctification. Can one set up more than one sign in one's Christian life and can one realize eternal life? And can one, in setting up signs, ever reach beyond Sunday's church attendance and the celebration of the Lord's Supper?

⁂

Actually, it is far from surprising that the decisive meaning of our topic extends itself so endlessly far. It is, not merely in a fundamental sense but also in a historical sense, an age-old problem. It already appears in the Bible.

---

8. Editor's note: Here Van Ruler is engaging critically with some tenets in neo-Calvinism. See also his reference to Abraham Kuyper in the text below.

For, on the one hand, we must firmly maintain that the preaching of God's kingdom is characteristic of Christianity in the biblical sense. In the gospels, Jesus' preaching of the kingdom of God or the kingdom of heaven is patently central. And, on careful scrutiny, it is no different in the letters of the apostles. Without doubt the apostles express themselves in different terms, at least mostly (for the word βασιλεία[9] is not confined to the synoptic gospels), but what is expressed in these different terms is in essence precisely the same as that which Jesus mostly captures in the word kingdom.[10] Therefore it is simply nineteenth-century myopia to discover, even in a single respect, an opposition between, for instance, Jesus' teaching and the Paulinian. And once we have been completely freed from this myopia, we have to say that the Old Testament, yet again and, in the full sense, though in different forms, deals with the same things. The categories, not in the formal-logical but in the material-theological sense, [namely,] of the fundamental relationships in the structure, remain the same throughout the entire Bible. We may as well say that, in spite of the vast difference in linguistic forms and in spite of the endless variation of accents and facets, the biblical witness constitutes a unity. And we can fittingly summarize this unity of content, at least of essence, in the idea of the kingdom of God.

But, on the other hand, we must equally firmly maintain that we cannot expunge from the biblical witness those elements that at first glance appear erratic. [These include] Word and people, witness and sacrament, confession and church discipline, divine service and offices, as givens that are on earth but that have been chosen, that is, chosen to be bearers on earth of the idea, the proclamation, the expectation and the reality of the kingdom. And these givens together constitute what may be called, in one word taken from the many words of the biblical witness, kāhāl-*ecclesia*, and what has become consolidated in history as the church of Christ.

In addition, the church then no longer seems to be an erratic entity within the preaching of the kingdom except at first glance. It is already an unbiblical misunderstanding of the idea of the kingdom when we

---

9. Βασιλεία: Kingdom.

10. [1] See K.L. Schmidt, "Die Wortgruppe βασιλεία κτλ. im NT." In *ThWNT*, *Band 1*, 584: "[...] that the kingdom of God implies the whole of the preaching of Jesus and His Apostles."

Translator's note: All translations of Schmidt in this essay follow the rather free translation of G.W. Bromiley.

think [that] we see that. In the biblical sense, the kingdom of God and the church belong together as self-evidently as divine patience and divine election do. It is true what Chantepie de la Saussaye[11] stated[12]—that the idea of the kingdom gives Christian faith an Israelite character in that it is drenched with the strong, dynamic vision that the final and highest reality is not Being [zijn] but a living, acting Person. But it is equally true that precisely the Israelite character of the idea of the kingdom can be protected only by the no less Israelite idea of the elected people of God as sign, guarantee, promise and bearer of the kingdom. [That is so] in the sense that even the fully sincere participation of one elected individual in the salvation [heil] of the kingdom is not the matter [zaak] itself, not even in a partial sense, but merely a sign of the matter, namely, that the kingdom shall come over all flesh. Without this idea of the church, the kingdom is once more stabilized in some or other form, robbed of its strictly dynamic, divine character, made static in an earthly-human dynamics, in a word, secularized. Undoubtedly the opposite can also be adduced, namely, that the election and sign character of the church can be protected only by the idea of the kingdom. Once the church is no longer oriented to the kingdom, it no longer consents to be *pars pro toto*, it flees from the eschatological perspective, it transmutes the promise into reality, it no longer understands itself as sign but as the matter [zaak] itself. Expressed in an exaggerated way, the kingdom without the church becomes history and the church without the kingdom becomes myth, while according to biblical categories the case is this: the kingdom is myth and the church is history.

※

In this way, some probability has been given to my negative statement, namely, that the kingdom of God and the church may in no way be parallelized, not in a coordinating nor in an antithetic sense. The kingdom of God may therefore not be seen as either standing *alongside* or standing *opposite* to the church. And after what has been said, it is surely obvious that, apart from this parallelizing, every identification should also be

11. Daniël Chantepie de la Saussaye (1818–1874), professor of theology in Groningen (1872–1874). Here Van Ruler draws on a quotation by Gerardus van der Leeuw (one of Van Ruler's teachers in Groningen), included in "Koninkrijk Gods en geschiedenis," in *Het oecumenische gesprek der Kerken* ('s-Gravenhage, s.a.), 103.

12. [2] Quoted by Dr. G. van der Leeuw, "Koninkrijk Gods en geschiedenis," in *Het oecumenische gesprek der Kerken*, 's-Gravenhage s.a. [1939], 103.

rejected. Neither the Roman Catholic idea that the kingdom of God is the *church* nor the sectarian idea that the church is the *kingdom of God*, does justice to the remarkable biblical tense, yet at the same time completely self-evident duality of the two figures. Should we wish to formulate this duality in more detail, we would have to say that it involves a relationship of relativity, of mutual involvement, that is on the one hand strongly perspectival and on the other strongly centric. By this I mean that the kingdom of God and church are never two forms [gestalten], entities, equivalent spheres, that can stand alongside or opposite each other, that can be compared to each other. Nevertheless, they are not one and the same so that that they can in some or other way be equated with each other. They stand in relationship to each other. The church is oriented to the kingdom. And the kingdom is oriented to the church. But not, in the two instances, in an identical sense. The church is oriented to the kingdom in a perspectival sense [zin]: the church here and now lives solely from the kingdom as perspective. That is the great light. And the kingdom is oriented to the church in a centric sense [zin]: the kingdom here and now lives solely in the center of the church. That is the great darkness. The church expects the kingdom. And the kingdom is present in the church in a hidden way. The secret of this duality lies in the great problem of pneumatology: the relationship between eschatology and election.

❦

The time is now steadily approaching for us to examine the question: What, in the last instance, should we understand by "the kingdom of God"?

Over the course of time, several questions have emerged around this question that have, in my view, all fallen short of reaching the heart of the matter in their posing of the question.

I am thinking, for instance, of the issue of kingship and kingdom. The word מַלְכוּת and also the word βασιλεία undoubtedly have, purely philologically, this double meaning in that they indicate, on the one hand, the status, the dignity, the authority of being king, and, on the other hand, the territory, the realm, over which the rule is exercised. In a word such as earldom we still discern this double meaning quite clearly: first, being earl and secondly the territory over which one is earl.[13] It is my opinion that

---

13. Translator's note: Van Ruler's example does not work perfectly in English, since "earldom" as "the status of being earl" is no longer in use.

we should not pay that much attention to this matter when we are dealing with an approach to the meaning of the expression "kingdom of God." It seems to me that, whatever solution ones comes up with, its application to the biblical-theological concept "kingdom of God" inevitably leads to a secularization of the concepts. [In one case it leads to] ethicizing and mysticizing (if the first meaning is chosen), [in the other] to ontologizing (when both meanings together are chosen). In that a radiation of the transcending content of the concept is already evident.

I am also thinking of the even more famous question: present or future? Twenty or thirty years ago, this question played an enormous role in theological discussions. *Is* the kingdom here or is it *coming*? This question is not as completely inadequate as the previous one when it comes to finding the biblical-theological sense [zin] of the concept. One can certainly not restrict oneself to saying that the kingdom is there. The Bible, also in its specifically New Testament parts, or rather, particularly in them, is too full of eschatological expectations to allow that. One can, however, just as little restrict oneself to saying that the kingdom is coming. The Bible, also in its specifically Old Testament parts, or rather, precisely in them, knows too much of the present reality of salvation [heil]. In this case, however, one can combine the two solutions and say that the kingdom is and is coming. And in that we then have a lovely paradox that mirrors the true characteristic of the kingdom beautifully. This characteristic I would then find in this definition: The kingdom is soteriological-eschatological in nature. When we pray in one prayer: "Thy kingdom come," *and*, "For thine *is* the kingdom," then exactly the same kingdom is meant in both cases. And that in both cases not only the same noun but actually also the same verb is meant, is expressed in highly compressed form in the almost untranslatable idea that the kingdom has "come near", with which this duality is brought under one heading. For the rest, we can safely state that we have advanced very little by means of this contrast, so that we may calmly let it go again.

In the third place, following K.L. Schmidt,[14] I draw attention to the remarkable fact that even the New Testament, in which the concept plays such an important role, is extremely sparing in attaching attributive or

---

14. Karl Ludwig Schmidt (1891–1956), German New Testament scholar who helped to establish the school of form criticism. He was a professor in Gießen, Jena and Bonn before he was removed from his position by the National Socialists in 1933. He then became a professor in New Testament studies in Basel (1935–1953).

predicative qualifiers to the kingdom of God.¹⁵ Schmidt mentions as attributive qualifiers only ἀσάλευτος (immovable), ἐπουράνιος (heavenly) and αἰώνιος (eternal) and as predicative qualifiers the comments that the kingdom, apart from being of God, is also of people, but then of those who are poor (of spirit) and persecuted (for righteousness' sake). The qualification "of heaven" can obviously be ignored, since has to be interpreted in the light of the late-Jewish use of "heaven" to avoid using God's name.¹⁶ This restraint in the further qualification [of the kingdom] is undoubtedly of great theological importance. It sets a boundary in the face of all immanentist misunderstandings of the concept. It also sets a guard against detaching the idea of the kingdom of God from the whole of the biblical witness and then using it as a manageable ideal in complete solitude, or rather, in extremely worldly company. All I wish to say is that, in the light of this restraint in characterizing [the kingdom], it is at best senseless to separate this idea of the kingdom of God from the strictly christological meaning of the New Testament, of the epistles *and of* the gospels. *If* our conscious thinking demands further fleshing out of this idea, it has to come from the context in which it occurs. And then one can reduce the matter quite simply to one formulation: The kingdom of God = the salvation [heil] in Christ.

❧

And with this I have come to the true core—the positive thesis that I would wish to defend. The kingdom of God = the salvation [heil] in Christ.

As proof of this thesis, I draw attention to the following points.

In the first place, I draw attention to the exorbitantly large place that the miracles occupy in the gospels, both quantitatively and qualitatively. Together with the words of Jesus and then obviously also the history of his suffering, death and resurrection, the miracle stories all but *fill* the gospels. And this in the closest possible relationship to the preaching of the kingdom. They are the illustration of this preaching; they are the demonstration of the kingdom itself. Not its realization. The kingdom itself is realized in the resurrection. But definitely the demonstration of it in the sense that flashes of the eternal light and of the eternal life that

---

15. [3] See K.L. Schmidt, "Die Wortgruppe βασιλεύς κτλ. im NT," 583.

16. Van Ruler derives this conclusion from K.L. Schmidt, "Die Wortgruppe βασιλεύς κτλ. im NT," 583.

commences with the resurrection even now—in the miracles—shoots through the darkness of this world. Now then, if it is true that it is precisely in the miracles that the kingdom is at present the most visible and real, then that already indicates the soteriological character of the kingdom, here specifically directed at the bodily side of life (but in the biblical sense bodiliness is indeed the essence of being human). And simultaneously with that the eschatological character of the kingdom is indicated, because [in the Bible] it remains, after all, a matter of a few miracles. Together they do not constitute the healing of the world, but merely delineate the field of signs that in themselves point beyond themselves. The kingdom is a salvation [heil] that is coming and is extremely close [to us].

In the second place, I point out that it is impossible to draw the kingdom of Christ and the kingdom of God apart in the New Testament witness—both figures are explicitly discussed.[17] Perhaps Old Testament studies have reason to find it difficult[18] to combine the two figures of the Messianic kingdom and the kingdom of Yahweh—I do not presume to pronounce any judgement about that, though it seems to me that Old Testament scholars need only push their way through a thin partition to reach the true, that is, the christological, meaning of the texts in this case too.[19] But in the New Testament it can very clearly be shown that there is mention of the intertwining and even the identity of the kingdom of God and of God's Christ. Well then, both the fact that there is mention also of the kingdom of Christ and the fact that it is one and the same as the kingdom of God indicate that it is simply to bypass the texts to seek the link between the kingdom and Jesus Christ only in the fact that Jesus is the bearer—or, even more meagerly—the preacher of the kingdom. I know that a number of further problems for New Testament studies are located here. Briefly formulated: "The fact that Jesus is king raises the question in what the Messiahship of Jesus consists."[20] But it is more than a New Testament problem; it is the dogmatic problem par excellence. Here indeed lies the great question of human life *qua talis*: What do you think

---

17. Van Ruler regarded the *regnum Christi* (the kingdom of Christ) as a modality of the *regnum Dei* (the kingdom of God). For cross-references to literature in Dutch, see Van Ruler's *Verzameld werk 5C*, 716, note 19.

18. [4] See G. von Rad, "'מֶלֶךְ und מַלְכוּת im AT." In *ThWNT, Band 1*, 566-67.

19. [5] Perhaps this pushing through the partition is reserved for the preaching in the congregation, in which case the preaching would then be more scientific, that is, more committed to the subject matter [zaak] that is at stake, than Old Testament studies itself.

20. [6] K.L. Schmidt, "Die Wortgruppe βασιλεύς κτλ. im NT," 578, 581-82.

of the Christ?[21] And from a New Testament perspective, everything is relatively clear here as well.

In the third place, I draw attention to the extremely rich network of synonyms in which the word βασιλεία occurs in the New Testament. I draw attention to: δικαιοσύνη, εἰρήνη, χαρά, παλιγγενεσία, σωτηρία, δύναμις, ἐξουσία, δόξα, ἐπιφάνεια, χάρις, ἐπαγγελία, ζωή, γνῶσις.[22] "In all these synonyms we may see that the concern of the βασιλεία as God's action towards men is soteriological."[23] Of course, we cannot say that all the cited concepts are completely subsumed under the concept βασιλεία. But, as opposed to the isolating and abstracting that is usually applied to the concept [βασιλεία], it is, nevertheless, of extraordinarily great importance to discover, first, that in Scripture the figure βασιλεία is effortlessly inserted in these series of words and functions excellently in this company, and, secondly, that the word [βασιλεία] is also, without more ado, used promiscuously with various of these words. And now it is surely beyond doubt that with these other words the New Testament intends to outline all the moments within the whole of the gifts and treasures that we have received in Christ. All these things, the peace, the joy, the liberation, the power, the glory, the revelation, the life, the knowledge, the righteousness, and together with that the kingdom, have come in Christ. It is particularly on the basis of this New Testament synonymics that I pose the following thesis: the kingdom of God = the salvation [heil] in Christ. One does well to relativize the word "kingdom of God" in this context, thereby robbing it of the fetish character through which it hypnotizes everyone, by considering that it too is merely a word, an image, just as all other words in their biblical usage. And, moreover, that in this case [we are dealing] with a way of speaking that was borrowed from the late-Jewish apocalyptic and the rabbis, even if its roots lie in Israelite prophecy.[24] We can undoubtedly speak of divine primordial words. In doing so, however, we must bear in mind that Scripture does not take up a single word from the treasury of the human vocabulary that Scripture does not drop again. And we must continually bear in mind that

---

21. See Matthew 22:42.

22. Δικαιοσύνη: Righteousness / justice; εἰρήνη: peace; χαρά: joy; παλιγγενεσία: regeneration; σωτηρία: saving / deliverance; δύναμις: power; ἐξουσία: authority; δόξα: glory; ἐπιφάνεια: epiphany / revelation; χάρις: grace; ἐπαγγελία: promise; ζωή: life; γνῶσις: insight, knowledge.

23. [7] See K.L. Schmidt, "Die Wortgruppe βασιλεύς κτλ. im NT," 583, 584.

24. [8] See K.L. Schmidt, "Die Wortgruppe βασιλεύς κτλ. im NT," 585.

Scripture promptly places each word that it takes up in a living whole of words that is, taken as a whole, extremely expressive and vivid. Therefore the expression "kingdom of God" cannot be stabilized, as if it could not be replaced by, for instance, the expression "righteousness of God" or the expression "eternal life." In the last instance, there is only one primordial word that abides and that is the name "Jesus."

In the fourth place, I point out that the kingdom of God, in as much as it is coming, is always and exclusively presented as God's gift. It is never described as the product of the natural development of things. And not as the result of human effort either. It comes because it pleases God to give it. Hence, from the human side: receiving the kingdom as a child,[25] with the attitude of expectation,[26] in the form [gestalte] of a heritage,[27] entering the kingdom through rebirth,[28] struggling to enter,[29] searching for the kingdom, and to that end renouncing all other things.[30] Sacrifice and patience are the foci of the ellipse of human possibility in the face of the kingdom. This turn is so abundantly familiar from the developments in theology of the last twenty years that I do not have to deal with it in detail. It once more, very forcefully, underlines both the soteriological and the eschatological character of the kingdom.

Finally, I point out that specific passages presuppose the equating of the kingdom of God with Christ. Schmidt cites a few of these passages and then remarks that these texts merely provide the lexicological basis for a conclusion that is already clear from "the obvious material fact": "that for Jesus the invading kingdom of God has come into time and the world in His person as expressed by John in his statement: ὁ λόγος σὰρξ ἐγένετο"[31, 32]. Origin formulated it beautifully when he spoke of the αὐτοβασιλεια.[33] And Marcion said: *in evangelio est dei regum Christus*

---

25. See Mark 10:15; Luke 18:17.
26. See Luke 23:51.
27. See 1 Corinthians 6:9, Galatians 5:21.
28. See John 3:3.
29. See Luke 13:24.
30. See Matthew 13:44–46.
31. Ὁ λόγος σὰρξ ἐγένετο: The word became flesh.
32. [9] See K.L. Schmidt, "Die Wortgruppe βασιλεύς κτλ. im NT," 590-91.

33. Αὐτοβασιλεια: Self-kingdom. The term αὐτοβασιλεία is derived from Origen's commentary on Matthew 18:23 (XIV.7): "καὶ ὥσπερ αὐτός ἐστιν ἡ αὐτοσοφία, καὶ ἡ αὐτοδικαιοσύνη, καὶ ἡ αὐτοαλήθεια, οὕτω μήποτε καὶ ἡ αὐτοβασιλεία" ("and as He is wisdom itself, and justice itself and truth itself, so He is perhaps also the kingdom itself."). Van Ruler derived this citation from K.L. Schmidt, "Die Wortgruppe βασιλεύς κτλ. im NT," 591, but elsewhere also criticizes the term.

ipse.³⁴ The incarnate, exalted Christ who is present in the church *is* the kingdom of God. Seen in this context, the fundamental given also becomes clear, namely that the kingdom of God is equated only once (Revelations 1:6) with Christians: Christ ἐποίησεν ἡμᾶς βασιλείαν.³⁵

↭

These five observations have, I believe, adequately demonstrated that the kingdom of God equals the salvation [heil] in Christ, just as the New Testament, indeed, the entire Bible attests. To summarize, I provide a quotation from Skydsgaard:³⁶

> When we pose the question, "What does Jesus want?", the answer is, "Jesus wants one thing: the kingdom of God." Everything in Him, his will and the very depth of his being, his proclamation and his miracles, were directed at one thing: the kingdom of his Father, the realizing of God's will, and the sovereignty and victory of the divine will. For that purpose He came: to overcome the violence of sin, death and the Devil, to wrest people from the power of the Evil One, from the meaninglessness, the fortuitousness and the bitter, unjust suffering of this world; to create a new heaven and a new earth.³⁷

The statement: The kingdom of God = the salvation [heil] in Christ has become clear with this. And also the more precise circumscription: and therefore the kingdom is soteriological-eschatological in nature. This essential characteristic, the sole valid one, is adequately illuminated by this. To explicate this further would involve an exposition of all the central biblical categories in Christian doctrine such as atonement and salvation, ascension and parousia, exaltation and outpouring of the Holy Spirit.

↭

It seems necessary to me, before we proceed to relate the concept of the kingdom to the idea of the church, to reject certain misconceptions by

---

34. *In evangelio est dei regnum Christus ipse*: In the gospel the kingdom of God is Christ himself. Van Ruler derived this citation from K.L. Schmidt, "Die Wortgruppe βασιλεύς κτλ. im NT," 591. The source is Tertullian's *Adversus Marcionem*, IV,33.

35. Ἐποίησεν ἡμᾶς βασιλείαν: [Christ] made us into a kingdom.

36. Kristen Ejner Skydsgaard (1902–1990), Danish Lutheran theologian and professor in dogmatics at the University of Copenhagen (1942–1972).

37. [10] Skydsgaard, "Godsrijk en kerk," *Onder Eigen Vaandel* 14 (1939), 116.

referring to the view of the idea of the kingdom of God that we have now developed.

In the first place, the ethicizing conception has to be considered. It transposes the center of gravity to moral ideals and norms and the dispositions of the people that orient themselves to these and try to realize them. This is already a very old misconception. Yet it is extremely remarkable that its origin is always traced to the Hellenistic world. This conception is not to be found in the Old Testament. Rabbinical teaching also does not reach it, even though it speaks of taking up the yoke of God's kingship, for it understands that to mean the confession of the monotheism of Judaism. But in the Hellenistic parts of the Septuagint the kingdom is already identified with the four cardinal virtues: wisdom, justice, goodness and courage. In Philo we find this ethicizing in its pure form: he makes the βασιλεία a chapter in teaching about virtue.[38] Similarly, we must also state: we do not find this conception in the New Testament. But the church had barely entered into the Hellenistic world before it adopted this ethicizing of the kingdom once more in the teaching of the church fathers. [It did this] by strongly emphasizing the idea of judgement, making the coming of the kingdom dependent on the conduct of the congregation and then seeking the solution in an ascetic-dualistic ethics of perfection.[39] And even now the way in which the figure of the kingdom of God is employed in theological debates illustrates in a most alarming way to what extent Christianity still remains strangled in the deadly coils of ethical idealism. People are, after all, in the habit of placing questions about Christianity and war, Christianity and society, Christianity and education under this heading! Both the fact that people believe they can arrange these questions under this heading and especially the fact that they seem to believe that the heading itself is exhausted in these paragraphs indicate to what extent the kingdom is identified with the idea of ethical normativity. This has fatal consequences for the relationship of kingdom of God and church. This ethicizing goes hand in hand with an individualizing way of thought, through which a correct view on the church concept is obstructed from the outset: everything is staked on the moral disposition of the individual. Along with this ethicizing comes, moreover, a degrading of preaching, which starts to lack all elements of prophecy and proclamation

---

38. [11] See K.G. Kuhn, "מַלְכוּת שָׁמַיִם in der rabbinischen Literatur." In *ThWNT*, Band 1, 571; K.L. Schmidt, "βασιλεία (τοῦ θεοῦ) im hellenistischen Judentum." In *ThWNT*, Band 1, 574-75.

39. [12] See K.L. Schmidt, "βασιλεία (τοῦ θεοῦ) in der alten Kirche." In *ThWNT*, Band 1, 594.

and slips away into propaganda and admonition. The church becomes an ancillary institution or—a step further—an obstacle to the kingdom. Of course, one cannot say that every ethical quality should be expunged from the idea of the kingdom. Still, this ethical quality takes its shape [gestalte] only in a theocratic relativism[40] around the sacrament of the Lord's Supper. The Sermon on the Mount and the civil code of justice do not really stand in diametrical opposition to each other. The Christian lives in the light of preaching and sacrament, in a humanly healthy sense, for moderation and bourgeois decency (compare the "ought to be" from the first question in the baptismal formulary).[41] That is most definitely not the kingdom itself. Perhaps one could formulate it in this way: It is an eloquent reminder (now at last really properly human!) of the signs of the kingdom, especially the sign of the Lord's Supper.

In the second place, I draw attention to the sociologizing of the idea of the kingdom. It is a variant of the ethicizing [approach]. We may think of the American notion of the "social gospel." We may also think of religious socialism and related currents. In this regard, we may, however, also think of Abraham Kuyper,[42] who made a mighty effort to demonstrate, both theoretically and practically, that the kingdom of God is a social force in all spheres of life. The same objections that I have brought against the ethicizing conception apply against this [conception] as well. And to these must be further added the great, fundamental objection that in this way the kingdom acquires its own sphere, its own form, alongside and over against the church. With that we become entangled in desperate problems when it comes to our topic (sovereignty in own sphere!).[43] In

---

40. Translator's note: This is what Van Ruler wrote. Even if the word is changed to "relativity", the meaning is not clear.

41. The first question in the classic Reformed baptism formulary reads: "So that it becomes public that this is your belief, will you then answer the question sincerely: Although our children are conceived and born in sin and are therefore subjected to all kinds of misery, indeed to damnation itself, will you confess that they are sanctified in Christ and should be baptised as members of this congregation."
Editor's note: No further bibliographical details are provided in the original.

42. Abraham Kuyper (1837–1920), prominent Dutch pastor, theologian, journalist and politician. He was a central figure in the *Doleantie*, that led to a schism in the Dutch Reformed Church (Nederlands Hervormde Kerk) that took place in 1886. He established the Vrije Universiteit te Amsterdam and was professor there from 1880 to 1901. He was a long-standing member of parliament and also served as the Dutch Prime Minister (1901–1905).

43. Van Ruler refers here to Abraham Kuyper's notion of sphere sovereignty. Van Ruler engaged critically with Kuyper's theology in a book entitled *Kuyper's Idee eener Christelijke Cultuur* (Nijkerk: G. F. Callenbach, 1940). For further cross-references to

opposition to this conception, I would wish to propose: Christianity is no social phenomenon; in as much as it is a phenomenon in the world, it is far rather a political phenomenon. In the field of signs, it erects a sign almost as important as the sign of the Lord's Supper: the divine authority of government as God's servants. We can indeed speak of "politischer Gottesdienst"[44] and, for example not, or much less easily, of the cultural service of God. And we may never will the latter without the former. The only gate that leads from salvation [heil] to culture is that of the political order.

In the third place, the mystical conception of the kingdom as spiritual realm, hidden deep in the hearts of people and consisting in spiritual communion with God, must be equally sharply rejected. One may arrive at the fascinating thought that in this, in the spiritual joy and intoxication of the soul, a fragment of the kingdom has become reality, thereby breaking down and exceeding the boundary set by the sign character of all things. Concerning the relationship of kingdom and church, we have then ended up in the conventicle. Here all those questions awaken that concern the work of the Holy Spirit. And there are few aspects of Christian thought in which everyone is so jovially and self-evidently heretical as in precisely this one. To be safeguarded against this mystic misconception of the idea of the kingdom requires extremely strict disciplining of our thought. We have to consider the providential *and* the conserving *and* the testifying character of the work of the Holy Spirit. Briefly put, we have to consider that the outpouring and the work of the Holy Spirit is, in the scriptural context, no more than pledge, firstling, in short, it is *the* sign par excellence of the kingdom. The spiritual joy that we feel in our hearts, that too is no more than a symbol in the biblical sense: a sign established by the election, filled with the matter [zaak], which is present in its hiddenness.

The fourth possible misconception, the ecclesiological one, I have already discussed. It identifies the kingdom with the church. I can pass by it by merely mentioning it.

---

literature in Dutch, see Van Ruler's *Verzameld werk 5C*, 797, note 58.

44. Van Ruler's source for this expression may be Karl Barth's Gifford Lectures, especially the 19th lecture under the German title "Der politische Gottesdienst." In *Gotteserkenntnis und Gottesdienst nach reformatorischer Lehre. 20 Vorlesungen (Gifford-Lectures) über das Schottische Bekenntnis von 1560, gehalten an der Universität Aberdeen im Frühjahr 1937 und 1938* (Zollikon, 1938), 203f. See also Barth, *The Knowledge of God and the Service of God according to the Teaching of the Reformation: The Gifford Lectures Delivered in 1937 and 1938* (Eugene: Wipf & Stock, 2005).

Finally, we are left with another remarkable case before us. I have in mind the ontological-metaphysical conception of the kingdom. Its point of departure is that it is self-evident that God reigns. It bases that on creation. And in order to link the biblical elements of soteriology and eschatology, which unmistakably inhere in the idea of the kingdom, it likes to distinguish between the realm of omnipotence, the realm of grace and the realm of glory. So extremely many problems arise here that I do not see it as possible to squeeze them into the limited scope [of a lecture]. Therefore I content myself with the observation that the cardinal fault lies in the point of departure. From the biblical perspective it is by no means self-evident that God reigns. On the contrary, precisely that is the cosmic question that holds heaven, hell and earth in breathless suspense and revolutionary movement. Regarding the relationship between kingdom and church, the question about the church's position in the world as such arises here, the question about the extent to which the world may be regarded as a fitting terrain for the church. For the real problem of our topic, however, this question is of no importance whatsoever.

In this way, I believe, my statement that the kingdom of God is, soteriologically-eschatologically, to be identified with the salvation [heil] in Christ can be maintained polemically-negatively as well.

And so, having come through this maze of problems, we now stand before the simple and wide land of the real matter [zaak]: the relationship between the kingdom of God and the church. Put briefly, we can define the relationship thus: the church is the *sign* of the kingdom of God. And we would have to make it more precise by saying: the church is the field of the signs of the kingdom of God. There resides, and there has to reside, in the church something of the disparateness, of the pluriformity, of the inconsistency of signs. They can be understood only as signs and are therefore robbed of a final sense [zin] and objectiveness. When one regards the signs as things [zaken], one does indeed stand with perplexity before a *Paradoxenhaufe*.[45] Then one can no longer handle the contradictions. And then we would have to make it more precise by saying: the church is the field of signs in which the kingdom of God is present in a hidden way. In the light of these remarks, we may now suddenly see [anew] the classic Protestant definition of the church in Lutheran symbolics: the

---

45. *Paradoxenhaufe*: Heap of paradoxes:

church is *communio* or *congregatio sanctorum et vere credentium, in qua evangelium recte docetur en recte administrantur sacramenta*.[46] All nothing more than signs. What a multiplicity of signs. But in this way we have the kingdom here and now. Skyngaard is correct when, in conclusion, he describes the relationship of the two figures in this way: the kingdom of God is partly critical boundary, partly divine content of the church.[47]

Approaching it from this angle, we must describe the church from the following perspectives:

1. The election;
2. The miracle;
3. The cross;
4. The sacrament;
5. Preaching.

About each of the five, a few further comments.

That there is a church, is a matter "posited by God and beyond the control of us men."[48] Election constitutes the heart of the church. This holds for the gathering of people, and for the sacraments, and for the preaching, and even for the liturgy, and definitely for the offices. Nothing in the church subsists in itself. Nor does anything have inherent permanence, objectiveness in itself. Everything is there because it has been instituted by God. This truth of the election underlines with great emphasis the sign character of the church. As long as one does not go on to reify the election. Seen from the angle of this truth of the election, it is surely not enough to talk of the church as gathering of the elect. We must go further and speak of the gathering of the true believers in Christ, even of the church as the *numerus praedestinato*rum.[49] As long as one does, however, keep in mind that this *numerus praedestinatorum* is only revealed and only becomes reality around the sacrament, the preaching and the

---

46. The church as *communio* or *congregatio sanctorum et vere credentium, in qua evangelium recte docetur et recte administrantur sacramenta*: The church is the communion or congregation of saints and true believers where the gospel is rightly taught and the sacraments are rightly administered. Van Ruler's source here is most probably Herman Bavinck's *Gereformeerde Dogmatiek*. See his *Reformed Dogmatics Volume 4* (Grand Rapids: Baker Academic, 2008), 287, where precisely the same formulation is found. It seems to be compiled from various Lutheran confessions.

47. [13] See K.E. Skydsgaard, "Godsrijk en kerk," 124.

48. [14] K.L. Schmidt, "καλέω κτλ." In *ThWNT, Band* 3, 511.

49. *Numerus praedestinatorum*: the number of the elect.

offices. And with this the sign character of the election-in-individual-sense too is emphatically maintained. The elect have no option but to cross themselves out and to speak of the universality of salvation [heil]. One constantly has to leap from the one sign to the other sign.[50] That is what we called playing leapfrog[51] in our childhood years. But this truth of the election does add to the attitude with which a person receives the kingdom another element. To the two previously mentioned elements, sacrifice and patience, a third element, sober obedience, is added. I have no option but to cling to all the signs that God instituted and my heart must expand to encompass them all.[52] Election drives a very deep love of the church into the expectation of the kingdom.

Alongside this element of the election, we must promptly place the element of the miracle. We currently—and rightly—speak of "the miracle of the church." Indeed, we can experience the church only in this way. *That* it is there, and that it is *still* there, and *what* it is—all of this is, in the light of the practice of the church, nothing but a visible miracle of God. That places the church on the same level as all the miracles reported in Scripture. And to grasp the meaning of this, we may consider one thing: Jesus rose from the dead, but in a glorified body. Lazarus,[53] the daughter of Jairus,[54] and the young man of Nain[55] rose from the dead, yet not with a glorified body.[56] In that the relationship of kingdom and church is supply expressed. And in principle that also says what the position of the

---

50. [15] Also the ordering of the covenant of grace: the faithful *and their seed* can then, for all the sincerity of their content, but be degraded *and* elevated to [being] signs instituted by God. Then the idea of the national church is to be maintained. For the rest, the relationship between the kingdom of God and the covenant is a separate topic, by no means an easy one.

51. Translator's note: The Dutch expression "scholletjes trappen" refers to the game of jumping from one ice floe to the next without falling into the water. The English above is not an exact equivalent.

52. [16] This is the meaning [zin] of article 28 of the Belgic Confession: "But all people are obliged to join and unite with it, keeping the unity of the church by submitting to its instruction and discipline," etc. It is about accepting and embracing, in obedience and love, *all* the signs that God has set. Only in this way can one be "high-churchly."

Translator's note: In the final sentence, Van Ruler apparently uses "hoogkerklijk" in a positive sense. Since he rejects the High Church stream in Anglicanism elsewhere, he seems to mean "high-churchly in the true sense". Inverted commas have been inserted to hint at this.

53. See John 11:1f.
54. See Mark 5:5:35f; Luke 8:49f.
55. See Luke 7:11f.
56. See Luke 7:11.

church in the world is: in the world the church is everything, the essential and the only, but—there is nothing special about it.

In the third place, alongside election and miracle, the cross. The church is congregation under the cross. The ascension returns the church to the situation of the cross. Christ is King and as King He rules, but: He rules from the cross. The crucifixion is a type of elevation, a type of ascension for Christ. The reverse also holds: the ascension is a type of crucifixion for his congregation. That serves as a strong reminder to the church: merely sign, not the matter [zaak] itself; merely sign of the kingdom, not the kingdom itself. The kingdom is the critical boundary around the church.

In the fourth place, immediately linked to that: undoubtedly critical boundary, but simultaneously divine content. Therefore we constantly have to mention alongside the figure of the cross also the figure of the sacrament. That is by no means a contrast. From our own formularies for baptism and the Lord's Supper we know how closely together cross and sacrament belong. Nevertheless, the emphasis is now shifted somewhat, the tone changed. The cross says: merely sign, "vilis et abjecta" (Calvin);[57] the sacrament says: but in that truly sign of the divine matter [zaak] and the church gets some share in the depth and glory of the kingdom.

Finally: preaching. For surely everything really issues in that, if we carefully think through all the connections and, in particular, if we see the church in the light of the kingdom. The very being [wezen] of the church consists in this—not in that it has sacraments—but in that it is bearer of the gospel of the kingdom. The church is church of the Word.

In conclusion I would state this as result of the argument: The kingdom of God is present only in the church—and then in a hidden way. The church is merely sign of the kingdom of God—and then as hidden sign. Therefore one cannot flee from the church into the kingdom. One can only, within the church, raise one's heart upwards, towards the kingdom.[58]

---

57. *Vilis et abjecta*: Worthless and despicable. The source is Calvin's commentary on John 1:14. Van Ruler's source may have been Karl Barth's *Kirchliche Dogmatik* I/2 (Zollikon/Zürich, 1932–1967), 167.

58. Here Van Ruler hints at the Reformed formulary for the Lord's Supper, i.e. the so-called "sursum corda."

The Millennium[1]
[ca. 1942]

Some thoughts evoked by the introduction colleague IJsseling provided to the topic of the convention, as an aid to a new introduction [to be offered] by Ten Boom.[2]

WHEN THIS TOPIC COMES up, something—even quite a lot—awakens in me. It would seem to be a topic of fantasy, beneath the dignity of scientific theology. It is by no means that. Theology has to engage with it in depth. About many questions the decisions are taken here. The topic holds Christian eschatology captive within the circumference of the apocalyptic. Biblically, that is necessary.

I do not claim that I know how to tackle the topic. I can merely provide some perspectives and some intimations about it. Gunning's dictum[3] that an incorrectly completed eschatology brought the Lord to the

---

1. The inventory number of the Dutch text, "Het duizendjarige rijk" is I,167. Van Ruler noted the following in his handwritten bibliography on this text: "A collection of comments in a discussion regarding the Hilversum Convent." He did not remember when this meeting took place. Because he placed this alongside other texts from 1942, this could be dated in that same year. The original consisted of eight hand-written pages. It was first published in Volume 5C of Van Ruler's *Verzameld werk* (2023), 799–804.

2. Paulus Cornelis IJsseling (1871–1958) was a Reformed minister. After his retirement he lived in Hilversum—which explains his participation in the Hilversum Convent. Willem ten Boom (1886–1946) was also a Reformed minister and worked in Amsterdam as a missionary for Israel (1925–12) and as secretary of the Hervormde Raad voor Kerk en Israël (1942–1946) ("the Reformed Council for Church and Israel). He also lived in Hilversum in his later years. Van Ruler wrote a preface for Ten Boom's book *Bloed en vuur: Symboliek der voornaamste oudtestamentische offerhandelingen* (Amsterdam, 1946), 6.

3. Johannes Hermanus Gunning (1829–1905), Reformed minister, also taught at the Universities of Amsterdam (19982–1889) and the Rijksuniversiteit te Leiden

cross comes to mind vividly. The doctrines regarding eschatology must, by their nature, retain something of the incomplete.

The discussion on IJsseling's introduction[4] moved roughly unanimously along the line of condemning Augustine's idea that the millennium has arrived with the dispensation of the church.[5] Since I am personally mostly inclined to favor this idea, it is obvious that I saw my role in the discussion as defending it. That placed me, willy-nilly, in a one-sided[6] position. What comforted me all the while was that this position has had the support of the overwhelming majority in the tradition of the church. That is no proof (consider the tradition of the immortality of the soul!), but it is a comfort. There is one element in the doctrine of the millennium with which I can *fully* identify, without any sense of unease: the strong emphasis it places on the earthly character of salvation [heil].[7] This idea is so thoroughly biblical that it is, to my mind, self-evident: salvation does not entail that we are wrested from the materiality of the earth and transposed to the spirituality of heaven, but that we, together with this entire earth, in all our materiality, are wrested from the powers of corruption, in particular, from sin and death. That has been aptly captured in the doctrine of the millennium. Therefore, the objection that this doctrine is conceived in an unspiritual way does not impress me in the least. The one objection that I do have is that this doctrine leaves the impression that it maintains the earthly character of salvation to "a thousand" years only. And what then? Is "bliss" spiritual after all? A thousand year is not long enough for me.

Alongside the earthly character of salvation stands the future character of salvation. With that too I can fully identify. The eschatological expectation does not merely belong to the structure of biblical-Christian

---

(1889–1899). Gunning was one of the leaders in the so-called "ethical" school in Dutch theology. The source of Gunning's dictum is J.H. Gunning Jr., *De prediking van de toekomst des Heeren* (Utrecht, 1888), 21. He stated that: "The congregation never forgets that it was a faulty eschatology that led to the crucifixion of the Saviour."

4. See note 2 above.

5. See Augustine, *De Civitate Dei*, XX.7.

6. Translator's note: This is what Van Ruler wrote, but he probably meant "isolated."

7. One of the core themes in Van Ruler's theology is that the Christian faith indeed hinges on (Dutch: draait om) Christ, atonement and justification, but that it is about (Dutch: gaat om) something else: the redemption of creation and the coming of the kingdom of God on earth. In this regard, Van Ruler would also say that, for God, it is about (Dutch: gaat om) this world, this earthly, life, ordinary life, humaneness, sanctification, and so forth. For cross-references to literature in Dutch, see Van Ruler's *Verzameld werk* 5C, 308, note 5.

thought; it *is* this structure. Only: it is now a matter of considering the concept "future" in its pure biblical sense. It is not *our* future or the future of our world, a future which could then be considered from the perspective of the present as the termination of the line that runs, with or without continuity (Schilder's "shock moment"[8]), from the present. This future is God's future that comes upon us.[9] The most essential thing that can be said about the God of the Bible is that God is *coming*. For this reason, the Bible does not start thinking at the beginning, from the present or from creation or from the abstract eternity of God before creation. The Bible begins thinking at the end, in the salvation-filled eternity of God at the ending, from God's ultimate intentions. And the Bible sees this God, with the divine salvific intentions, coming towards us, intrusively, overwhelmingly, thrusting Godself into our reality. That is the kingdom of God that is there because it (overwhelmingly) comes. We expect it and in this way we stand within it. Jesus Christ, the theocracy in Israel, the church—all these are modalities of the kingdom of God. And while we are standing within it, we may consider that we have not yet even *dreamt* of the kingdom of God—that exceeds everything. And thus everything remains as expectation. Now, it seems to me that this category of the future is seriously impaired by the doctrine of the millennium.[10] It operates with a conception of the future that is categorically conceived from the present. It makes it impossible to consider the presence of the kingdom of God in the present, or at least to recognize the plerophory and the reality of it: it does not arrive at the πλήρωμα of God[11] in the modality of the flesh in the present. And it has no understanding of the fact that we cannot even dream of the kingdom of God in the modality of the creature; it does dream of it.

---

8. Klaas Schilder (1890–1952), Reformed minister and professor at the Theological Seminary of the Reformed churches (Gereformeerde Kerken) in Kampen (1933–1944). In 1944 he was dismissed by the general synod of the Gereformeerde Kerken and then became professor of the Theological Seminary of the "vrijgemaakt" (liberated) Reformed Church. The source of Schilder's "shock moment" is K. Schilder, *Wat is de hemel* (Kampen, 1935), 122f.

9. Translator's note: There is a wordplay in the Dutch original between "future" (*toekomst*) and "come upon" (*toe-komt*).

10. Elsewhere Van Ruler wrote: "Chiliasm shows a tendency towards a docetic divinization of the flesh: it desires a visible divine glory of human nature as adopted through the incarnation of the Word" (translation—EMC). See his doctoral thesis, *De vervulling van de wet* (Utrecht, 1947), 90.

11. Πλήρωμα: Fullness.

That brings me to an extremely important matter: how does the kingdom of the millennium relate to the kingdom of glory? Concerning the characterization of the kingdom of God in the tension between future and present that I have just given, no problems arise in this regard. But when we locate a millennium between the present of grace and the future of glory, then we ask ourselves: Where does it belong, within the grace or within the glory? The tradition of chiliasm says: Within the glory! But must we then think of a duality in the glory of God? Once we proceed with the idea of chiliasm, does God's glory not become hazy? Must we then conceive of it as spiritual?

To my mind the structure of the Apocalypse does not force us to adopt the doctrine of the millennium. IJsseling advances the notion of repeated delay: in the Apocalypse things move towards the end, but the end is ever again retarded. In Chapter 20, then, we are indeed roughly at the end. In my view, however, the Apocalypse should be seen as a kaleidoscope in which all the facets of God's historical-eschatological activity constitute the pieces of glass. Each chapter deals anew with the same thing, namely the 'history' (from ascension to parousia), but the kaleidoscope has been turned a fraction of a revolution: all the particles are still there, but they are positioned differently each time. In Chapter 20 the same history is dealt with, but in the image we see predominantly the blessed *power* of the church in the life of the [various] cultures. When the kaleidoscope is turned, the fearsome power of the beast in the life of the various cultures predominates. Still, in both cases the same things are dealt with.

The rule of the church in relation to the ἔζησαν of Revelations 20.[12] On this point too, I would want to come up for Augustine. We only have to think about the highly remarkable position of the *ecclesia triumphans*[13] in Christian thought. It is not to be identified with the *regnum gloriae*. That is one of the worst confusions that can occur in Christian thinking. The *ecclesia triumphans* too is waiting. And in that, and not only in that, it is at one with the *ecclesia militans*[14] on earth. What the *ecclesia triumphans* is in the form of death, the *ecclesia militans* is in the form of the Lord's Supper. When it is said that the church *is* the millennium, then this form of the *ecclesia triumphans* must be included positively. In it resides all

---

12. Ἔζησαν: And they lived.

13. *Ecclesia triumphans*: The church triumphant. For cross-references to literature in Dutch, see Van Ruler's *Verzameld werk 5C*, 803, note 13.

14. *Ecclesia militans*: The church militant.

that is triumphant about the millennium. And because it resides in that, it also resides in the church *tout court*. That only the *martyrs* are mentioned is logical: the church is nothing but a martyr church; the church is unimaginable in any other way. But just as Jesus Christ triumphed on the cross (crucifixion = elevation and glorification), so the church triumphs in its martyrdom. It establishes comfort in the present. One of the worst things that I heard in the discussion was the constant observation: This era really does show clearly that there is no millennium. This observation struck a painful blow to my heart. It befits an idealistic philosopher of culture, but not a Christian who lives from God's promise. God's whole πλήρωμα dwells among us bodily in Jesus Christ.[15] Bodily: in the flesh, in the hiddenness, in the grace and the mercy.[16] That is the *regnum Christi*. The *regnum Christi* is the *regnum Dei* in a particular mode, namely, the mode of the flesh, in the existence of the created things as such, with its majesty and its glory. The *regnum Dei* itself is the *regnum gloriae*:[17] then God rules openly, without the *velamen* (Calvin) of the flesh.[18] Therefore: the *regnum Christi* is exhausted: nothing whatsoever can be added to it. Now, in the God forsakenness of this world, God is close to us in Christ. He has never been as close to our hearts as in these most terrible horrors of the war. The earth proceeds along "Christian" lines. All this is indeed the diametrical opposite of the talk of the bourgeois complacent, of which the church á la Augustine stands accused. To grasp at a League-of-Nations-style of rest on earth and then to say that one sees nothing of the millennium—*that* is bourgeois-complacent talk. The church calls that building the tower of Babel.[19] Well, this profound Christian comfort in the present is taken from me, if not entirely, then at least partially, by the doctrine of the millennium: the real core is taken from it.

To return once more to the reproach concerning the bourgeois-complacent attitude of the church. We have to free the identification of church and millennium from its rigidity. As if this identification is given but once, only in one form! Christian Europe is one example of it. But the Great Skater may change direction and reduce the whole of Christian

---

15. See Colossians 2:9.

16. Van Ruler regarded the *regnum Christi* (the kingdom of Christ) as a modality of the *regnum Dei* (the kingdom of God). For cross-references to literature in Dutch, see Van Ruler's *Verzameld werk 5C*, 716, note 19.

17. *Regnum gloriae*: The kingdom of glory.

18. *Velanum*: Veil. The sources in Calvin includes his *Institutes* III.2.20; II.XIV.3.

19. See Genesis 11:1–9.

Europe to ruins, ploughing under completely not only its earthly form but also its Christian spiritual-moral foundations (as it goes in our times), profaning and desecrating and destroying even the church, his own heritage.[20] And start anew in Papua. As He did with Asia Minor and North Africa. Perhaps Augustine and Calvin did not see that as clearly as we do. That is not surprising: they lived amid the chaos of the nationalities in Europe and had their hands full ordering it to be a Christian culture—while we live in the time of the decline of the West.[21] That they did not see it and that we do is in both cases only what is to be expected. We do not have to reproach them and to claim an advantage over them.

Then: the characteristic of the millennium is the restraining of Satan. In this regard, the church has always referred to Constantine the Great. We pass all too lightly over this reference. As if that was not the restraining of Satan par excellence! That the state, experienced and celebrated everywhere in heathendom as product and dwelling of the gods, was de-demonized and made into a servant of God through the proclamation of the truth derived from revelation. We take the problem of the state much too lightly. It is the sphinx of human existence. That this sphinx was demystified is the event of salvation par excellence. We cannot claim that this demystification in Christian Europe succeeded completely. The church is *also ecclesia militans*. And Christian Europe is one of God's experiments. Yet *what* has happened since the baptism of Constantine and Clovis is important enough to discover the truth of Revelations 20 in it. Along with this demystification of the state as sphinx of existence goes the ordering of human life, caught in the chaos of sin, through the commandments and rights and institutes of the Lord. The barbarians of the migration of peoples [Völkerwanderung] became the bearers of human culture through the discipline of the church. That has been the fruit of twenty centuries of Christianity. When these fruits no longer hang on the tree of the confession of Christ, they rot.

One more concluding remark: To me it seems an arbitrary restriction to reserve the term "chiliasm" for the effort of the aggressive Anabaptists of Münster in 1535. By "chiliasm" we normally understand

---

20. Translator's note: In this section where the image of the Great Skater is used, inclusive language could not be maintained without rendering the text practically unreadable. Van Ruler's non-inclusive language is used here.

21. This is probably a reference to Oswald Spengler's *The Decline of the West*. See Spengler, *Untergang des Abendlandes: Umrisse einer Morphologie der Weltgeschichte* (München, 1919).

that view which regards the millennium as a separate period in history, distinct from the present one of grace. To that has to be added that this view has not been advanced only by the sects; it also has a line of venerable representatives among orthodox teachers of the church.[22] The church itself has, however, never taken this course. And rightly so, to my mind. All that the church can do to settle the outstanding account of the sects is to develop its doctrines anew and to do that, "with a progression moving backwards" (Gunning),[23] from the biblical notion of the kingdom of God that it has so sadly neglected.

---

22. Herman Bavinck (1854–1921), minister in the Christelijk Gereformeerde Kerk ("Christian Reformed Church"), professor of theology at the Theologische School te Kampen (1883–1902), and at the Vrije Universiteit te Amsterdam (1902–1921). See Herman Bavinck, *Reformed Dogmatics Volume IV: Holy Spirit, Church, and New Creation*, translated by John Vriend and edited by John Bolt (Grand Rapids: Baker Academic, 2008), 655–58.

23. The source in Gunning is his *De prediking van de toekomst des Heeren* (Utrecht, 1888), 87.

Editor's note: What Gunning says is that doctrine should be developed from the eschaton, that is, "backwards" from the future and not "forward" from the past. Van Ruler's text does not make this clear.

The Meaning of the Mosaic Law[1]
[1947]

I WOULD ASSIGN A fourfold meaning to the Mosaic law in Christian existence: a kerygmatic, an existential, a functional and a material meaning.

Under the *kerygmatic* meaning of the Mosaic law I understand [the following]: When it is a matter of proclaiming Jesus as the Christ, we have to borrow the terms, contents and forms we use from the Mosaic law in particular: we have to speak the "language of Canaan."[2]

Under the *existential* meaning of the Mosaic law I understand [the following]: It is the Mosaic law in particular that has necessitated the Messiah's sacrifice of atonement. Thereby the entire Christian existence has acquired a Mosaic, specifically a cultic, structure. We have to find our bliss [zaligheid] in the cross of Golgotha.

Under the *functional* meaning of the Mosaic law I understand [the following]: It is the Mosaic law in particular that describes the function within the whole of the kingdom of God of all the forms [gestalten] that the Spirit calls into being in the Christianizing of the world. The shadows of the kingdom fall along the walls of existence.

Under the *material* meaning of the Mosaic law I understand [the following]: It is from the Mosaic law in particular that we have to borrow the basic principles and the material [that we use] when, in the

---

1. The inventory number of the Dutch text, "De Betekenis van de Mozaïsche Wet" is I,216. This was based on a lecture at the Faculty of Divinity at the Rijksuniversiteit te Utrecht, 12 May 1947. It is included in Volume 5C of Van Ruler's *Verzameld werk* (2023), 805–15.

2. Editor's note: The expression the "language of Canaan" is used by Karl Barth in his *Evangelical Theology* (Philadelphia: Fortress Press, 1985), 171–83. Barth derives it from a work by H.F. Kohlbrugge entitled *De Taal Kanaäns* (Den Hertog: Houten, 1986), who in turn derives it from John Bunyan's *The Pilgrim's Progress*. Van Ruler uses the expression frequently in his writings.

aggressiveness of the work of Christianizing, it is a matter of ordering the world along Christian lines. A "Christian" state manifests distinctly Old Testament traits.

Now I would want to restrict myself to illuminating these four theses.

I

First, then, the kerygmatic meaning of the Mosaic law. It provides the concepts and forms of expression for the proclamation of Jesus as the Christ. Jesus is *our* Passover [lamb] that has been slaughtered. He is the atonement for our guilt.[3] He is the Lamb of God that takes away the sins of the world. Through Him and through his sacrifice God's just claim [recht[4]] is established: the atonement takes place through satisfaction. Thus He is King of Kings and Lord of Lords: the political form of human existence too is involved in the *regnum Christi*.[5] And from his great, historical cultic act—the sacrificial act of God on Golgotha—flows not only justice [recht], but also love. We would not be able to express what love is without reference to the sacramental vehicles of love as they are described in the law.

We cannot do without the Mosaic, Old Testament forms when we truly want to proclaim Jesus the Christ. We cannot make do with the speech forms of common human consciousness [alone]. Undoubtedly, we shall have to exert ourselves to the utmost to translate the kerygma into common human speech. But we shall have to keep it in mind that we shall never succeed completely. Even the word "sin" is no common human word. The law had to be added, Paul says, on account of sin, to make the sin into sin, to bring sin itself to light as sin, that is, as transgression and guilt.[6] Guilt is an Israelite affair. The atonement entirely so.

---

3. The understanding of sin as guilt and of reconciliation as atonement for guilt are core motifs in Van Ruler's theology that are expressed throughout his oeuvre. In this regard, he gives preference to Anselm's understanding of atonement as satisfaction. For cross-references to literature in Dutch, see Van Ruler's *Verzameld werk 5C*, 127, note 28.

4. Translator's note: See the glossary on the Dutch word "recht". Here its meaning is not clear from the context. "Recht" can refer to God's rights (the honor of God's name), or to the need to put things right in God's world, or to both.

5. *Regnum Christi*: Reign/kingdom of Christ.

6. See, for example, Romans 5:20.

We should never imagine that we indicate common human concepts with these and similar words. Because world-historically that is not true. In world history it is the people of Israel that God put and kept in [a state of] guilt by means of the law. In the Christianizing of a culture that happens anew. The Mosaic law has to be added to it if there is to be significant talk of guilt and atonement. It creates the *language* of both theology and the kerygma. It creates the language of Canaan and without this we would be unable to accomplish the proclamation of the Messiah Jesus. The word "Messiah", for instance, is already part of the "language of Canaan". To my mind the word "christological," as compared to "Messianic," already smacks too much of translation into the [language of] common human consciousness.

In other words, in the Mosaic law a broad foundation for salvation [heil] has been provided in this world. A basis, a work-floor, has been laid, upon which God's work, the work of salvation [heil], of rescuing us from being lost in guilt and death, could be accomplished. This is how we have to put it, particularly from a Messianic angle. From the perspective of the Messiah and his work, the Mosaic law acts as groundwork to the salvation [heil] of the Lord in this world. From the perspective of the sanctifying and Christianizing work of the Holy Spirit, the Mosaic law acts rather as the extension of the salvation [heil] of the Lord in this world.

Naturally, this is no opposition. The groundwork itself is already an extension. In the Mosaic law a basis for the work of salvation [heil] is broadly spread out in the world. In both regards, as groundwork and as extension, the Mosaic law must be understood as mediating instance between revelation (as presence of God) and existence. Revelation is the height of particularity; it is the presence and engagement of God in and with existence. Existence is the height of ordinariness. Between these two a mediation has to be brought about. What is at stake is that the salvation [heil], given in the revelation, should achieve its extension and representation in the ordinary forms of existence. In this mediation, the law of God plays its role. It is the mediating instance between revelation and existence.

It is abundantly clear that it [the law] already has this function in its kerygmatic meaning. The [preached] word stands between, on the one hand, the presence of God, unfathomably deeply hidden in the flesh and in the latter's rebelliousness and contradictions, and, on the other hand, the ordinary forms of existence, which are the very essence of superficiality and simplicity.

Preaching is the first phase of the mediation between revelation and existence. It still teems with the particularity of revelation. It takes place in the language of Canaan. Revelation itself brings it its own medium along [to engage] with existence. The law too belongs to the material of revelation that God gave to Israel and through Israel to the world. It is a gift of grace. The mediating instance is not derived from existence and its rationality. On the other hand, however, preaching already enters into the ordinary forms of existence. It wishes to be understandable. The Reformed church's language of Canaan is also, *sprituali modo*, in the way and in the power of the Holy Spirit, more understandable than the Latin of the Roman Catholic church.

This mediation, however, continues. It starts with preaching. But quite a lot comes into being alongside it. I have in mind the sacraments, the offices and the liturgy. I also have in mind the Pneumatic morality [manifested] in good works and spiritual experiences in the heart. I also, and in particular, have in mind the great apostolic pursuit of the church in the Christianizing of the culture and the theocratizing of the state. Particularly in spiritual experience and in culture we approach most closely the ordinary forms of existence, though here too the eschatological vision is never permanently and completely reached.

We do have to consider that the Mosaic law has *acquired* this kerygmatic meaning. This meaning does not encompass the original and the ultimate, the eschatological sense [zin] of the law. The law has *become* (γέγονεν) to us a pedagogue to Christ.[7] In itself it is not that. That involves a certain alteration in the law.

Eschatologically the law is not the means and Christ the end—precisely the opposite.[8] It has acquired this function of kerygma concerning Jesus the Christ only historically, in the historical acts of God, in God's

---

7. See Galatians 3:24.

8. One of the core tenets in Van Ruler's theology is that special revelation, the election of Abraham and of Israel, the incarnation, the covenant, the suffering of Jesus, atonement, justification, the church, the offices of the church and so forth, are not ends in themselves but only means.

Editor's note: The argument of this essay is that the Mosaic law is not included in this list; it has an eschatological significance as law of the kingdom. By contrast, the gospel is necessary only for the sake of the fulfilment of the law. See also Van Ruler's doctoral thesis on the fulfilment of the law, entitled *De vervulling van de wet*.

deed of fulfilling the law. Eschatologically it is the law of the kingdom.[9] *That* is what it is about: not about Jesus Christ and not about the Holy Spirit but about the kingdom. And then not only about the kingdom but also about the law, God's justice [recht] and the image [of God] in existence, and then [the latter] in its ordinary forms. The law, then, is more eschatological than the gospel. It partakes in the self-sufficiency of the kingdom, in the very being [wezen] and the future of God.

We can, however, have no knowledge of this in the present except via the Messianic and the Pneumatic, via the incarnation of the Word and the indwelling of the Holy Spirit. That is why we can never understand the law fully as the law of the kingdom and have to be satisfied with understanding it as the mediating instance between revelation and existence, even though we may never forget its eschatological nature, also and particularly when it functions as mediating instance between revelation and existence. Then too we have to be stubbornly focused on the *ordinary* forms of existence: not on the church but on the world, not on the sacrament but on ordinary life, not on the ecclesiastic liturgy but on religious experience and culture, not on church polity but on the state.

II

Some things become even clearer when we now turn to what I called the existential meaning of the Mosaic law. It made the cross, the sacrifice of atonement, necessary. That Jesus, the Messiah, had to go the way of sacrifice to accomplish the work of salvation [heil] on earth can, after all, be understood only from the Mosaic law. Here we obviously have to think mainly of the ceremonial parts of the Mosaic law. As soon as we let go of the Mosaic determination of the gospel of Jesus Christ and try to understand the cross in terms [derived] from common human consciousness, we are bound to come to the worst and most dangerous misfortunes.

The history of theological thought about the mystery of the cross as cross of atonement serves to prove this. Soon people start finding in the sacrifice on the cross an absolute necessity grounded in the very being [wezen] of God, a theological, even an eschatological necessity. Or people find in it an anthropological necessity grounded in human consciousness: the cross is then merely a depiction of God's attitude. I believe that

---

9. Elsewhere Van Ruler describes the law as a form [gestalte] of the kingdom of God, indeed as *the* form of the kingdom of God. For references to the relevant literature in Dutch, see Van Ruler's *Verzameld werk 5C*, 814, note 11.

we should find in the sacrifice on the cross nothing but a historical-soteriological necessity. That is to be understood only in Mosaic terms. The atonement of guilt is as much an Israelite affair as the guilt itself.

Meanwhile the Mosaic ceremonies have now acquired a historic accent through the cross of Golgotha. With that existence as such is ceremonially structured: we find our entire salvation [heil] in the historic cultic act of love. In that [way] the ceremonial law of Moses has, through its fulfilment in Jesus Christ, acquired absolute authority for all times and for all people.[10] In comparison to this, it would have been child's play had the apostolic Christianization of the peoples consisted in enforcing the Mosaic ritual on the people. The heathens would easily have been able to assimilate the Mosaic rituals. But the cross of Golgotha they have never assimilated.

Nor *can* it be assimilated. Through the cross the ceremonies have acquired a historical accent. The *means* of salvation [heil] has become *fact* of salvation [heil]. The Mosaic law has not been abolished by that. On the contrary. By that it has come into force in the most painful way. We may consider the spiritual suffering of Kierkegaard and Pascal regarding the *historical* cross that can never be fully processed. For the sake of this suffering, which is salutary—to retain it as such in Christian existence—we should not carry the cross as human symbol into the church. We should leave it, as spiritual reality, to stand in history. At this point Rome and the Reformed [branch of the] Reformation part ways.

This historical character of the cross also reminds us of the historically determined character of the Mosaic law. I expressly speak of the Mosaic law and not only of the law of God. It is a figure [gestalte] from history with all the fortuitousness and eccentricities that are typical of such things. We constantly have to keep that in mind when we want to engage with the problems of God's law in a theological and not a philosophical way. Theology orients itself, up to its most systematic pinnacles, to the historical-eschatological acts of God and not to the eternal conditions of being of reality.

Therefore the law of God cannot be absorbed into ethical rationality either. It cannot be identified, even and precisely not regarding its

---

10. See Van Ruler's doctoral thesis, *De vervulling van de wet*, 164. He explains what the "fulfilment" of the law truly means: "bring into effect, empower, filled with power, in Kraft setzen ..." The basic thesis of this dissertation is the following: "that the living God filled God's law with Spirit through the Messiah means that God in the Messiah and through the Spirit made the law applicable for all peoples and all ages" (translation—EMC). See *De vervulling van de wet*, 319.

content, with the *lex naturalis*[11] and not even with the common human moral law. To illustrate that, it suffices [to note] that the Mosaic law really does not have only moral parts and aspects but also ceremonial and juridical ones. Yet that is not even the most important [consideration]. What is decisive is that the essential content of the law is not in any way to be found in ethical or any other rationality, but only and exclusively in the presence of God. The law of God is historically determined because revelation is a historical act of God. The living God was and is present in Israel, in Jesus Christ. In God's law it is about God and about God *only*.

Therefore it is impossible to conceive of God's law as a formal instance. What matters is the content. What matters is God's just order [recht] that wants to be established in the flesh. One can unceasingly add to and subtract from this. It is subtracted from when, for instance, the prophetic criticism of the law come to the fore and at a specific point denies that the cult had been instituted by God. It is added to when, for instance, the baptism of John is classified under the just order [recht] of God.[12]

The law is a historically determined configuration [gestalte] in that it is an entirely mobile entity. Involuntarily, the idea of a continuing revelation arises here. Regarding the gospel, we would have to reject this idea. Regarding the law, it is fully worthy of consideration.

This mobility of the law of God is seen most clearly in the fact that [the law's] fulfilment—the gospel of Jesus Christ—can be canonized, so that the New Testament is simply added to the Old Testament by a divine act.

All of this entails that the gospel of Jesus Christ is Mosaically determined in a radical and decisive way. It is Israelite in character. Its uniqueness has to be respected. It can never be assimilated into common humanity. It is even less possible with [the gospel] than with the Mosaic law. It is less eschatological. It knows more realities and dualities. The law retains more reminders of the kingdom—in its structure, nature and intent—than the gospel. That, then, is why the gospel is temporal and the law eternal.[13] The incarnation of the Word as a whole and the indwelling of the Holy Spirit as a whole are an intermezzo.[14] Eschatologically they

---

11. *Lex naturalis*: Natural law.

12. See Matthew 3:15.

13. Van Ruler was influenced by Bavinck in this regard. See Bavinck's *Reformed Dogmatics Volume 4*, 450. See Van Ruler's *De vervulling van de wet*, 473.

14. Van Ruler regarded the incarnation, the indwelling of the Spirit, the ascension,

are undone.[15] Eschatologically what is at stake is the kingdom and created reality. The Messiah and the Pneuma were given solely for the sake of the kingdom. The gospel is there for the sake of the law.[16]

In order to retain a grip on this, we do well to accentuate the duality of the messianic and the pneumatic in the gospel. Certainly, we cannot express the gospel reality only pneumatologically. Jesus Christ remains the center of Christian existence. But nor can we express the gospel reality only christologically. Around Jesus Christ the Spirit creates all of history.[17] This duality of the christological and the pneumatological accentuates the temporary nature of Christian existence in its Christianness. It creates an intrinsic relativity.

If we respect adequately this duality, relativity and temporary nature of the messianic-pneumatic reality, we would not easily come to the point where we accentuate the element of the ontological, of the new and of the definitive to such an extent that we regard the Old Testament as outdated. [We would not] understand Jesus Christ only *senkrecht von oben*[18] and find in the Christian situation only a continuation of Jesus Christ. By the Word that has become flesh,[19] I would wish to understand the Word that God spoke to the fathers.[20] The element of the ascension[21] within the messianic reality entails that the Christian situation is to be understood as an incidental repetition of the people of Israel and not as a permanent continuation of the incarnation. Therefore, through the fulfilment in

---

heaven, the church, the New Testament apostolate, theocracy, and so forth as an intermezzo. This is closely related to his view that special revelation, the incarnation, the church, the offices of the church, and so forth are God's emergency measures. For cross-references to literature in Dutch, see Van Ruler's *Verzameld werk 5C*, 176, note 89.

15. Elsewhere Van Ruler defends the thesis that the Son return the kingdom to the Father in the eschaton so that the incarnation and the indwelling of the Spirit are cancelled in the eschaton. For cross-references to literature in Dutch, see Van Ruler's *Verzameld werk Deel 5C*, 745, note 73.

16. See Van Ruler, *De vervulling van de wet*, 474.

17. In Van Ruler's oeuvre one finds four variants of this thought, namely a) that God creates history; b) that the Word of God creates history; c) that the Holy Spirit creates history and d) the revelation creates history. For cross-references to literature in Dutch, see his *Verzameld werk 5C*, 170, note 29.

18. Here Van Ruler is opposing the views of Karl Barth. The expression "senkrecht von oben" (vertically from above) is derived from Karl Barth. See, for example, his *Der Römerbrief* (second edition) (Zürich, 1989), 6.

19. See John 1:14.

20. See Hebrews 1:1.

21. For Van Ruler's views on ascension, see his *Verzameld werk 5C*, note 133.

Jesus Christ, the Old Testament and the Mosaic law have come into force for the whole of Christian existence.

III

With this we come to the third [aspect] that I named: the functional meaning of the Mosaic law. It describes the function (within the whole of the kingdom of God, seen as God's historical-eschatological actions) of the forms [gestalten] that the Spirit creates in the historically produced existence around the Messiah, the crucified Jesus and the Jesus exalted to heaven.

If we see these forms in a one-sidedly christological way, then we must surely see Christian existence as a whole and in all its facets in terms of its identity with the incarnate Word. Then, moreover, [Christian existence] gets a completely ontological quality. Then no room remains for the future of God. The eucharistic sacrifice becomes identical with the sacrifice on the cross. The liturgy is seen as a heavenly reality. The priest is an *alter Christus*.[22] The good works of love are no longer to be distinguished from the work that Christ has accomplished once and for all. Culture has to be brought under the roof of the church and sanctified there. Ordinary life is made sacral. The emperor receives his sword from the pope. People are after the whole of Christ. And everything ultimately falls in this category. Existence is brought to a halt in the *nunc aeternum*.[23] There is no place for the Spirit. Nor is there any place for history. Because there is essentially no place for God, for God's future, for God's kingdom and God's law.

We must not see the forms of Christian existence in a christological way either. The truth of the ascension resists that. We have to see them pneumatologically. The Spirit creates them within the chaos and from the nothingness of existence lost in guilt. The Spirit creates history. It is the work of sanctification and Christianizing.

We must not think about this in a one-sidedly ecclesiological way, as if the true and only work of the Spirit is to be found in the church. The church is not the only creation of the Holy Spirit. We must think about

---

22. *Alter Christus*: Another Christ.

23. *Nunc aeternum*: The eternal now, the dimension of eternity that is present in a single moment in the here and now. This is a classic term used in mystical and philosophical circles. For Van Ruler's views in this regard, see the cross-references in his *Verzameld werk 5C*, 815, note 32.

this much more broadly; we must think about it apostolically. Where the doctrine of the church usually appears in the traditional ordering of the dogmatic loci, I would place the doctrine of the apostolate.[24] This undoubtedly also embraces the doctrine of the church, of the offices and of the sacraments. But it much more pertinently embraces the teaching about the ethos, spirituality, culture, the state and the colony.

When we think in this broad way, we would not so easily slip into the objectionable identification with the messianic reality. We would, particularly, not lightly identify a Christianized culture and a theocratized state with Christ as a whole. All these and similar figures are no more than shadows of the eschatological reality that falls along the walls of existence. They are Mosaic. After all, the Mosaic law describes the shadow of the things to come.

The image and the body are from Christ. Therefore, the fulfilment of these shadows does not consist in their being abolished because "reality" has come to replace them. In the fulfilment reality has not come in their place. That happens only in the consummation. In the fulfilment, the shadows have received an embodiment. In that way they have gained substance, durability and bodiliness. In this way they have come into force. In the Christ all God's promises are "yes" and "amen."[25] The shadows are not vain and empty; Jesus Christ is their truth.

So it is through the knowledge of the fulfilment of the shadows in Jesus Christ that we receive the courage and joy to live—in the pneumatically filled existence—in the shadows of the eternal kingdom. Then that is no longer too little for us. Nor does it appear senseless and vain to us. We no longer despair of human existence or reality. They are shadowy across the board. We live our entire lives symbolically and figuratively. The Spirit creates the image of God within existence. The Spirit establishes the just claim [recht] of God in the flesh. In that, we are not oriented to Jesus Christ but to the kingdom of God. Christ is, however, the guarantee that we are not pursuing a fata morgana.

This shadow character, this symbolic-figurative [character], is inherent in all of Christian existence. That obviously holds for the church, the offices, the sacraments and the liturgy. However, it also holds for ethos. The entire sanctification is nothing more than a symbol of the salvation [heil]. The pneumatic morality too. Even all of humanness. It is really not

---

24. See Van Ruler's *De vervulling van de wet* where he observed that the church is apostolic. Her very being is the apostolate (p. 75).

25. See 2 Corinthians 1:20.

the eschatological reality itself but shadows called up by the Spirit. And spiritual experience as well. In that the deepest shadow falls along the most intimate walls of existence. In spiritual experience[26] the kingdom is erected in the dark passions of the blood. Yet we should not imagine that the important matter, what it is all about, is a reborn person who knows though spiritual experience the just order [recht] and love of God. It is to a far greater extent about the sacrifice of Golgotha. And to an even greater extent about the future of God.

We do have to remember—in close connection to the shadow character of the Mosaic law—the commandment character of God's law. We do not do well to transmute the entire law of God into promises: "you shall" instead of "you must," We can plead that the law of God and the counsel of God, the will of the command and the will of the decision, constantly coincide.[27] Indeed, I do not see how we can maintain the biblical teaching about the law and its fulfilment in its purity without ever again confirming this coinciding. The law is spiritual and only Godself can legitimately handle it. But then we must also carefully leave the command character of the law intact. What is liberating about the biblical teaching is precisely that the counsel of God comes to human beings in the imperative form as well. [This implies that] human action has been taken up in God's action. So a field of historical and moral freedom is created around human beings in which they can busy themselves, in accordance with their calling, with their task—the task of being human. This freedom that is introduced by the imperative form of the law of God breaks through all fatalism and all determinism regarding existence. Through this, people who despair of everything and are in danger of perishing of dejection are raised up from their death.

We can even go one step further and speak not only of the commandment character but also of the work-covenant character of the law. "Do this and you will live"[28]—that is indeed the deepest truth that can be expressed about the relationship between God and humanity. *That is what it is all about: that all God's words will happen in existence.*

26. For Van Ruler's views on spiritual experience (Dutch: bevinding), see the extensive cluster of texts on "The experience of salvation [heil]" in Van Ruler's *Verzameld werk 4B*, 497–808.

27. Van Ruler hints at the classic distinction in Reformed theology between the will of God's decree (*voluntas decreti vel beneplaciti*) and the will of God's command (*voluntas decreti vel beneplaciti*). Van Ruler often refers this distinction. For cross-references to literature in Dutch, see his *Verzameld werk 5C*, 718, note 53.

28. See Luke 10:28, Leviticus 18:5.

Therefore we shall be judged also according to works. That is why we should not preach and believe grace without justice.

Now it is the commandments in particular that call forth the shadows of the eternal kingdom. All of existence is called into being by the creative, that is, the commanding, word of God. The gospel too derives its appeal form from the law. The gospel is proclaimed so that it may be both believed and *confessed*. This confessing, this confessional character of Christian existence is form and image, is shadow. The confession is, after all, the epitome of explicitness and externality. This confessionality permeates the whole of sanctification and the whole of Christianization.

IV

With this I have approached the final [aspect]. The functional meaning of the Mosaic law automatically passes over into the material [meaning]. The Mosaic law describes the function of the figures [gestalten] that the Spirit creates in Christianizing existence. We can also say: The Mosaic law describes not only the function but also these figures [gestalten] themselves. From the Old Testament we know not only who Jesus the Christ is; from the Old Testament we also know what the human being, what the cosmos, what history is. The whole of existence comes forth out of the Thora: marriage, sexuality, property, jurisprudence [recht], punishment, the state, and so forth. If it is a matter of ordering the life of the individual and of the community in a truly Christian way, that is, according to the knowledge of the Lord, the Lord's salvation [heil] and the Lord's justice [recht], then we would have to apply the Mosaic law to and impose it on all the peoples of the earth. The Mosaic law too belongs to the revelation of the living God to Israel and—in Israel—to the world. It is truly *no quantité négligeable*.²⁹

In this regard, we have to keep in mind the historically determined and—what goes along with that—mobile character of the law. The notion of continuing revelation comes to the fore. The entire Thora returns in Christian existence, but it returns in a divine way. In the human sense of the word there is not that much to be said for continuity. We may consider what has happened with the ceremonies. We must therefore eschew the narrow-mindedness and desperate clutching of the sects that believe continuity can be detected only when the entire Thora return in

---

29. *Quantité négligeable*: Something that one does not need to reckon with.

the literal sense, in all its rational forms. We have to take our stand in history and to remain open to every new historical situation. We have to act in a pneumatic-historical way. And therefore not fear compromises.

Regarding the mobile character of existence, we must keep in mind that we have to act according to times and circumstances. How far can we go in firing the gun of Christian existence with Mosaic ammunition?[30] In how many instances can we, according to the Thora, apply the death penalty?[31] In the Mosaic law it applies, for instance, also to homosexuality. That we cannot follow now. The commonwealth does not tolerate this holiness of the Lord. But then we should not say that we are too civilized for it. We would do better to bewail the level of unholiness of our commonwealth. We do, however, have to take the weakness of the times into account.

The entire apostolic work of Christianizing is marked by one enormous ambivalence. It is marked by aggression on the one hand and by synthesis on the other. With the knowledge of the Lord, of the Lord's salvation [heil] and of the Lord's just claim [recht] as point of departure, unremitting and fierce aggression is directed at the basic passions of pagan existence. In that the Mosaic law has its full material meaning. This aggression is always the beginning, the point of departure. We cannot be directed at the synthesis *a priori*. Then we would cripple ourselves with regard to our apostolic resilience. The synthesis is always *a posteriori*. It is not the purpose but the result. A mixing of revelation and heathendom occurs.[32] That is what we call Christiandom.

However, although we cannot say *a priori* that this synthesis is located in the apostolic intention of the human being, we do have to say *a posteriori* that it is located in the historical-eschatological intention of God. This mixing of revelation and heathendom implies that salvation [heil] loses its distinctiveness in the long run and is taken up into the ordinary forms of existence. An intrinsically Christian world is not easily imagined, not only not in practice but also not in principle. The living

---

30. Translator's note: This sentence, literally translated, reads: "How far can we go in drawing the bow of Christian existence in a Mosaic way", where "draw the bow" is a Dutch expression for "shoot". Even in Dutch the sentence is a bit forced but the meaning is clear from what follows: "To what extent can we impose the Mosaic law on Christian existence."

31. See Leviticus 20:13.

32. Such a synthesis or mixing of revelation and heathendom (or variants thereof) is a theme that frequently occurs in Van Ruler's oeuvre. For citations to such literature in Dutch, see Van Ruler's *Verzameld werk 5C*, 746, note 82.

God is ultimately concerned with the human being and nothing else. God's concern is with humanness.

Naturally, the same danger that overcame the people of Israel also threatens the Christianizing of the world. Would the [other] peoples not also violate the law of God, attempt to establish their own righteousness, forget the Lord, fall into guilt and crucify Christ? To all these questions the answer has to be in the affirmative. In a Christianized culture Christ is indeed crucified anew. Yes, Christianizing *is* crucifixion. Christianizing takes place so that people may become sinners. And the essence of history consists in the entanglement—one that cannot be disentangled—of guilt and atonement. In this mystery, however, the law of God has its meaning, a meaning that cannot be annulled.

The Kingdom of God and History[1]
[1947]

IT MAY BE SAID of every sub-section of academia that the researcher and lecturer, precisely in the disruption of modern consciousness, constantly and rightly feels the need to gain an insight into the relationships linking his or her area of academic work with the whole of academia and the cultural world. For theologians this holds to a particularly high degree. On the one hand, the nature of the object of their research entails that they constantly have to penetrate to the last and deepest questions concerning being human before God and in the world. They have this in common with philosophers. On the other hand, by virtue of the curiously specific form of their research, they have for long and quite naturally shared in a deeply concerned way in the crisis in the conception of science that has shocked our culture over the last decades.[2]

---

1. The inventory number of the Dutch text, "Het Koninkrijk Gods en de geschiedenis" is I,225. This was Van Ruler's inaugural lecture in accepting the position of professor on the behalf of the Nederlandse Hervormde Kerk at the Rijksuniversiteit te Utrecht on 3 November 1947. It was published as a brochure by G.F. Callenbach in Nijkerk. It was also included in the posthumous volume *Verwachting en voltooiing: Een bundel theologische opstellen en voordrachten* (Nijkerk, 1978), 29–42. For this edition Ms van Ruler made some changes to the text that are indicated in annotations where appropriate. The footnotes numbered in square brackets were provided by Van Ruler himself. In them, references to Dutch and German sources are therefore maintained throughout. This essay is included in Volume 5C of Van Ruler's *Verzameld werk* (2023), 816–841.

2. [1] G. van der Leeuw, *Inleiding tot de theologie* (Amsterdam, 1935).
Gerardus van der Leeuw (1890–1950), Dutch Reformed (Hervormde) minister at 's-Heerenberg (1916–1918); professor in history of religion, phenomenology of religion and Egyptology at the Rijksuniversiteit te Groningen (1918–1950); Minister of Education, Arts and Science (1945–1946). He taught Van Ruler when the latter studied at Groningen.

This need is felt the more strongly when one has been called to work in three separate areas in theology as disparate as biblical theology, national church history and missiology.[3] The problematic of the relationship between theology and the sciences and the crisis of the relationship between science and culture then combine to leave one with an irresistible urge to find a synthesis in which one can cast some light on the unity of one's material. How can biblical theology, national church history and missiology be united in anything resembling a harmonious whole? To rephrase, how do we fit Abraham, the father of the faithful, Voetius,[4] a central figure in Dutch theology at this illustrious university, and the people of Papua, as objects of mission, into one field of vision? Still differently, stated in the language of the visionary theologian Hoedemaker,[5] what relationships are there between the apostolic gospel, national theology and the Christianizing of the world?

I do not know of a better way to do justice to this need for and urge towards orientation and synthesis than to spend this hour with you delving into the question of the relationship between "The Kingdom of God and History."

Within this theme, the Bible, the church and mission find their place without coercion. And it cannot but have an enlightening effect regarding the relationship between theology and the other academic disciplines when a theologian deals in a serious way with the phenomenon of history.

In this regard, I can heartily endorse the following dictum of Huizenga[6]: "For us, history is as much a form of truth about the world as

---

3. Initially, Van Ruler was charged with teaching biblical theology, national church history and internal and external mission. When his colleague S.F.H.J. Berkelbach van der Sprenkel retired in 1952, Van Ruler's teaching responsibilities were changed to dogmatics, Christian ethics, the history of the Nederlandse Hervormde Kerk, her symbols and liturgies, and church polity.

4. Gisbertus Voetius (Gijsbert Voet; 1589-1676), Dutch Reformed (Gereformeerde) theologian, professor of theology and Eastern languages at the University of Utrecht.

5. [2] Ph.J. Hoedemaker, *Het apostolisch evangelie en de nationale theologie* (Amsterdam, 1876). From the same author, also see *De Reformatie en de Gereformeerde Kerk* (Amsterdam, 1878), especially p. 29f.

Philippus Jacobus Hoedemaker (1839-1910), Dutch Reformed (Hervormde) minister, professor at the Vrije Universiteit te Amsterdam (1880-1887), and later again a minister in Nijland and Amsterdam (1890-1909).

6. Johan Huizinga (1872-1945), Dutch historian who lectured at the universities of Amsterdam (1903-1905), Groningen (1905-1915) and Leiden (1915-1942). Among his well-known books are *The Waning of the Middle Ages* (1919), *Erasmus* (1924) and *Homo ludens* (1938).

philosophy and the natural sciences are."[7] In the phenomenon and the science of history, we have been given an indispensable tool to fathom, or at least approach, the riddle of reality and specifically of being human.

We would, however, have to go a step further and speak of history as an unavoidable tool, not merely an indispensable one. Particularly since Troeltsch,[8] we have become deeply aware of the historical character of all of our thinking and our entire existence. He spoke of historicizing as a foundational motif, alongside the mathematical naturalization, of the modern spirit [geest].[9] Under "historicizing" he did not primarily understand the accumulation of the material of our historical knowledge or the entry into our field of vision of so many strange historical phenomena and cultures. His problem was not the relativism and skepsis of the comparative study of history, but precisely the fundamental incompatibility of each new, individual figure [gestalte] in historical life. Spirit [geest] itself, with its rationality and normativity, became historical to him. And in the face of the superior force of this metaphysical essence of history, he no longer found it possible to rely on abstract values, ideals, norms and ideas. The riddle of reality and of being human appeared to lie in the category of history—in the unceasing arising of ever new positions and ever new figures [gestalten].[10]

The academic study of history, particularly what Troeltsch himself called the "formale Geschichtslogik" (formal logic of history)[11] and the "materiale Geschichtsphilosophie," (material philosophy of history)[12] will have its work cut out wrestling with this insight into "die innere Natur der Geschichte" (the inner nature of history)[13] that he developed. It touches

7. [3] J. Huizinga, *De wetenschap der geschiedenis* (Haarlem, 1937), 106.

8. Ernst Troeltsch (1865–1923), German philosopher, historian of religion and sociologist of religion. He was professor of theology in Heidelberg and of philosophy in Berlin.

9. [4] Ernst Troeltsch, *Gesammelte Schriften, Dritter Band. Der Historismus und Seine Probleme. Erstes Buch: Das logische Problem der Geschichtsphilosophie* (Tübingen, 1922), 9 et *passim*.

10. [5] I described some of these in more detail in my contribution "Historische cultuurvorming" in the volume *Geschiedenis: Een bundel studies over de zin der geschiedenis* (Assen, 1944), 200–21.

11. *Formale Geschichtslogik*: Formal logic of history. The source is E. Troeltsch, *Gesammelte Schriften, Dritter Band: Der Historismus und Seine Probleme: Erstes Buch: Das logische Problem der Geschichtsphilosophie* (Tübingen, 1922), 27–67.

12. *Materiale Geschichtsphilosophie*: Material philosophy of history. The source is E. Troeltsch, *Gesammelte Schriften, Dritter Band*, 67–83.

13. *Die innere Natur der Geschichte*: The inner nature of history. The source is E. Troeltsch, *Gesammelte Schriften, Dritter Band*, 165.

on virtually all positions in the sciences and culture. He himself also did not escape from it, in spite of his synthesis of a-prioritizing formal thought and psychologizing philosophy[14] of life, and in spite of his harking back to Leibniz's monadology and Spinoza's identity speculation. Nevertheless, I think that one does an injustice to the seriousness of his statement of the problem if one should, following Huizenga, manage to discern in the historicizing of the life of the mind only "a disastrous bewitchment."[15] Troeltsch himself had explicitly argued that his "historicizing" is not to be identified with the skeptical relativism and the aesthetic-contemplative pessimism of what he called the "bad historicism".[16] And it is highly questionable whether the German title of his posthumous book, *Der Historismus und seine Überwindung*, was accurately chosen.[17]

However that may be, it can hardly be said of the theological development since the demise of Troeltsch in 1923 that it has seriously grappled with the problem that he raised. Karl Barth, whose first great book appeared in a second, completely reworked edition in 1921,[18] very soon came to dominate the field in the development of theological thought. On account of his totally new approach, people lost interest in the phenomenon of history in their theological deliberations. He concentrated the attention of theologians on the eternal point of calling and election. F. Gogarten[19] did still make some attempts to go into and take seriously

---

14. [6] The book *Der Historismus und seine Problem* is dedicated to the memory of Wilhelm Dilthey and Wilhelm Windelband!

15. [7] J. Huizinga, *De wetenschap der geschiedenis*, 91.

16. The source is E. Troeltsch, *Gesammelte Schriften, Dritter Band*, 122f.

17. [8] Ernst Troeltsch, *Der Historismus und seine Überwindung*. The content consisted of five lectures prepared for England (see. F. von Hügel's "Einleitung"). The English title was: *Christian Thought: Its History and Application*. See "Bibliographie der von Troeltsch im Druck erschienen Schriften," in Ernst Troeltsch, *Gesammelte Schriften, Vierter Band. Aufsätze zur Geistesgeschichte und Religionsgeschichte*, herausgegeben von Hans Baron (Tübingen, 1925), 872. F. von Hügel thought that the second part of *Der Historismus und seine Probleme* is found in this work. More detailed analysis suggests that it offers no more than a summary of the first part! Karl Heussi, *Die Krisis des Historismus* (Tübingen, 1932), 14, also cast doubt on the aptness of the title.

18. [9] Karl Barth, *Der Römerbrief* (München, 1922).2 [Van Ruler made an error in the note to indicate the date as 1922. The date in the text above, i.e. 1921 is nevertheless correct—DvK].

19. [10] Friedrich Gogarten, *Die religiöse Entscheidung* (Jena, 1924); *Illusionen. Eine Auseinandersetzung mit dem Kulturidealismus* (Jena, 1926) (The title already says a lot!); *Ich glaube an den dreieinigen Gott. Eine Untersuchung über Glauben und Geschichte* (Jena, 1926); *Glaube und Wirklichkeit* (Jena, 1928).

the life work of Troeltsch.[20] Yet, on the one hand, his thought was determined to too great an extent by the critical-ethical category of the personal decision for him to be really open to the theological relevance of the figures [gestalten] of history. On the other hand, his theological work got swept up in the whirlpool of National Socialism. K. Barth undoubtedly did eventually free himself from the existentialist individualism of Kierkegaard, the great enemy of all philosophy of history,[21] but he did not go beyond the church.[22]

Culture, the state and history still did not attain any worthy place in his theological field of vision. That may well be because he saw the essence of the church as exclusively concentrated in proclamation. Ecclesiologically, he still found it difficult to accommodate phenomena such as church polity[23] and church history.[24] In his theological mode of thought, the word cannot become any image and the judgement does not pass over into form.

Structurally this "critical" theology fully fits into in the period that commenced after the previous World War and that Bornhausen[25] characterized as one of "deliberate neglect of further work along the lines of Ernst Troeltsch"[26] For theology such abandoning of the problems posed by and even the problems of Troeltsch had the result that it progressively

---

20. Friedrich Gogarten (1887–1967), German Lutheran theologian, at first a member of the school of dialectical theology. Professor at the universities of Breslau, Bonn (in 1935 as replacement for Karl Barth who was dismissed) and Göttingen (1935–1955). In 1933 he joined the so-called "German Christians."

21. [11] Sören Kierkegaard, *Philosophische Brocken* en *Abschließende unwissenschaftliche Nachschrift*, 2 Bände (Jena, 1925). On Kierkegaard, see especially Hermann Diem, *Philosophie und Christentum bei Sören Kierkegaard* (München, 1929) and Eduard Geismar, *Sören Kierkegaard* (Göttingen, 1929).

22. [12] Since 1932 Barth wrote his magnum opus under the title of *The Church Dogmatics*!

23. [13] Karl Barth, *Christengemeinde und Bürgergemeinde* (Zollikon-Zürich, 1946); id., *Die Schrift und die Kirche* (Zollikon-Zürich, 1947).

24. [14] Karl Barth, *KD*, I/1, 3: "What is called Church history does not correspond to any independently raised question concerning Christian talk about God, and it cannot therefore be regarded as an independent theological discipline. It is an auxiliary science indispensable to exegetical, dogmatic and practical theology" (as translated by G.W. Bromiley, see Barth's *Church Dogmatics* I/1, 5).

25. Karl Eduard Bornhausen (1882–1940), German theologian and professor in Frankfurt (1934–1937). After initially being a representative of liberal theology, he became an advocate for Hitler's rise to power and a member of the NSDAP.

26. [15] Karl Bornhausen, "Geschichte: II. Geschichtsphilosophie, geschichtlich?", in *Religion in Geschichte und Gegenwart*2, Zweiter Band, 1103.

lost contact with other academic disciplines and was no longer able to contribute to an encompassing vision on cultural existence as such. Missiology alone should have restrained us from this atrophy of theological attention. When we but glance once at the recent literature in missiology, we are astonished at the perspectives, not only world-wide but world historical, that it opens.[27] Mission is engaged in a fundamental way in the world-historical process. We see this all the better when we do not shy away from the interconnectedness of all mission work and the formation of culture. Then, indeed, perspectives are opened on the position of Christianity in the global commonwealth.[28]

☙

One can explain in other ways as well why theological studies should devote particular attention to the phenomenon of history and to the problems brought forth by it. To this end one could point to church history.[29] One could, with even stronger emphasis, point to biblical theology and biblical studies in general. The material of theological studies is historically determined across the board. Even the most systematic of the theological disciplines, dogmatics, does well, if it is not to pass over into philosophy, to keep the historical character of God's being [wezen] and works constantly in mind.[30]

Nevertheless, theology is in no way a study of history. Nor can it understand itself as a component within this study unless it is willing to surrender all its presuppositions, yes, its very self. Now to express, on the one hand, this specificity of theology and to manage to retain, on the other hand, its openness to historical reality, we have to turn, at this point, to the other term of our theme: the kingdom of God.

---

27. [16] H. Kraemer, *The Christian Message in a non-Christian World* (London, 1938). See also the impressive report by J.C. Hoekendijk, *De wereldzending in oorlogstijd 1940-1944* ('s-Gravenhage, 1946).2

28. [17] See the comment by H. Kraemer, *Van godsdiensten en menschen: Reisindrukken van een Tambaram-ganger* (Nijkerk, 1940), 200: "When one listens carefully, one gets the feeling that there is an unarticulated need among a people who are becoming Christianized such as the Batak, that reached towards a *"corpus Christianum,"* towards a religiously sanctified order of life."

29. [18] J. Lindeboom, "Der Historien Claghe," in *Vox Theologia* 7/1 (October 1935), 26-31.

30. [19] In my book *De vervulling van de wet: Een dogmatische studie over de verhouding van openbaring en existentie* (Nijkerk, 1947), I tried to illustrate this statement.

It is one of the most important results of the modern study of the Bible that we have come to see that in the idea of the kingdom of God we have a curious and irreplaceable concentration of the kerygma of the synoptic gospels.[31] The roots of this synoptic proclamation of the kingdom are to be found in late-Jewish apocalyptic and eschatological conceptions, in age-old Arian, specifically Iranian, complexes of ideas and in the Old Testament's prophetic-messianic preaching on God.[32]

Terminologically the word appears only a few times outside the Synoptic gospels: it is generally replaced by a large number of synonyms. Still, one can maintain with Karl Ludwig Schmidt[33] that at the level of content the entire proclamation of Jesus Christ and his apostles is summarized in the figure of the kingdom of God.[34] If we further take into consideration that the Old Testament is also filled with the proclamation of the kingship of Yahweh,[35] that one of the most important roots of the Israelite Messianic expectation has to be sought in the problematic of the earthly kingship,[36] and that the people of Israel and their Torah is to be understood as the Herrschaftsbereich Gottes,[37] then the conclusion lies at hand that the kingdom of God is not only the central datum in the Synoptic and New Testament proclamation and teaching but—with

---

31. [20] Albert Schweitzer, *Geschichte der Leben-Jesu-Forschung* (Tübingen, 19264); H.M. Matter, *Nieuwere opvattingen omtrent het koninkrijk Gods in Jezus' prediking naar de synoptici* (Kampen, 1942).

32. [21] Rudolf Otto, *Reich Gottes und Menschensohn: Ein religionsgeschichtlicher Versuch* (München, 19402) emphasized the Asura-religion in the Vedas, Parseeism, and the book of Enoch (p. 2, 7, 11, 69). The old-Israelite Messianism is absorbed in that. Karl Ludwig Schmidt, "Die Wortgruppe βασιλεύς κτλ. im NT," in *ThWNT, Band 1*, 585, sought the roots more in apocalyptic and rabbinism, while he saw prophetism as standing in the background. See also G. van der Leeuw, *De primitieve mensch en de religie: Anthropologische studie* (Groningen/Batavia, 1937), 182; and Wilhelm Friedrich Mundle, "Reich Gottes: I. Im AT und NT, " in *Religion in Geschichte und Gegenwart2, Vierter Band*, 1817-1822.

33. Karl Ludwig Schmidt (1891–1956), German New Testament scholar and an early exponent of the so-called form criticism school. He was professor of New Testament studies in Gießen (1921), Jena (1925) and Bonn (1929) and was dismissed by the national-socialists in 1933. He then became professor of New Testament studies in Basel.

34. [22] Karl Ludwig Schmidt, "Die Wortgruppe βασιλεύς κτλ. im NT," 584–85. See also his *Die Polis in Kirche und Welt: Eine lexikographische und exegetische Studie* (Zürich, 1940).

35. [23] Gerhard von Rad, " מֶלֶךְ und מַלְכוּת im AT," in: *ThWNT, Band 1*, 56–69.

36. [24] A.H. Edelkoort, *De Christusverwachting in het Oude Testament* (Wageningen, 1941), esp. 111ff.

37. [25] Wilhelm Friedrich Mundle, "Reich Gottes: I. Im AT und NT," 1817.

many modifications—in the proclamation and teaching of the Bible as a whole.[38]

With this result of modern biblical studies, much has been gained for the [understanding of] the problem of the relationship between theological studies and history, revelation and existence.

First of all, surely this, that this central placement of the proclamation of the kingdom of God creates a space, in the theological sphere of interest and Christian confession, for history in its broadest extent. Here we touch upon the relationship between the eschatological emphases in the biblical teaching on the one hand and the christological and pneumatological emphases on the other. With a degree of caution, one could say that what is at stake in the Bible, also in the New Testament, is not in the final instance the gift of the Messiah and of the Pneuma but the coming of the kingdom of God on earth, however much the coming of Jesus Christ and the work of the Holy Spirit are unconditionally necessary for that. From this perspective, the element of truth in the statement, otherwise highly contestable,[39] of A. Harnack:[40] "Not the Son but only the Father belongs in the gospel as Jesus proclaimed it"[41] can be discerned. The kingdom of God encompasses the gift and the work of the Messiah and the Pneuma; it is concentrated in these and is especially in this way present on earth as historical reality. Yet in its true, eschatological essence it [the kingdom of God] goes beyond these and embraces *more*.[42] There-

---

38. [26] In the works of Ph.J. Hoedemaker, *De kerk en het moderne staatsrecht, Eerste stuk: De kerk naar goddelijk recht* (Amsterdam, 1904); id., *Handboek van het Nieuwe Testament, deel 1: Christus naar de vier evangeliën* (Amsterdam, 1906); id., *Handboek voor het onderwijs in het Oude Testament ten dienste van de catechisatie, het huisgezin en de zondagsschool, tevens leidraad bij het onderzoek der Heilige Schrift* (Amsterdam, s.a. [1886]); id., *Zonde en genade: De tijd der Richteren* (Amsterdam s.a. [1887]); id., *Genade en recht: Israël onder de regeering van Saul en David* (Sneek s.a. [1893]), there are important notions and suggestions relating to this problem. They have, up to now, not received the attention they deserve. These may be made fruitful for the question of "the kingdom of God in the Old Testament," and also for the no less important question of "the Old Testament in the kingdom of God."

39. [27] See G. Sevenster, *De christologie van het Nieuwe Testament* (Amsterdam, 1946).

40. Adolf von Harnack (1851–1930), German Lutheran theologian and professor of church history in Berlin. He is well-known as the author of three volumes of the *Lehrbuch der Dogmengeschichte*.

41. [28] Adolf von Harnack, *Das Wesen des Christentums* (Leipzig, 1902), 91. The German text quoted by Van Ruler reads: "Nicht der Sohn, sondern allein der Vater gehört in das Evangelium, wie es Jesus verkündigt hat, hinein."

42. [29] See the distinction between the *regnum Christi* and the *regnum Dei* in Oscar Cullmann, *Königsherrschaft Christi und Kirche im Neuen Testament* (Zürich, 1941); id.,

fore the preaching of the Christian church and, in connection with that, theological studies will not be allowed to restrict itself to the proclamation of Jesus the Christ but—with that as point of departure—will have to devote its loving attention to the whole of reality, particularly historical reality,

To that has to be added that the biblical concept of the kingdom of God has a particularly dynamic content and, in that respect, not only leaves room for history but is at its core very definitely laden with an awareness of the historical dynamic. This insight too can be accepted with thanks as a result of modern biblical research. The kingdom of God is not to be understood in a static-ontological sense as another spatial entity, sphere or world alongside or above our temporal-spatial world, but as God's action with this our reality.[43] This central notion corresponds to the core of the biblical teaching about the being [wezen] of God. It is, after all, typical of the biblical teaching on God that it does not see the living God in God's very being [wezen] as an eternal, self-sufficient Being [Zijn] but as Will.[44] God acts as Lord in the field of reality and *makes* existence historical. On viewing the Bible as a whole in its difference from non-biblical religions, one is even inclined to declare that the Bible takes God to be, above all else, a historical power. At least, we owe to this knowledge of God and expectation of the kingdom our European conception of history in itself. It is in this that we may, following Sprey,[45] find one of the

---

Christus und die Zeit: Die urchristliche Zeit- und Geschichtsauffassung (Zürich, 1946) and the important notion, derived from 1 Corinthians 15, that the Son will hand over the kingdom to the Father.

Van Ruler regarded the *regnum Christi* (the kingdom of Christ) as a modality of the *regnum Dei* (the kingdom of God). For cross-references to literature in Dutch, see his *Verzameld werk 5C*, 716, note 19.

43. [30] For this insight I am indebted to Heinz-Dietrich Wendland, *Die Eschatologie des Reiches Gottes bei Jesus: Eine Studie über den Zusammenhang von Eschatologie, Ethik und Kirchenproblem* (Gütersloh, 1931), esp. 16–18.

44. [31] For some years now this has been emphasized among us by J. de Zwaan, for example in his *Paulus als geestelijk hervormer* (Amsterdam, 1932). This insight is now common in biblical studies. Cf. Ludwig Köhler, *Theologie des Alten Testament* (Tübingen, 1936), 12

45. Karel Sprey (1897–1979), classicist and teacher at the Christelijk Lyceum in Hilversum. In the text quoted here Sprey writes, "What is remarkable is *that a view of the future is lacking* [in Plato; DvK]. I say that in spite of the *Politeia*, which, on closer scrutiny, turns out not to be an ideal for the *future* [...], noting at the same time that he is not alone in this. Instead, one of the most fundamental differences between Greek thought as a whole and the contemporary European experience of life is, to my mind, revealed here " See K. Sprey, "Plato en de geschiedenis," in H. Honders, e.a. (reds), *De zin der geschiedenis* (Wageningen, 1944), 44; emphases by Sprey).

most fundamental differences between the whole of Greek thought and the current European experience of life.[46] The cycle of nature has been breached and reality is directed at its future; expectation has come in the place of anamnesis. The idea of entelechy[47] and process is perceptively attacked, precisely also in modern science and the philosophy of history, by the problem of the "new" that constantly breaks through spontaneously.[48] It has to be said that, without any doubt, the Bible understands God's actions with God's world as ultimate actions, that, in other words, the kingdom of God is inherently eschatological. Yet this transcendence of the being [wezen] of God is, nevertheless, to be understood in a qualitative sense only, as a hidden superiority over all opposition.[49]

Therefore there is so little contrast between the eschatological kingdom of God and history that it should far rather be said that it is precisely God who creates history.[50] [This] God comes at us from God's eschatological being [wezen],[51] from God's future, and overwhelms us.[52] Ac-

---

46. [32] K. Sprey, "Plato en de geschiedenis," in H. Honders, e.a. (red.), *De zin der geschiedenis* (Wageningen, 1944), 44.

47. Entelechy: The Greek term ἐντέλεχεια was introduced by Aristotle in *De Anima* II.1, 412a9. Its meaning in Aristotle is debatable. Van Ruler uses it to describe a goal that is immanent in a particular reality—like the oak is present in germ in the acorn.

48. [33] On the problem of the "new" see Ernst Troeltsch, *Der Historismus und seine Probleme*, 167; id., *Der Historismus und seine Überwindung*, 39; id., "Die Bedeutung des Begriffs der Kontingenz," in id., *Gesammelte Schriften, Zweiter Band: Zur religiösen Lage, Religionsphilosophie und Ethik* (Tübingen, 1913), 769-78.

49. [34] Heinz-Dietrich Wendland, *Die Eschatologie des Reiches Gottes bei Jesus*, 20, speaks of a "weltüberlegene Weltmächtigkeit des Reiches." On page 22 he observes that one should not see such transcendence as negative but as positive, not as "Abseitig," aloofness but as "Allmächtigkeit" omnipotence. Cf. Paul Althaus, "Reich Gottes: II. Dogmatisch," in *Religion in Geschichte und Gegenwart 2, Vierter Band* (1923).

Translator's note: [W]eltüberlegene Weltmächtigkeit des Reiches is untranslatable. The idea is that the kingdom is a world power, a power in the world, that is nevertheless superior to the world and goes beyond it.

50. In Van Ruler's oeuvre one finds four variants of this thought, namely that it is (1) God, (2) the Word of God, (3) the Holy Spirit, and (4) revelation that creates history. See the cross-references to literature in Dutch in Van Ruler's *Verzameld werk* 5C, 170, note 29.

51. Translator's note: There is a word play here in Dutch involving "coming towards" [toekomende] and "future" [toekomst].

52. [35] I provided a more detailed justification and explanation for this understanding of God in my *De vervulling van de wet*. Cf. the conclusion of K. Sprey in "Plato en de geschiedenis," 57: "Plato taught that a philosophy of history in the true sense of the word is only possible for one who has an eschatology."

cording to biblical teaching, God does this particularly in God's deed of revelation. This is historical, an event in the true sense of the word.

Therefore it belongs to the structure of the Christian faith that it is bound to historical facts, these being understood as acts of God. And particularly when we distinguish between the Messianic and the Pneumatic moments with the necessary consistency, it turns out that this structure of Christian faith has sufficient elasticity to encompass the phenomenon of history in its broad scope. As soon as we place some emphasis on the work of the Holy Spirit, [it is seen that] Christian faith is not bound only to evangelical and biblical history but embraces church history and mission history as well. In [doing] that, it impinges—in its way—on the history of the human race. The Christian confession then inevitably displays aspects of a philosophy of history and theology is [then] approaching (on its way towards) the other academic disciplines and philosophy.

But there is more. The eschatological kingdom of God not only leaves room for the reality of history in connection with special revelation and not only thrusts humanity into the dynamics of history. If we are to get to the bottom of the connection between the kingdom of God and history, it is also of the highest importance to note that the biblical idea of the kingdom includes a tendency to expansion, starting from the eternal point of calling and election in the temporal reality. As soon as the idea of the kingdom fully breaks through in Christian proclamation and becomes completely dominant, the word is expanded to image and the judgement to form. The image of God[53] comes to surround the Word of God and the form of life the final judgement. Here we can consider the problem of how we should translate *malkuth* and βασιλεία, as king*ship* or king*dom*. However much the first meaning may stand in the foreground because of the dynamic being [wezen] of God in the Bible, it is beyond doubt that the second meaning is an indispensable association of the main concept.[54] Here we may also consider the central problem of biblical studies as a whole: the relationship between gospel and law and, related to that, the relationship between the Old and the New Testament. The expectation and the proclamation of the kingdom entail the necessity

---

53. [36] See G. van der Leeuw, *Het beeld Gods* (Amsterdam, s.a. [1939]).

54. [37] Rudolf Otto, *Reich Gottes und Menschensohn*, 12–13, 17, 37; Wilhelm Friedrich Mundle, "Reich Gottes: I. Im AT und NT," 1817, speaks of a "notwendige Wesenbestimmung" ("necessary determination of the essence"). I depart here from Heinz-Dietrich Wendland, *Die Eschatologie des Reiches Gottes bei Jesus*, 15, who declares: "However, this secondary meaning of the word is not relevant for grasping the concept of the kingdom of God."

that, in the existence in which the proclamation of the gospel of grace has been established, God's law—as the law of the kingdom—should be seen to be working towards the sanctification of all that exists.[55] Sanctification intends the restoration and preservation of the image of God in human life. This immediately brings to the fore the question about the meaning of the Old Testament, and the national-symbolic form of life of revelation contained in it, for the kingdom of God in the history of the human race.[56] The church-historical and missiological disciplines of theological studies already have their hands full with the problem of what shaping has taken place and can take place in this regard during the process of Christianization. It should, however, be explicitly mentioned that there are problems here and that in these moments of the image and the form the most intimate relationship between the kingdom of God and history are indicated.

Let us now take stock.

Our first result is that we have come to see that the kingdom of God surrounds history as its margin. The kingdom is the eschaton of history. What that means I can best express in the words of Van der Leeuw. He said: "History is eschatologically determined. It cannot be understood or even experienced from within itself. Its meaning [zin] lies in the acts of God that are in place before there can be talk of history and after history will have been completed. "The kingdom of God is nothing else but the entry of God into history. Therefore it has come, it is coming and it will come."[57]

Our second result is that, according to biblical-Christian teaching, the kingdom is revealed: in its presence in history, in the Messiah and the Pneuma, in the gospel and the law, in the Old and in the New Testament, in the sacrament and in a Christianized culture. The historical, dynamic and then also relative character of all these figures [gestalten] of the kingdom of God have to be fully acknowledged.

55. [38] On the meaning of the word "sanctification" in distinctive biblical language, see K.H. Miskotte, *Bijbelsch A.B.C.* (Nijkerk, s.a.2).

56. [39] I discussed this question in my *De vervulling van de wet*, and in my *Religie en Politiek* (Nijkerk, 1945), 123–49.

57. [40] G. van der Leeuw, "Het koninkrijk Gods en de geschiedenis," in *Het oecumenische gesprek der kerken* ('s-Gravenhage s.a. [1939]), 104, 109. Also cf. his *De primitieve mensch en de religie*, 183.

Our third result is that we have come to see clearly that, considered theologically, history itself and as such, with all its enigmas, lies as a broad margin around revelation. We came very deeply under this impression when we studied E. Stauffer's[58] book *Die Theologie des Neuen Testaments*[59] that appeared in 1945. He summarizes all the theological material of the New Testament under the heading "Die christozentrische *Geschichts*-theologie des Neuen Testaments," ("The Christocentric theology of history of the New Testament")[60] and therefore sees New Testament theology and biblical theology in general as a struggle with the riddle of history. This becomes most palpable when the problem of the state comes under discussion. The state is a central datum in profane history. But Stauffer avers that people of the Bible had, often with an extremely risky self-denial, engaged with the logic of the imperial idea of Egypt, Assur-Babylon and Persia.[61] They did not restrict themselves to the figures [gestalten] of revelation but grappled in history itself with the problem of God's acts and the demonic forces. We have learned a similar respect and an identical seriousness in face of historical reality from our deliberations concerning the relationship between the kingdom of God and history.

History as one of the forms of the truth about the world: this form of truth is not that of theologians. That they will have to leave to researchers in other academic disciplines. They are, however, highly interested in it. They can, moreover, make a contribution to the problematic of this form of truth by concentrating in all their work on the question concerning the meaning [zin] of the historical character of human existence. Why *is* this world there and why does it *endure*? I can finally conclude my exposition by a concise consideration of this question.[62]

The wonderment, the θαυμαζεῖν, about the fact that the world is there and that it endures is not only the womb of all philosophy, science and culture. It returns to an exacerbated degree, as astonishment, at the

---

58. Ethelbert Stauffer (1902–1979), German theologian, professor in New Testament in Bonn (1934–1948) and Erlangen (1948–1967).

59. [41] Ethelbert Stauffer, *Die Theologie des Neuen Testaments* (Genf, 1945). Cf. W.C. van Unnik, *Hedendaagsche problemen in de nieuw-testamentische wetenschap* (Nijkerk, s.a. [1947]).

60. This is the title of the second part of Stauffer's *Die Theologie des Neuen Testaments* (Geneva, 1945), 34ff.

61. [42] Ethelbert Stauffer, *Die Theologie des Neuen Testaments*, 64.

62. Translator's note: A play on words in Dutch, which cannot be replicated in English, renders this sentence somewhat awkward in translation.

hour of birth of theological reflection. Christian theology is surprised that the world is *still* there, partly because of the corruption in which it lies submerged, partly because of the salvation [heil] that has appeared in it. And it searches with the deepest interest, along with all of humanity, for an answer to the question: Why? It searches for a theodicy.

Theologically one can look for the meaning [zin] of history in the time granted to human beings to be converted to the kingdom of God. That, briefly put, is the position of Barthian theology. Historical reality then appears under the category of the patience of God. As such it would stand outside the actual eschatological-soteriological activity of God. It [historical reality] can at most be appreciated as a secondary sphere of power within the *regnum Christi*.[63]

One can, in immediate contrast to that and following the theology of Coccejus[64]—a theology in the baroque style!—seek, in a periodizing and rhythmic way, the meaning [zin] of history in its *perfectio*, its completeness, and find in this *perfectio* of the historical process a reflection of the *perfectio* of Holy Scripture, yes, of the being [zijn] of God.[65] In a later century, Kuyper[66] sought, in a corresponding way, its meaning [zin] in the collective display of the image of God.[67]

One can also, again in directly contrast to *that*, entertain the idea that K. Heim[68] once floated: that the necessity and to that extent also the meaning [zin] of history lies in the incarnation of Satan, in which the rebellion against God became complete and manifest, that is, became visible.[69] In view of texts such as Luke 21: 22, 24—where there is mention of

---

63. [43] This view is defended in all the writings of Karl Barth and his followers.

64. Johannes Coccejus (1603–1669), Dutch professor of sacred philology, Hebrew and theology in Bremen, Franeker, and Leiden (1650–1669).

65. [44] See Gottlob Schrenk, *Gottesreich und Bund im älteren Protestantismus, vornehmlich bei Johannes Coccejus: Zugleich ein Beitrag zur Geschichte des Pietismus und der heilsgeschichtlichen Theologie* (Gütersloh, 1923), 220–21.

66. Abraham Kuyper (1837–1920), prominent Dutch pastor, theologian, journalist and politician. He was a central figure in the *Doleantie*, that led to a schism in the Dutch Reformed Church (Nederlands Hervormde Kerk) that took place in 1886. He established the Vrije Universiteit te Amsterdam and was professor there from 1880 to 1901. He was a long-standing member of Parliament and also served as the Dutch Prime Minister (1901–1905).

67. [45] A. Kuyper, *De gemeene gratie, Tweede deel: Het leerstellig gedeelte* (Kampen, 1932³), 630.

68. Karl Heim (1874–1958), German Lutheran theologian in Münster (1914–1919) and Tübingen (1920–1939).

69. [46] Karl Heim, *Jesus der Weltvollender: Der Glaube an die Versöhnung und Weltverwandlung* (Berlin, 1937), 239.

the fulfilling of the times of the pagans and of the days of vengeance—it becomes hard to deny that this terrifying idea fits into the New Testament kerygma structurally. [70]

Yet another aspect comes to the fore when one declares with Z.W. Sneller:[71] "The meaning [zin] of history is the realization of the kingdom of God,"[72] or, somewhat more carefully, with H. Bavinck,[73] that the kingdom of God is, in spite of much that militates against the idea, the essential content, the core and purpose of the whole of world history.[74] As we know, this idea has been the submerged tendency in all Christian-European reflection on the riddle of history since Augustine.[75] [This has been so] even though [the latter's] contrast between the *civitas Dei* and the *civitas terrena*[76] has undergone major modifications[77] over the course of the centuries, particularly at the hands of the Reformation, and though the dream of the kingdom of God persists among us only in its many secularized forms.[78]

Starting from what we have found as result of our discussion of the relationship between the kingdom of God and history, we should now deal carefully with all these answers to the question about the meaning [zin] of the continued existence of the world and of the historical character of existence. When we speak theologically, there should be, before

---

70. [47] These dark tones are also heard in A. Kuyper, cf. *De gemeene gratie, Eerste deel: Het geschiedkundig gedeelte* (Kampen, 1931³), 215-16: "Assuredly it was *grace* [common grace that made the continued existence of the world possible –AAvR], but a frightened grace, an anxious grace, a grace that makes the soul shudder when it contemplates what an ocean of human sorrow is opened up along with that." See also his view on common grace as a stimulus and perfectioning of sin. See in this regard also my *Kuypers idee eener christelijke cultuur* (Nijkerk, s.a. [1940]), 37, 126, and S.J. Ridderbos, *De theologische cultuurbeschouwing van Abraham Kuyper* (Kampen, 1947), 59ff.

71. Zeger Willem Sneller (1882–1950), Dutch historian, professor of Dutch economic history at the Nederlandse Economische School te Rotterdam.

72. [48] Z.W. Sneller, "De zin der geschiedenis," in H. Honders, e.a. (red.), *De zin der geschiedenis* (Wageningen, 1944), 32.

73. Herman Bavinck (1854–1921), minister in the Christelijk Gereformeerde Kerk ("Christian Reformed Church"), professor of theology at the Theologische School te Kampen (1883–1902), and at the Vrije Universiteit te Amsterdam (1902–1921).

74. [49] H. Bavinck, *Kennis en Leven* (Kampen, s.a.), 51.

75. [50] See O. Noordmans, *Augustinus* (Haarlem, 1933).

76. *Civitas Dei*: City of God; *civitas terrena*: earthly city.

77. [51] D. Nauta, "De geschiedbeschouwing der Reformatie," in H. Honders, e.a. (red.), *De zin der geschiedenis* (Wageningen, 1944), 140-60, esp. 152-55.

78. [52] Walter Nigg, *Das ewige Reich: Geschichte einer Sehnsucht und einer Enttäuschung* (Zürich, s.a.).

all else, a deep respect for the secret of God in the existence of the world in itself and in history in particular. We have to admit with Huizinga that it is God who determines history and that the "how" of things is therefore unfathomable; so that humans have to content themselves with the "that."[79] But that does not alter the fact that the kingdom of God, certainly not as a static theocracy but definitely as a militant sanctity that revolutionizes this world, is not immanent in the world, but breaks into and breaches it imminently.[80] R. Otto[81] has described in an impressive way[82] how it is present in our time as *mirum* and μυστήριον.[83] We have also said that we do not do justice to the Bible if we see this presence of the kingdom in history christologically only. We should at least also see it pneumatologically.[84]

Then history is to be understood as the enthronement of God. Without any doubt there is something festive about that. It also belongs to the essence of the Christian-European experience of life that people derive from expectation of the kingdom of God the courage to enter into history. Nevertheless, in using the word "festive", we are saying too much. The enthronement of God is not primarily a festival but rather a struggle. It is [a matter of] ruling *in medio inimicorum*[85] (Psalm 110; 1 Corinthians 15). In the historical process all the rebelliousness of humanity against God's rule is revealed.

The one side of the enthronement of God is thus to be found in the guilt of humanity. Hegel sought in freedom the final goal of the world in

---

79. [53] J. Huizinga, *Hoe bepaalt de geschiedenis het heden? Een niet gehouden rede* (Haarlem, 1946), 11.

80. [54] G. van der Leeuw, *Gemeenschap, gezag, geloof* (Groningen/Batavia, 1937), 53, 66.

81. Rudolf Otto (1839-1937), German theologian and religious studies scholar, professor in Breslau (1915-1917) and Marburg (1917-1937). He was especially famous for his book *Das Heilige: Über das Irrationale in der Idee des Göttlichen und sein Verhältnis zum Rationalen* (1917).

82. [55] Rudolf Otto, *Reich Gottes und Menschensohn*, passim.

83. *Mirum*: Extraordinary, wonder; μυστήριον: Mystery.

84. [56] Cf. H. Faber, *De geschiedenis als theologisch problem: Een studie naar aanleiding van Ernst Troeltsch "Der Historismus und Seine Probleme"* (Arnhem, 1933); and id., *De leer van den Heiligen Geest: Studie over eenige actueele vraagstukken der moderne theologie* (Arnhem, 1941).

85. *In medio inimicorum*: Amid the enemies. The expression is found in the Vulgate in Psalm 109:2: "Virgam virtutis tuae emittet Dominus ex Sion: dominare in medio inimicorum tuorum." See also 1 Corinthians 15:25.

its historical process and found this freedom in becoming conscious.⁸⁶ Paul also sought God's purpose in the history of God's great paradigm, the people of Israel, in becoming conscious, but then in becoming conscious of guilt.⁸⁷

This human rebelliousness and guilt could not, however, prevent God from ascending to the throne. On the contrary! The other side of the enthronement of God is, in turn, to be found in the atonement for guilt. God's throne is the cross.

The riddle of history is not solved but summarized in these two—guilt and atonement.⁸⁸ History is to be understood as a permanent syntax of guilt and atonement and the cross as the most essential form of life of the kingdom of God in history.

This view does not allow us to fit together [the parts of] history as if it were a jigsaw puzzle: the kingdom of God does not render it transparent. We can, however, draw courage from it to take our stand in history; to busy ourselves in it though contemplation and action; to confess to the kingdom of God; to respect the superiority of destiny to the deed and all knowledge; to accept the ambiguity of all the work of Christianization as both aggression and synthesis; to persevere within this relativity, and simply to be ourselves.

Only in this way can we become what we were meant to be, namely human. And with that God's intention with history will also have been achieved. For however much the kingdom of God is eschatological by nature, it is to no less an extent soteriological and directed at *this*: that humanity, *in* its historical existence, be saved.⁸⁹

---

86. [57] Georg Wilhelm Friedrich Hegel, *Sämtliche Werke*, herausgegeben von Georg Lasson, *Band VIII: Die Philosophie der Weltgeschichte, Erste Hälfte, 2: Die Vernunft in der Geschichte. Einleitung in die Philosophie der Weltgeschichte* (Leipzig, 1930), 41.

87. [58] See my *De vervulling van de wet*, 367–408.

88. The understanding of sin as guilt and of reconciliation as atonement for guilt are core motifs in Van Ruler's theology that are expressed throughout his oeuvre. In this regard, he gives preference to Anselm's understanding of atonement as satisfaction. For cross-references to literature in Dutch, see Van Ruler's *Verzameld werk 5C*, 127, note 28.

89. In the final part of his inaugural lecture, Van Ruler addressed words of thanks, appreciation and respect to various groups and individuals in the audience. This part was omitted from the published version in the volume *Verwachting en voltooiing* and is omitted here as well.

Law and Gospel[1]
[1948]

THE QUESTION ABOUT THE relationship between law and gospel[2] is as old as Christendom. It arises immediately once the Messiah enters the Torah to fulfill it in a divine fashion—up to the last tittle and jot.[3] Perhaps the tension is also already present in the Old Testament. I am thinking of the rough interface between the Mosaic religion and prophetism that can never be evened out. I am also thinking of the fact that within the Mosaic law itself the problem of the relationship between God and humanity has not been solved, at least not for [our] rational consciousness. But in the New Testament the problematic rapidly breaks forth fully, to such an extent that Christianity and Judaism already stand in opposition to each other in the New Testament canon. With that the theological problem acquires its (indispensable) religio-historical and even cultural-historical form. Paul and James, John and the author of the Epistle to the Hebrews have wrestled with [the problem] in a grand manner. One can safely say that the center of all apostolic thinking and reflection lies here: how this duality in the gift and act of God—the Torah and the Messiah—is to be understood. Once the Word of God acts in the world of pagans, the problem acquires all its theological, religio-historical and cultural-theoretical complications. Christianity is understood as *nova lex*;[4] Gnosticism alle-

---

1. The inventory number of the Dutch text, "Wet en Evangelie" is I,234. This was a lecture for a society for Evangelical Lutheran pastors in Amsterdam on 8 April 1948. The original consisted of 28 hand-written pages. This essay was published for the first time in Volume 5C of Van Ruler's *Verzameld werk* (2023), 842–857.

2. Van Ruler later portrayed the relationship between law and gospel as a "deadly Lutheran dialectic". See his "Perspectieven voor de gereformeerde theologie," in *Theologisch Werk* 2 (Nijkerk, 1971), 87.

3. See Matthew 5:18.

4. *Nova lex*: New law.

gorizes the Old Testament; Marcion[5] wishes to abolish it. Here too Roman Catholicism embarks on its majestic synthesis of the *mandata Dei*, *consilia evangelica* and *ius naturae*;[6] the Old Testament becomes nothing more than a non-binding *illustration* of the totally new reality that is given in the incarnation of the eternal Logos. Luther, in turn, brought the gospel radically to the forefront and did not know what to make of the law—it merely brings people to their knees and is an *opus alienum Dei*[7] that really belongs in the town hall. Calvin, starting from the New Testament, harks back radically to the Old Testament as *more* than illustration, as fully and *constitutively* Word of God in the world. Kohlbrugge,[8] taking things to an extreme, declares that what matters for all time and eternity is nothing but the law of God.

In the face of such a deluge of problems, we cannot but feel helpless when we have to explicate the relationship between law and gospel within the brief time allotted [to a lecture]. And not only the history but also the actual situation of the church confronts us with a multitude of problems. The development of modern Protestantism and the National-Socialist crisis of our Western culture have competed to table the question: Does the church do well to continue even now to lug the ballast of the Old Testament with it?[9] Old Testament studies reveals time and again that the book as a whole is a world apart, in which everything is interwoven with everything else in a highly peculiar way, so that one can in *no* instance disentangle the ethos from the cult and the legal order [recht]. The problem of Jewry, of the continued existence of the synagogue alongside the church, in short, the question of Israel, emerged in a highly urgent way— in political, missionary and theological contexts. Finally, [there was] the rediscovery of the apostolicity of the church, the place, the function and the task of the church in the passage of God's Word through the centuries

---

5. Marcion (ca. 110-160) was born in Sinope along the Black Sea as the son of a bishop. He arrived in Rime around 140 where he defended he statement that the God of the Old Testament was not the same God as the Father of Jesus Christ. For his views, he was excommunicated in 144.

6. *Mandata Dei*: God's commandments; *consilia evangelica*: evangelical counsels; *ius naturae*: natural law.

7. *Opus alienum Dei*: The alien work of God.

8. Hermann Friedrich Kohlbrugge (1803-1875), initially a Lutheran auxiliary preacher in Amsterdam, after further studies in Utrecht became a minister in the Niederländisch-Reformierte Gemeinde Elberfeld (1848-1875).

9. See Adolf von Harnack, *Marcion:. Das Evangelium vom fremden Gott: Eine Monographie zur Geschichte der Grundlegung der katholischen Kirche* (Leipzig 19242), 217.

and the peoples of the earth, and, along with this, the apostolic meaning [zin] of history, the question of the Christianizing of culture, the *corpus christianum* and the theocracy, [This] led to a completely new assessment of the relationship between law and gospel. In my view, the old solutions fail us almost across the board in this new situation. We can no longer get our arsenal even from Calvin, and certainly not from Kohlbrugge, when we have to fathom the position of the church in the world theologically in a truly timely way.

As a result of this state of affairs, I see no course open to me (within the brief allotted time) but to provide some more or less loose comments on a subsection of the theme. These comments will for most part concern the character and meaning of the law of God in its distinctness from the gospel of God.

⌘

In the first place, I speak of the *form* character of the law. By that I mean more than one thing. I am thinking particularly of the distinction between the form element and the judgement quality in the Word of God. In all the pronouncements of God to human beings, the side in which the judgement quality comes to the fore the most strongly is the gospel. It is the predication that God gives to existence. It stands within the vertical dimension. The whole of human existence is seen as both messianic and pneumatic, not only in its relationship to God but *as* relationship with God. Only when we consider that the Word of God is not only gospel but also law does it become clear that the Word of God is also inherently creative and that the existence predicated in the gospel does indeed *exist* in some or other way and does so in a *specific* way, in [specific] forms. The law also creates the horizontal dimension. It confers extension and delineation to God and God's salvation [heil] in human beings and their existence. It calls up forms.

With this, however, I have not completely outlined what I mean when I speak of the form character of the law. This distinction between the form element and the judgement quality merely indicates one side of the matter, the one in which the law displays to us particularly the reality character of the existence created and predicated by the Word. As exact opposite to that, however, it must also be maintained that the law is also form in that it transcended and constantly transcends the realities and dualities posited by the gospel. I have in mind the duality of the Messiah and the Pneuma, of the *regnum Christi* and the *regnum Dei*,[10] of God's grace and God's glory, of the gospel as opposed to the law. I also have in mind the realities of the incarnation and the outpouring [of the Spirit], of our flesh in heaven and the indwelling of the Spirit in our hearts, in short, of Jesus Christ and the Holy Spirit. *Of that* Judaism and the synagogue have no knowledge. But, according to modern biblical studies, Moses and the prophets *too* had no such knowledge. And it seems to me that it is high time [for us] to pay careful attention to the stubborn resistance of Old Testament scholars to the christological interpretation of the Old Testament. Are there in this no insights into the kingdom of God that we would disregard only to our disadvantage? Does not the law of God indeed *tend*, beyond all Messianic and Pneumatic determination and specificity, to the ordinary forms of existence?

In this regard too, the law is dear to me for its form character. We should also consider how much weight the matter of form carries. A person must *live*. We do not find ourselves only in the *nunc aeternum*[11] but in time, and even this—not only space—entails the necessity of form, if only for the sake of continuity. It is not in accordance with the measure of love merely to say to people: Believe in Christ and put your trust in the guidance of the Holy Spirit. They would then find themselves only in the vertical dimension of the judgement and salvation [heil] of God. They have to, however, also find themselves in the horizontal dimension of form and their own existence. The full measure of love is reached only when the law erects the building of love around the gospel that surrounds the framework of God's just order [recht]. It was not *simply* an error and a misunderstanding when the apostolic and old Catholic church saw Christianity as *nova lex*. John and James already started doing so.

And it is not only a person who must live; a people must also live. The church must to some extent be organized in the world. Yet that is still a minor matter compared to the other matter: that the world has to be organized in the church in some or other way. To what end does the Word of God operate in history? Surely not so that immortal souls may be rescued from the earth and [taken up] in heaven. Yet surely also

10. Van Ruler regarded the *regnum Christi* (the kingdom of Christ) as a modality of the *regnum Dei* (the kingdom of God). For cross-references to literature in Dutch, see his *Verzameld werk 5C*, 716, note 19.

11. *Nunc aeternum*: The eternal now, the eternal dimension that is present in a single moment of the here and now. This is a classic term used in mystical and philosophical circles. For cross-references to literature in Dutch, see Van Ruler's *Verzameld werk 5C*, 815, note 32.

not to save some people for eternity. But only and exclusively to preserve humanity and the world for and from within the kingdom of God that comes towards us from the end.[12] Only *that* is a genuinely eschatological existence in the biblical sense of the word: to have courage and joy, to state one's stand within the chaos of guilt and perdition, within the circle of God's presence, [living] from God's salvation [heil] and with God's justice [recht]. It is not eschatological to desire to be removed from the present. That is idealism. And in contemporary Christianity, quite a lot of pagan idealism hides beneath the cloak of the biblical expectation of the future. The biblical preaching of the kingdom of God takes its stand entirely within the chaotic present and brings with it salvation [heil] for this earth. An order is erected between God and humanity, between salvation [heil] and existence and, moving from there, also an order *within* existence. Also in communal existence. Even in politics. In Scripture revelation has a national-symbolic form of life, a dream of the ruler as servant of God and shepherd of the people. In it a fiercely aggressive attack is directed at the state as it understood itself in heathendom. The peoples of the earth should live in the light of this salvation [heil] and this justice [recht]. Therefore the great apostolic work of [proclaiming] the Word amid the states, peoples and cultures is not possible unless the law, precisely also in its form character, is included [in the preaching of] the gospel as an essential component. [This applies] particularly in our time, now that we are experiencing, on the one hand, the dissolution of the Christianized societal forms and, on the other hand, the rising tide of heathendom from the East, imparting its passions and forms to the institutions of the global commonwealth. Particularly in such a time, it is to my mind *betrayal* of the cause pure and simple when the church simply states that the time of the *corpus christianum* is past, withdraws itself, prepares itself for the catacombs and cease even to *struggle*, with the kingdom of God as point of departure, to get the state in its sights as an object of Christianization. In this way the church will *certainly* not land up in the catacombs! It has turned itself into far too innocent an entity for that to happen. Hoedemaker[13] already stated that the plea for

---

12. For cross-references to literature in Dutch, see Van Ruler's *Verzameld werk 5C*, 855, note 13.

13. Philippus Jacobus Hoedemaker (1839–1910), Reformed minister, professor at the Vrije Universiteit te Amsterdam (1880–1887), and later again a minister in Nijland and Amsterdam (1890–1909). Van Ruler's source is possibly Ph.J. Hoedemaker, "Gevaarlijke wapenen": *Leerrede over Matth. 26:52*, Sneek, 1897, 21.

theocracy does not arise from the church's craving for glory; instead, the abandoning of theocracy is connected to the aversion to suffering.

⌾

In the second place, I would wish to make some comments about the *commandment* character of the law. We would have to maintain the commandment character of the law and, along with that, the law in and of itself—if only for the sake of the gospel. After all, the appeal form of the gospel cannot be understood without the law. The living God is not merely present—deeply hidden—in the interest of our salvation [heil]; God does not merely act, noiselessly. God also speaks. That is the gospel: the proclamation of the presence, God's being-there and being-busy in the interest of our salvation [heil]—in the flesh. The gospel is inherently proclamation. In spite of everything and everyone, over against everything and everyone, above everything and everyone, it is proclaimed that God is on earth and is busy saving it. That is the deepest joy of the sermon. But the gospel is *more* than proclamation. It is also appeal. It calls people from their lost state. The being and the acts, the deeds and the intentions, the words and the promises of God are proclaimed so that God may be praised and professed. Through the gospel existence is made confessional. The confession and the dogma are the first forms of Christianized existence. But it *comes* to this only when people are called to it, in other words, when what goes forth is not only a proclamation but also an appeal, a calling, an order, a commandment. The gospel in and of itself already has the form of the law. Therefore we cannot possibly let the law and its commandment character slip—in the interest of the gospel.

But for the sake of humanity too we cannot do that. The distinctiveness of human beings, the scope of their moral and historical freedom, the agential character of their existence—all of that is not merely respected, but definitely also created, restored and preserved in the commandment character of the law. Something is entrusted to them. A command goes out to them. In that, what comes to them is not merely the most particular aspect of the being and acting of God, God's salutary presence in the flesh in the Messiah and through the Spirit—that is still no more than the calling of the gospel, which makes their existence confessional. In that there also comes to [human beings] the most essential about God's being and acting. God's eschatological being that comes towards us, God's kingdom and God's full righteousness, God's eternal counsel.

And that in the form of the commandment! In *this* way, that is, that God's action is taken up in the actions of human beings. And in this way that the entire historical process is accounted for in the eternal counsel. Then no darkness remains in eternity anymore. Godself enters into existence[14] in the commandment form. Here—and only here fully—all elements of fate in existence and in the relationship between God and humanity are overcome definitively.

We should not regard this as trivial. Also from a purely practical and pastoral perspective there are highly important moments here. Through this biblical proclamation of the gospel *and* the law, and of the law in its commandment character, in which the counsel of God passes over into the actions of people, through this biblical proclamation, tired modern people are shocked from their despair-of-everything and from their bondage to fate, which is finally all that remains to them. They arise to joy.[15] Israel understood this better and held on to it more than the church does. Even Jews cling to this more than Christians. The sole difference between Judaism and Christianity may be that Christians have discerned more clearly that this passage of the counsel of God into active existence via the commandment character of the law does not take place without guilt, yes, that through this all of existence is made into guilt. I shall return to this later.

But this guilt character of existence must not scare us away from the commandment character of the law. On the contrary! Unless we pass completely through guilt, we shall never arrive at genuine humanity and, along with that, at [the One who is] truly *God*. *That* is what it is about in these things: about humanness and the biblical God.

One of the most fatal things in our time is that people on both sides impose an opposition between Christianity and humanism.[16] It is one of the main symptoms of the dissolution of our Christianized form of life. As if these were *two* things! As if humanism in the true, European sense of the word can be understood and maintained otherwise than as a form of Christianity. The moment we detach it from its historical roots in the confession of the personal God of the Bible and turn to new religious and metaphysical roots in classical thought, we *necessarily* lose the human

---

14. See A.A. van Ruler, *De vervulling van de wet,* 293.

15. "Joy" is a core motif in Van Ruler's theology. For cross-references to literature in Dutch, see his *Verzameld werk 5C,* 869, note 65.

16. On the relation between Christianity and humanism, see the cluster of texts in Van Ruler's *Verzameld werk 6B,* 711–79.

being in its true humanness. Then it [humanity] is in the end squeezed to death in one great, all-encompassing, divine relationship of Being [zijn], whether it be that of reason, that of the state, that of nature, or that of the stars. Only the God of the Bible, the Unique One, the God who is truly personality—only God creates around this human being the scope for moral and historical freedom in which the human being can be truly human. With what else is the biblical God concerned but with human beings and their humanity? This, however, can be maintained only when we cling to the law, and in particular its commandment character, and carefully respect it in all of our thinking and speaking. In this way alone do we save not only humanness but also the pure biblical kerygma about God. In this, after all, lies the real aroma of the biblical teaching: that God abandoned Godself to human existence to such an extent that God did not stop at erecting, opposite to, with and in humanity, a particular figure [gestalte] of Godself in the incarnation [of the Logos] and the indwelling [of the Spirit]. [God] even poured out, in the commandment form of the law, God's entire counsel, kingdom, righteousness and eschatological being in the *deed* of human existence, thereby *becoming* the song of the human creature. Within this eschatological range *everything* is *light*!

In the third place, the *shadow* character of the law.[17] Here we touch on one of the most intimate problems of the New Testament in its relationship to the church on the one hand and to the Old Testament on the other. To my mind, we will have to make a conscious choice at this point between the Catholic and the Reformed understanding of Christian existence, and to do so more clearly than this was done in the sixteenth century.

First, the Catholic perspective. By the word "Catholic" I mean primarily but not only Roman-Catholicism, but also Anglicanism, particularly in its Anglo-Catholic tendency, and to an extent also, *mirabile dictu*, Lutheranism. From a Catholic perspective one passes directly from the New Testament into the church. It is a complete succession. That is possible because, according to the Catholic conception of the New Testament, particularly in the New Testament fact par excellence, the incarnation, something that is in principle new has been given. In a certain sense the link with what had gone before is severed. The ancient fathers from

---

17. See Van Ruler, *De vervulling van de wet*, 286–91.

the Old Testament remained, up to the coming of the new, in the *limbus inferni*[18] and the Old Testament itself functioned, after the coming of the new, only as more or less random illustration, possibly with the aid of the means of allegory. The incarnation itself is understood exclusively vertically: the Logos that came in the flesh[19] is the eternal Logos and *ratio* that is also discussed by philosophers. The incarnation is an ontological event or even reality in the most extreme sense of the word. And it creates a situation that remains definitive in all eternity: the dogma of the two natures provides the definitive structure of the reality between God and humanity. From this Catholic vision on the incarnation as the gift of something that is in principle, absolutely, ontologically and definitively new, it follows naturally that there would be no place here for the shadows of the law any longer. The eternal reality has come to *replace* it. The relationship of Christian existence to this Messianic-Pneumatic presence of God—or, as we should then rather say, the christological synthesis of the divine and the human—this relationship would necessarily have to be determined only in the category of identity. The church is then seen as the permanent continuation of the incarnation. Its liturgy is identical to the heavenly liturgy. The essence of the sacrament lies in the sacrifice and this sacrifice is the repetition or representation of the sacrifice of Jesus Christ—in any case identical to it. The priest is an *alter Christus*.[20] Good works are an impulse in the stream of sanctity that started flowing on Golgotha. And all of this continues for all eternity: the *ecclesia triumphans* and the *regnum gloriae*[21] can no longer be separated.

Unless I am mistaken, it is only the *Reformed* branch of the Reformation that brought forward at least the germ of a radically different view of Christian existence. It took seriously the truth that in the end the Son returns the kingdom to the Father, lays off the cloak of the flesh, returns from the office of Mediator to the eternal Sonship, with the result that Triune God dwells with humanity. For it [the Reformed branch of the Reformation], the incarnation is not definitive but temporary.[22] It also

18. *Limbus inferni*: The edge of hell.
19. See John 1:14.
20. *Alter Christus*: Another Christ

21. *Ecclesia triumphans*: Triumphant church; *regnum gloriae*: reign of glory. For cross-references to literature in Dutch, see of Van Ruler's *Verzameld werk 5C*, 855, note 35.

22. For the thesis that the Son will return the kingdom to the Father in the eschaton and that the incarnation will be cancelled, see the cross-references to literature in Dutch in Van Ruler's *Verzameld werk 5C*, 745, note 73.

took it seriously that in the incarnation the eternal Son did not pass into a synthesis of the divine and the human that may be considered as normal. Instead, [the Son] took upon Himself the *officium*[23] of Mediator solely on account of the incident of sin, so that in Jesus the Christ it clearly is and remains a matter of God, the Triune, the Lord. To it the incarnation is not an ontological reality but an incidental function. Therefore it also took it seriously that the Messiah really and truly ascended to heaven, with the result that, without any doubt, we have *our* flesh in heaven. But with the result, too, that Jesus Christ, the Son of God in the flesh, is not on earth but in heaven, this being the intermezzo par excellence in the entire messianic-pneumatic intermezzo in God's actions.[24] Here the Reformed suspicion that Lutheranism is after all still busy tilting back towards Catholicism becomes acute. In the Reformed view, all depends on placing a pure and heavy emphasis on the ascension.[25] This entails that the earthly situation—in which Christian existence takes place—is to an extent exempted from the "christological reality". The altar stands in heaven. It also stood on Golgotha. But there is a tendency in Reformed thinking, in the footsteps of the letter to the Hebrews,[26] to regard the first as more important than the second. The altar in heaven is the true Pneumatic reality. The altar on Golgotha in its cultic character, however essential it is, in its historical character, within God's atoning action, always retains something of the Mosaic shadow. The sacrificial act of God on Golgotha—this historical cultic act of love—is both the concentration of all the ceremonies of the law and, given its necessity, to be understood only from the Mosaic and within the frame of the Israelite stamp of revelation. Therefore it is itself to some extent "shadow". In accordance with this, one would then be inclined to understand the Logos in the prologue to the Gospel of John, in accordance with the Gospel itself, as the word that God had spoken to the fathers. In any case, these fathers were never stuck in limbo, but always experienced bliss [zaligheid]. And in any case, we are travelling along with them, just as they are not perfected, that

23. *Officium*: Office.

24. Van Ruler regarded the incarnation, the indwelling of the Spirit, the ascension, heaven, the church, the New Testament apostolate, theocracy, and so forth as an intermezzo. This is closely related to his view that special revelation, the incarnation, the church, the offices of the church, and so forth are God's emergency measures. For cross-references to literature in Dutch, see Van Ruler's *Verzameld werk 5C*, 176, note 89.

25. For Van Ruler's views on ascension, see the cross-references to literature in Dutch, in Van Ruler's *Verzameld werk 5C*, 415, note 133.

26. See Hebrews 9.

is, completed, without us. We too stand wholly in the promise character of salvation [heil], just as they do. And it is not as if the church were a permanent continuation of the incarnation. Instead, the Christianized commonwealth, in its duality of church and state, is an incidental repetition of the people of Israel.[27]

We live in the shadows of the coming things. The body and the image are of Christ. Through Him the shadows have gained bodiliness, substance, durability and solidity. They have been full-filled, that is, a body has entered them and in that way they have come into force.[28] Just as all God's promises became "yes and amen" in Jesus Christ,[29] so that in the present we tolerate it, through Christ, to live and rest wholly and exclusively in the promise, just so we tolerate, through Christ, the shadowy nature of Christian existence, the entire symbolic-figurative aspect of being human, of the world and of all reality. Through Christ we know and are assured that that we do not exist in [a world of] phantoms but in the struggle of God to express Godself in created reality.

It is no more than form. Here I hark back from the shadow character to the form character. It is no more than form. That holds for the moral as well, not only for the cultic and the juridical. The cultic resides in the cross of Golgotha as the center of redeemed humanity, to an extent in the church but far more in the duality of church and state and most of all in the Christianizing of life as the work of praising God, as the true liturgy.[30] The juridical resides in the comprehensive ordering that the law introduces in the individual and the communal existence. What else but form is all this? The theocracy, the Christianizing of culture, the digesting [vertering]—through the Spirit!—of all vitality in the historical process, the sacraments and the liturgy, all of being church and being Christian—what else but form is all this? [Consider] even spiritual experience, the deep emotion in the blood about the Lord,[31] the Lord's

---

27. For cross-references to literature in Dutch, see Van Ruler's *Verzameld werk* 5C, 856, note 62.

28. See Van Ruler's *De vervulling van de wet*, 164. There he explains the deepest meaning of "fulfilment": bringing into force, endowing with power, filling with power, *in Kraft setzen*. The basic thesis of his dissertation is this: "That the living God has fulfilled God's law in the Messiah through the Spirit means that God has, in the Messiah through the Spirit brought the law into force for all peoples and all times" (translation—EMC).

29. See 2 Corinthians 1:20.

30. For cross-references to literature in Dutch in this regard, see Van Ruler's *Verzameld werk* 5C, 117, note 52.

31. For Van Ruler's views on spiritual experience (Dutch: bevinding), see the

salvation and the Lord's justice [recht]—there we touch on the truest, the genuine, the eternal reality. But can the children of God with such spiritual experiences understand themselves and their community other than as forms and shadows? Would they not become intolerably fanatical if they understood themselves otherwise? And do they not depart from love then? But what holds in this way in sacrament and liturgy, in church and in politics, in culture and in mystical experience, also holds in ethics. The ethos, which is without doubt called forth by the law in its commandment character, is no more than form and shadow either. It, too, is really not the essential and only thing that have to do with. What we have to do with, what is really to *be done*, is in the last instance only about the very Lord.[32] And all sanctification, also [sanctification] in the ethos, is never more than a symbolization of the salvation [heil], even though it is not we who, in our powerlessness and insufficiency, erect symbols that are ultimately but empty ones. [It is] God who, in God's sovereign power and astonishing, incomprehensible abundance, erects symbols—full, filled, fulfilled, laden with the salvation [heil] and the kingdom—in our (in many respects recalcitrant) existence. Precisely this is our deepest joy: that God did not scorn our lost and doomed existence but justified and sanctified it.

※

I come to a fourth point: the *historical* character of the law. The core of this lies in in the fact that the law of God is always also the law of Moses. I would not wish to stop with Moses, however much I would want to make him my permanent point of departure. I note that even in the Bible there is already one continuous protest against this ossification to which the people of Israel fell prey. They wished to stop with Moses. Directed against this was already the prophetic protest, born of a new [sense of the] presence of God. Also directed against this was the reproach of the gospels: if one really wants to remain true to Moses, one must accept the Messiah. Finally, directed against this was the apostolic *anáthema*: accursed is the one who wants to hold on to Christ and, *besides* Him, also still to Moses (as an additional authority! as a second or even first authority!). This protest, reproach and *anáthema* entailed that the law of

---

extensive cluster of texts on "The experience of salvation [heil]" in Van Ruler's *Verzameld werk*, 497–808.

32. Translator's note: "Have to do with" / "to be done" is an attempt to reproduce the wordplay in the Dutch.

God appeared in ever new forms: in the Sermon on the Mount and the *paraenesis*, in summary and fulfilment.

But however that may be, in a divine way Moses was faithfully honored through all this—up to the mount of transfiguration[33] and the song of Moses and the Lamb.[34] The law of God is also the law of Moses. It also has this specific, historical character. We shall not be allowed to get rid of that. Theological study is not busying itself with the abstract, absolute and eternal truth. That we leave to philosophy—to the extent that we can make any sense of it at all. Theology, across the board, even in its most systematic disciplines, deals with historical *fata*, *data* and *facta*, with words and deeds of God, with what God has done and spoken in the world.[35] As theologians, Christians and human beings we shall have to exercise ourselves thoroughly and daily in the relativity of the material of theology that flows from this. We must take leave of all philosophical absolutes.

This presses on us the more when we consider that this historical specificity of the law of God is not to be understood as merely accidental but as essential. History is not to be seen as a contingent form of the revelation, depending only on God's accommodation to the historical form of human existence. Human existence is not all that historical. It is, rather, natural. Heathendom did not place being human in the category of history but in that of nature. Existence becomes historical only through the revelation. *Then* something happens only when God reveals Godself. The Word creates history.[36] This relates, in particular, to the necessity of seeing revelation as the presence of God. [Revelation] cannot be conceived of apart from its election character and its particularity. In Israel—and only there, amidst all the peoples of the earth—God is present. That is why the law of God is, ever again also and always in its original and primary sense, the law of Moses.

This presses on us the most when we consider finally also that revelation and Torah, God and God's law cannot be separated and set over against each other. *Godself* is the sole content of God's law. In the ethos as a whole, in the cult as a whole, in the legislation [recht] of the Mosaic law as a whole, it is solely a matter of Godself, God wanting to be present

33. See Matthew 17:1–8; Mark 9:2–8; Luke 9:28–36.

34. See Revelations 15:3.

35. For cross-references to literature in Dutch regarding the historical situatedness of the Christian faith and the church, see Van Ruler's *Verzameld werk 5C*, 249, note 16.

36. For cross-references to literature in Dutch in this regard, see Van Ruler's *Verzameld werk 5C*, 170, note 29.

among God's people, imparting salvific grace. And the opposite must also be said: in Israel the law is the only form of God in as much as God is present. The tables of the law lay in the Ark of the Covenant and the ark of the covenant is to be seen as the face of God. God is present in Israel in this way: in God's law. Here all philosophical distinctions between form and content, temporary and eternal, absolute and relative, simply come crashing down helplessly. In God's law God expresses Godself, God's very being, to God's people.

With this it is also confirmed that the law is a gift of grace. It is not an attempt by human beings to reach God through their own resources. It is not human beings who determined in their thoughts what the good and the true and the beautiful is. Instead, the law was *given* to them. And through the law God gives Godself—justifying and sanctifying. "Be holy, for I am holy,"[37] God said. And also: "I am the Lord, who sanctify you."[38] This Old Testament basic structure of the law, in itself and in the whole of the covenant and revelation, will have to be carefully respected when, in our theological deliberations, we deal with the problem of the law of God, also as Mosaic law, from the perspective of the New Testament assessment of the law. Our theological approach to and assessment of the law would then have to display far greater subtlety than is commonly the case.

But that is not what I mainly wish to point out in this context. What concerns me now, regarding the historically determined character of the law, is that the law is the major content of revelation that was entrusted to Israel and that the ends of the earth should await this "teaching", this Torah. In other words, any identification of the law, even if it is only of the Decalogue, with the *lex naturae* is forbidden[39] to us in a purely *theological* context of thought. These ideas of the *ius naturae*, the *lumen naturale* and the *lex naturalis*[40] tend towards pantheism: from the given reality beams a light with a rational and moral structure, which not only lights up the whole of existence, but in which God and humanity find each other. [Even if we disregard] all the general theological objections that must be lodged against this absoluteness, we would have to distance ourselves carefully from this identification particularly in view of the biblical conception of

---

37. See Leviticus 11:44f., 19:2, 20:7; I Peter 1:16.

38. See Leviticus 21:8. Van Ruler does not quote verbatim here.

39. Translator's note: The translation reads "verboden" (forbidden) for the printed "verbonden" (compulsory). Though the latter makes sense, the context rules it out.

40. *Ius naturae*: Natural law; *lumen naturale*: natural light; *lex naturalis*: laws of nature.

the law. The law is too patently gift of grace and the content of revelation; in the Decalogue the moral is too patently entangled with the ceremonial elements. [In it] all of existence, not only the religious [aspects] but also the moral [ones], is generally seen from the perspective of the particular presence of God. (Love of the neighbor differs in principal from general love of humanity because the neighbor stands within the circle of light of this specific God and in God's presence.) Moreover, the Decalogue is too patently entangled with the entire Torah, with the whole of Scripture and with all of Israel. Finally, the true and sole content of the entire law is too patently this specific God, the very Lord, for us to regard only the form of the law as Mosaic and Israelite and the content as commonly human and "*nat*ur*a*l".

We should not think of the law of God in the terminology of nature but in that of history. Thus, in the cloak of this specific law, God acts in existence. In as much as the law is to be seen as the mediating instance between revelation and existence,[41] revelation does not derive the means for its interaction with existence from the rationality of existence. Instead, it brings forth these itself in the shape of the law. [The latter] is intrinsically designed to engage in this mediation. It is included in the transition from the outset. This has the most far-reaching consequences for our insight into the essence of salvation [heil]. When the salvation [heil] [brought by] the revelation wants to pass over to existence and to be taken up in existence in this fundamental way, then it is not as *nova creatio*[42] and also not as μεταβολή.[43] It is to be seen solely as atonement and rescue [redding]. And the relationship between salvation [heil] and reality is not to be placed in the category of synthesis but solely in that of sanctification. But, leaving that aside for now, the law is the gift of revelation and in this capacity it provides revelation with its *trait-d'union* with existence, If we reflect on this somewhat more deeply, we shall quite soon reach the conclusion that we do the law an injustice when we think of it only as mediating instance between revelation and existence. Then it merely performs its feudal duties[44] among the really important things, those that matter—salvation [heil] and existence. In

41. For cross-references to literature in Dutch, see Van Ruler's *Verzameld werk 5C*, 856, note 56.

42. For cross-references on Van Ruler's views on the term "nova creatio," see his essay on "Limits to Eschatologizing" included in this volume.

43. Μεταβολή: Change.

44. Translator's note: The Dutch "hand- en spandiensten" originally referred to feudal duties and later included other obligatory, menial duties.

the Christian context, that is, in our Messianic-Pneumatic situation, we shall never overcome this idea. Yet there *is* something that reminds us that the law does not merely perform its feudal duties, but that the law itself matters, for all time and eternity, that the law is not merely the medium between revelation and existence, but is, above and beyond all revelation *and* all existence and all mediation, the expression of the kingdom of God, God's justice, indeed the eschatological being of God. This breathtaking thought runs throughout the entire Bible. As far as I can see, only Kohlbrugge in the Christian church had sensed something of this.[45] But in our time, every conversation with Israel will be fruitless unless the Christian church indicates that it has at least some intimation of this perspective. In a purely theological consideration [of the matter], the historically determined character of the law and the eschatologically determined character of the law vie for priority. But they do not stand in opposition to one another. The historical and the eschatological belong with each other. In any case, we must say that the historical *follows from* the eschatological.

This eschatologically qualified character of the historical further entails that we have to talk not only of the historically determined but also of the historically mobile character of the law of God as the law of Moses.[46] I have already pointed out that we cannot stop at Moses. That is why it is *Moses*. We are not driven away from him by rough violence from the outside. But to remain standing *with* him, to remain standing with *him*—the *mediator* between God and God's people, who spoke to Jesus about his *departure* at Jerusalem[47]—that means precisely: entering into history. In all the Mosaic forms it is about the very Lord. All the fire of the prophetic criticism blazes freely through us, and also through the Mosaic law, when we forget this, when we no longer understand the Mosaic forms in a Mosaic way. The Lord desecrates the Lord's [own] heritage, destroys the temple, shatters the holy city. So fragments fall away from it. And the baptism of John, the law of Christ, the Sermon on the Mount and the apostolic *paraenesis* are simply added to God's legal order [recht]. The law, the Torah, was never a formal authority, meticulously

---

45. That would be why Van Ruler refers very frequently to Kohlbrugge in his thesis, *De vervulling van de wet*, e.g. 265, 268v., 294, 343, 370, 381v., 401, 404, 459, 491, 497, 505v., 509, 511.

46. See Van Ruler, *De vervulling van de wet*, 270, 273–283, 316v., 321, 353, 405, 475–478, 479, 519v., 532, 534.

47. See Luke 9:31. In using "departure" (uitgang), Van Ruler follows the Statenvertaling, which, in turn, translates the Greek (ἔξοδον) literally.

delineated and objectively laid down. The law, the Torah, is a material reality: it is identical to God's own legal order [recht]. Only in this way can the strange mixture of positive and negative assessments of the law in the New Testament be understood. Only so, too, the most curious fact of the New Testament: that the Messiah, with absolute Messianic and divine sovereign authority, positions Himself within the law and [still] says: "But I say unto you" and that He maintains that He did *not* come to abolish [the law] *but* to fulfil [it].[48] So, too, is the extraordinary use of the word "law" by Paul—in some ten meanings—to be understood. [He talks] about the law of sin and death,[49] the law that brings wrath,[50] the law that is in my members,[51] the law of the Spirit of life in Jesus Christ,[52] the law of Christ,[53] the law in which I delight in my inmost self,[54] the law of works[55] and the law of faith[56]—but it is still one and the same law of God, the law of Moses (moral, juridical and ceremonial) that is holy, just and good.[57]

The law of God is historically determined, it stands and places in history, it drives humanity into history. The notion of the historical character of existence was born in the Mosaic religion. When we consider these things and try to bring them together in a comprehensive conclusion, the theologoumenon of the continuing revelation[58] irresistibly intrudes. The law of God as historically determined figure [gestalte], as the material reality of God's just order [recht] on earth drives [us] into history, it creates, by way of speaking, history ahead of itself. It is ceaselessly added to and subtracted from. How should that happen in the history of the Christian church? When God's just order [recht] is erected amidst the heathendom of the peoples of the earth? When an individual and a communal form of life is being created? What shape does the law of God take in the church's apostolic work of Christianizing?

48. See Matthew 5:17.
49. See Romans 8:2.
50. See Romans 4:15.
51. See Romans 7:23.
52. See Romans 8:2.
53. See Galatians 6:2.
54. See Romans 7:22.
55. See Romans 3:27.
56. See Romans 3:27.
57. See Romans 7:12.
58. For Van Ruler's views on continuing revelation, see the cross-references to literature in Dutch in his *Verzameld werk 5C*, 856, note 72.

As was said, we should not leave these questions hanging. Pietism did that. And even in Pietism God's law acquired a new shape. Nor shall we be allowed to leave these questions to the state. That, more or less, is what Lutheranism and, somewhat more consistently, Eastern Orthodoxy did. Then too the law of God acquired a new shape. National-Socialism in Germany went on to speak of the *nomos*[59] of the people. Nor should we, along the lines of Roman Catholicism, limit ourselves to a simple synthesis. This solution is highly popular: one simply places the *mandata Dei*, the *consilia evangelica* and the *ius naturae* next to one another. The theory about the relationship between nature and grace later gives this popular solution an important dose of geniality. We would have to deal with this more subtly. On the one hand, we should not forget that salvation [heil] does indeed enter into heathen existence and tends to be subsumed under its ordinary forms. Heathendom gets its place in the kingdom of God. It is rescued, de-demonized and sanctified. In that there resides, if one insists on using the word, a certain synthesis. On the other hand, we may not overlook that the law of God has its historically determined character, that it is the law of Moses, that revelation itself brings with it the means of its engagement with existence and that the law of God is about the Lord and nothing else. God gets God's place in heathendom. God is glorified in it. That entails, over and above all synthesis and, in any case, preceding all synthesis, a radical aggression against all passions and forms of heathen existence. [This springs from] the true knowledge of the Lord, the Lord's salvation [heil] and justice [recht], and therefore also from the Mosaic law. That is why I say that I would not want to stop at Moses but that I believe I would ever again have to start with him and make him my point of departure. Not Aristotle but Moses is the origin of a Christianized culture!

All of this entails that the church's work of Christianizing runs its course in one massive ambivalence. We should not bewail that. In Christianity we must once and for all abjure all absoluteness and idealism resolutely and completely. This ambivalence is an essential part of the historical character of God's law. It intrinsically belongs to the duality of revelation and existence and the mediation between the two. Yes, it belongs to the relationship between God and humanity as such. The living God does indeed *struggle* to express Godself in created reality.

---

59. *Nomos*: Law.

Finally: All these considerations and categories together intend but one thing, namely, to outline the *spiritual* character of the law. For we know that the law is spiritual, Paul says.[60] We found this spiritual character of the law most clearly when we became aware of its historical character. The Spirit and history stand close to each other in the biblical knowledge of God. History is seen as the work of the Spirit,[61] who plays and struggles with the nature of pagan existence. We were naturally dealing with the spiritual character of the law equally much when we discerned the elements of the form, the commandment and the shadow in the law of God. It is the Spirit who calls forth, from the end, from God's kingdom, from God's being [wezen] coming towards us,[62] through the law, the shadows of the kingdom along the walls of existence, thereby shaping the human, individually and collectively, into the image of God. The spiritual character of the law also lies in the fact that the law of God is about Godself, that God is the only legitimate content of God's law and that God expresses Godself, justifying and sanctifying, in human existence through the law.

But when we consider all of this together, then the spiritual character of the law comes to a point in that Godself, with God's full righteousness—and to *God* alone the righteousness and the holiness is due!—approaches humanity and confronts humanity through the law, rendering humanity guilty by means of the commandment. Humanity abuses the law. It takes the law into its own hands and erects for itself. with the aid of it, its own righteousness and holiness. That is abuse of the law of God. But the inducement to this abuse lay in the law itself, specifically in its commandment character. In this way, sin gets something to grab hold of at the start of its great deception of humanity. That is how it went with Israel. The living God not only cast the people into guilt[63] through the law but kept them in guilt. And in Paul there appears, alongside this world historical effect of the law in the great paradigm of the people of

---

60. See Romans 7:14.

61. For cross-references in this regard, see the Van Ruler's *Verzameld werk* 5C, 170, note 29.

62. Translator's note: There is a wordplay in the Dutch original between "future" (*toekomst*) and "come upon" (*toe-komt*).

Editor's note: Here Van Ruler may well be pre-empting later German discourse on a proleptic eschatology: God is coming towards us from the future, i.e. "Gottes zein ist im Kommen."

63. See the glossary on "schuld." Here and in the rest of the paragraph, the translation "debt" or "indebtedness" would fit the context better than "guilt."

Israel, the depth-psychological effect of the law in the struggles that each heart has with God. We must then ask ourselves whether the most typical insight provided by the New Testament is not this: that the apostolic work of Christianization takes place also and mainly so that humanity will fall into guilt and not so that humanity and the world should become better. Indebtedness is the most characteristic aspect of the relationship between God and God's creation. And history is to be understood only in this way: the cart of the kingdom of God has to make its way through the deep mud of guilt.[64] In this crushing of guilt, the human being becomes truly human for the first time. In other words, in it true humanity is found.

History is not only the process of guilt and penance but also the totally new possibility of the atonement for guilt. Therefore, history in its fullness can be defined only as the permanent syntax of guilt and atonement,[65] around and from out of the enthronement of God. All of that would become understandable from [a full treatment of] the theme of law and gospel. But in this treatise, I restrict myself to a few remarks on one subsection. That in the process especially the moment of guilt should come to the forefront should not be taken as a shortcoming. Guilt is so deeply ingrained in the situation in which God and humanity interact that in all our thinking in theology, cultural theory and philosophy of history we never have done with our pondering of the question: "Quanti ponderis sit peccatum?"[66] And as long as we have not discovered the *felix culpa*,[67] we do not realize what is really at stake between God and humanity.

---

64. The metaphor of a cart is possibly derived from a Dutch folk song that starts with the line: "A cart on the sandy path did ride; the moon was bright and the road was wide; the pony trotted merrily" (translation—DGL). Van Ruler uses this metaphor often.

65. *Syntaxis*: Combination.

66. *(Nondum considerasti) quanti ponderis sit peccatum*: (Have you not considered) how weighty sin is. This is an implied reference to Anselm's, *Cur Deus Homo*, I.21

67. *Felix culpa*: Happy fault. For cross-references to Van Ruler's use of this term, see the Dutch edition of Van Ruler's *Verzameld werk 5C*, 857, note 83. The expression is derived from the "Exultet" (the hymn formerly sung to the Easter candle as symbol of the risen Christ during the Easter eve celebration). It contains the line: "O felix culpa, quae talem ac tantum meruit habere Redemptorem!" (O happy fault that deserved to have a Redeemer of such quality and greatness.") It is cited by, among others, Thomas Aquinas, *Summa theologiae, III*, q.1, a.3, ad 3.

I Believe in Eternal Life[1]
[1948]

"I believe in eternal life"—this article of faith means in the biblical and Christian sense of the words in the first place that I should take death seriously. It is the last enemy to be conquered.[2] And not to be conquered at the end of my life, in my struggle with death. In that death is not overcome; I am overcome. Death reigns and triumphs. *That* is why it is called the *last* enemy that has to be conquered, because it is eliminated only at the end of this dispensation, at the parousia of Jesus Christ, at the inauguration of the kingdom of glory. Its power may have been broken, the sting may have been taken from it, for us it may have lost its deepest terror, but it does still reign unchecked. Its definitive overthrow and elimination—from what is and happens—awaits the last days.

That is how it stands with all the forces that have pounced on God's good and beautiful creation: death, disease, suffering, transience, vanity, sin, hunger, and so on. They can be experienced as forces. But from the moment that one experiences reality and the glory of it, that there is überhaupt something, the New Testament loses its aura of the primitive and the fantastic when it speaks in this regard of principalities, thrones and authorities.[3] There are hostile forces. They corrupt the good earth. The kingdom of Christ has been erected in the midst of them. He reigns

---

1. The inventory number of the Dutch text, "Ik geloof een eeuwig leven" is I,237. This was a lecture for a conference organized by the Centraal-Bond voor Inwendige Zending en Christelijk Maatschappelijk Werk (a society for internal mission and social work in the central region of the Netherlands). This essay is included in Volume 5C of Van Ruler's *Verzameld werk* (2023), 858–870.

2. See 1 Corinthians 15:26.

3. See Colossians 1:16.

amidst his enemies. He subjects them all under his feet.[4] And the last enemy that is done away with is death.[5] Then the kingdom of Christ is also at its end. Then God will be all in all.[6] The kingdom of Christ precedes this.[7] *That* we can, therefore, have only in the contradiction: of his reign in the midst of his enemies, of the Spirit and the flesh, of the cross and heaven. We do have to consider this contradiction when we deal with death and eternal life now. We must not suddenly strike through the one term to retain only the other one. We have to take death seriously.

Christ reigns in death, being embraced by death. And God is a match for it. But not the creature. *That* is the point that we usually overlook when we consider these questions: the difference between the Creator and the creature. And we do it easily, as if the creature is also a match for death. As if it has something within itself that is unassailable by death. When death appears, then—so we are wont to think—a part of the human being is irretrievably delivered up to it, but the essence of the human being, its soul or spirit, is still perfectly able to escape its grip.

What, after all, is really so terrible about death? When one considers carefully only this distinction between the two components that make up the human being and at that moment stress that the one is ancillary and the other essential, then one soon has to reach the conclusion that death is in essence a good thing. It is a liberation of the essential from the nonessential, of the soul from its dungeon, of the bird from its cage. That, too, is the conclusion reached by all heathendom and all philosophy. It is Christianity that made death so terrible. It stands for the unity of human nature. The soul and the body—if we may use these words in a loose way—belong together. There is no dualism of value between matter and spirit. That this visible and palpable reality exists is not a bad but a good thing. And that we eventually have to take leave of it feels terrible. The *earth* is, after all, our dwelling. *That* is where we are at home. And not in heaven.

What else is the immortality of the soul but one bloody underlining of the terror of death: body and soul belong together and the one is immortal while the other lies rotting in the grave. Also what, according to

---

4. See 1 Corinthians 15:25.
5. See 1 Corinthians 15:26.
6. See 1 Corinthians 15:28.

7. Van Ruler regarded the *regnum Christi* (the kingdom of Christ) as a modality of the *regnum Dei* (the kingdom of God). For cross-references to literature in Dutch, see Van Ruler's *Verzameld werk 5C*, 716, note 19.

the Christian confession, happens to us in the intermediate state between our death and the parousia of Christ, namely, that the body is preserved in the grave (that is, in the quarry of decomposition!) and the soul in heaven is but a detailed description of death's rule over us. Even the kingdom of Christ is not a match for that: through the power of his resurrection we are *preserved* in the grave and in heaven, that is, in death.

Christianity accentuates death in that it stands for the unity of human nature. Also in that it stands for the meaning of the body and the goodness of the earth. It does that across the board in its confessions. It knows God as Creator of heaven *and* earth; it knows about the cross of Jesus Christ, in the full and terrifying reality of the incarnation, essentially placed in the world, as historical factum, and it expects, beyond the ruin [ondergang] of the world, a new one. That is, not *another* but a radically renewed *earth*, which even has sociological forms so that righteousness may dwell in it. When we take this base line of all Christian confessing seriously, we also have to take death, as an enormous disruption, seriously. We do not come to terms with death just like that. We believe in *eternal* life as the true intention of God and death is in no way whatsoever to be squared with that.

This accent on death becomes more intense when we consider yet another aspect. Death is God's judgement. God, the Eternal, says to the children of men: return to the crushing [verbrijzeling], you children of men;[8] and: you are dust and to dust you shall return.[9] There is a pulverization of the creature by God. Therefore we should think often and seriously about the grave. What happens there is terrible and it is God's act.

Obviously, we touch on an extremely difficult problem here. Things are still relatively simple as long as we are able to keep them neatly separate: on the one side, God's sunny intentions with the earth and humanity, and, other the other side, the hostile forces that have pounced on God's good creation and have darkened and corrupted it. But in the long run, we cannot keep them thus neatly separated. This hostile force of death is a judgement of God.

It is probably putting it too mildly when we say that God uses death, along with all other forces. That God merely allows it is certainly putting it too mildly. The living, active, dynamic God of the Bible is never

---

8. See Psalm 90:3.
9. See Genesis 3:19.

a spectator. God is constantly at work in whatever happens. God is involved in the distress and struggle of the historical process of becoming human. In that process, God tackles everything, also the worst. At the least we should say that God uses war, hunger, suffering, sin and death. But there is always something disconcerting about that. In Psalm 90, the crushing of the human being proceeds directly from the holy mouth and the eternal being of God. God pronounces the death sentence on us and that is why we die. God lays us in the dust of death (Psalm 22).

From behind that, the entirely different dimension of guilt arises before us![10] It is all about the guilt of the creature. And the core of the matter is whether, in the relationship between creature and Creator, it could have been other than thus, that the creature becomes guilty before the Creator. And human beings become guilty not only *before* God but also *to* God, yes, through God.[11] God has decided to place[12] them under [the category of] disobedience. That is a yet deeper crushing than in death: when we are broken in guilt before God. That is already something of bliss itself. Here eternal life begins to dawn: in the admission that we become entirely *guilty*, entirely before, to and through God.

From this angle light is also shed on the other very murky problem: whether death is to be understood only as punishment for sin, or whether it may also be taken as a natural given. Did the leaves also fall from the trees in paradise? Since the struggle between Augustine and Pelagius, the Christian confession has maintained that death is not natural but is punishment for sin. However, Niebuhr rightly points out that, while the core of the problem of death lies in guilt, there is, concerning guilt, a margin of destiny concerning death in the Bible. Now I would like to say that this margin of destiny does not first appear in death.[13] It already appears in

---

10. The understanding of sin as guilt and of reconciliation as atonement for guilt are core motifs in Van Ruler's theology that are expressed throughout his oeuvre. In this regard, he gives preference to Anselm's understanding of atonement as satisfaction. For cross-references to literature in Dutch, see Van Ruler's *Verzameld werk 5C*, 170, note 28.

11. Translator's note: This enigmatic sentence becomes somewhat clearer if one considers that the Dutch "schuld" means both "guilt" and "debt". Humans stand guilty *before* God because they are indebted *to* God. As Van Ruler tentatively hints in the previous and following sentences, this guilt / indebtedness may be inherent in the unequal relationship between Creator and creature. In that sense humans are guilty *through* God.

12. Translator's note: Van Ruler seems to play on two meanings of the Dutch "besloten", namely "decided" and "closed, enclosed".

13. Reinhold Niebuhr (1892–1971), American Reformed theologian and professor at Union Theological Seminary in New York (1930–1960). Van Ruler's formulation

guilt itself. Before *God* the creature could not but become really guilty. From this also stems the curious motivation for God's forgiveness found in Psalm 103 and Isaiah 57: God takes into account how we were formed and that we are dust, therefore God is gracious to us and forgives us. The curse of death is a circle within the broader context of the damnation of guilt.

No person is a match for these things. That that is how it is regarding guilt, we leave aside for now. We return again to the problem and the reality of death. No person, nothing in a person, is a match for that either. That is why we stand so utterly helpless in the face of it. What do we know about what really happens when somebody dies? Death is a very thick and dense arras that hangs from the ceiling to the floor and behind which we cannot look. Nobody has ever come from behind death, not even Lazarus,[14] the daughter of Jaïrus,[15] and the young man of Nain,[16] because they did not pass through death but were simply retrieved from death to return there later. In the face of death everything is lost to us. We are also lost to ourselves. We are entirely cast upon God.[17] God pronounces the sentence of death. God lays us in the dust of death. And, when we die, we can place our trust only in God. God alone is a match for this terrible dominance of death. God can preserve us in death. God can also retrieve us from beneath death and make us arise from it. But regarding this we cannot imagine or even think anything. We can only love God and life. All our concepts, images, ideas, feelings, desires and impulses fall short in the face of death and are no match for it. We can summarize all of this in one concise formula with this content: there "is" no hereafter (unless it be that the word "hereafter" is no more than a concise indication of "being in death"), but we are entirely delivered up to God and to what God wants to do with us.

Therefore I do not see why there should be any problem or difficulty in the well-known fact that the Old Testament knew of no hereafter, no immortality, no life after life. The Old Testament loves only God and life,

---

could be a summary and interpretation of Reinhold Niebuhr, *The Nature and Destiny of Man: A Christian Interpretation, Volume 1: Human Nature* (London, 1946), 178–189. Van Ruler possessed a copy of this book.

14. See John 11:1f.

15. See Mark 5:35f; Luke 8:49f.

16. See Luke 7:11f.

17. For cross-references to literature in Dutch on the phrase "cast upon God", see the Dutch edition of the *Verzameld werk 5C*, 868, note 31.

and struggles, within life, with God concerning the enormous problem of death. It does not take it upon itself to solve the problem, as all pagans and philosophers do. It leaves it in God's hands. It befits us to do the same. And it would be highly desirable that Christians should, concerning death and eternal life, think along the lines of the Old Testament and let go of their heathendom and idle philosophy. At this point too it holds true that we should learn to understand the New Testament not from the perspective of Plato but from that of Moses.

Does the New Testament know of a hereafter, an immortality, a life after life? It knows God; it knows Jesus Christ; it knows about the power of God in the resurrection of Jesus Christ and of heaven as Messianic intermezzo.[18] Heaven is the place where Jesus Christ is for the time being and where salvation is preserved and hidden. In the New Testament heaven is not an ontological and certainly not an eschatological category: not another world or sphere of being alongside, outside and above the visible and palpable reality; also not a final goal in which everything will in the end come into its own or even to which it returns because it had come from it. Heaven has a role only because a pause intervenes in Jesus' Messianic mission between his resurrection and his parousia. The mystery of eternal life is preserved as such—as mystery!—in heaven. And on earth the Spirit is poured out so that we should also be preserved. And everything—in heaven and on earth—is aimed at that which God will in the end do with the earth. Now and then even the souls under the altar in heaven are overcome by impatience and call out: "O Sovereign Lord, holy and true, how long before thou wilt judge and avenge our blood on those who dwell upon the earth?" (Rev 6:10). Then they are brought back into the pause, in the state of rest. So we see that in the New Testament too the hereafter is strictly christologically determined and does not solve the problem of death in any way. We remain strictly dependent on what *God* does with things.

It is fitting here to devote some time to the problem of the forms of thought and representation that we have to use when we speak about death and eternal life. These have, without doubt, a mythical structure. I am thinking of the ascension of Christ. He ascended to heaven in the body and is, also according to his human nature, seated at the right hand

18. Van Ruler regarded the incarnation, the indwelling of the Spirit, the ascension, heaven, the church, the New Testament apostolate, theocracy, and so forth as an intermezzo. This is closely related to his view that special revelation, the incarnation, the church, the offices of the church, and so forth are God's emergency measures. For cross-references to literature in Dutch, see Van Ruler's *Verzameld werk 5C*, 176, note 89.

of the Majesty. I am also thinking of the idea of the separation of body and soul that occurs when one dies: the body that is preserved on earth and the soul that is preserved in heaven. Obviously, I am thinking most of all of the idea of the resurrection of the flesh, the uniting of soul and body and the new earth on which righteousness dwells. Can we represent something of this to ourselves? Can we imagine something of this in thought? I would want to answer that we can feel something concerning this, namely, a deep sense of being touched by the Lord, the Unique, the God of salvation and of life, who keep things in God's grip and is busy with them. We are completely cast upon God alone.

Now we might say that the word "God" is also a mythical form of thought and representation. But if we wish to be preserved from nihilism and insanity, we must certainly not imagine that this is saying everything. For instance, God, the God of the Bible, is also a historical force. God is far closer to us. God is also far more human and ordinary than we tend to think in our paganism and our philosophy. And when we know God in spiritual experience, true mythical thinking becomes to us the most spontaneous[19] thing on earth. Then, in dealing with the problems of death and the eternal image, we are dealing with God's mysteries. And they are indeed mysteries: it is about what *God* does with things and especially about what God *will* do with things. But when we know God in our religious experience, we have the unction of the Holy Spirit, we "know" the whole truth and speak wisdom among the perfect. Therefore we can—albeit with timidity and reverence, circumspectly and with "fear and trembling"—walk in these mysteries. The mythical forms of thought and representation are our playthings along this walk.

Why, after all, should we elevate purely discursive thought absolutely above the myth? We should far rather say that myth is the sole legitimate access to the vital things concerning God and humanity and the whole of reality. After all, the pagans and the philosophers too babble on about these things in myths, which engender an infinite melancholy about this world in our hearts: the immortality of the soul, the flood of endless light, nirvana,[20] the twilight of the gods, and so on. The Bible

---

19. Translator's note: The precise meaning is unclear because the Dutch word "eigene" has several meanings. When Ms Van Ruler-Hamelink published this piece after Van Ruler's death, she changed the word to "persoonlijke" (personal), but this does not seem to fit in the context.

20. For Van Ruler's view on nirvana, see the cross-references to literature in Dutch in Van Ruler's *Verzameld werk 5C*, 868, 51.

gives us knowledge of the Lord and this joy fills all our forms of thought with a never-ending hymn about the earth, the body, life and all things. We should also consider that this "walking in the mysteries" hold not only for the eschatological sections of the Christian confession, but most definitely across the board. We cannot utter a single true word without being overcome by timidity and joy over God.

This is what is important: that we refer the matter of eternal life, in whatever form we imagine it, strictly to God, to God's being and acts. It is not "something" in itself. It does not "exist" as another reality somewhere else than in our present reality. It does not in any way belong to the constituents of created reality as we know it. We are delivered up to death—that is all. Eternal life, however, is what the *living* God intends and does with God's creation. Therefore I can base my hope exclusively and solely on God and on nothing else in the entire universe. God's is the kingdom and the power and the glory in all eternity.[21] "Once God has spoken; twice have I heard this: that power belongs to God" (Ps 62:11). God is a match for the guilt of sin—that is atonement. And God is a match for the corruption of death—that is the resurrection of the flesh. And together that constitutes eternal life.

That is why God is called the God of life. Or also the God of salvation [heil]. What is at stake in the question about eternal life is the conception of God. We must not equate God to the essence of reality. Then life and death are degraded to nothing but phases in the metaphysical process of God's being. God is distinct from the whole of created reality. God is the Lord above life and death. But nor should we separate God from the reality of creation. Then life and death are degraded to meaningless, capricious twists of fate that befall creatures. God is busy with God's creation. God enters into it. God comes to its aid, judging and saving, sifting and healing. God saves it from all destruction, from the destruction of the nothingness and chaos, of vanity and senselessness, of guilt and death. When we know God in this pure biblical way, in God's distinctness from the essence of all things *and* in God's engagement with all distress, then the question of eternal life has been decided in this knowledge of God.

Therefore I am deeply convinced that, though the Old Testament knows of no hereafter, or knows of it only in very spectral forms, it very thoroughly and fully knows of eternal life. After all, it knows God the Lord and God is the strength of humanity. That is why the risen Christ

---

21. See Matthew 6:13.

could "prove" his resurrection to the travelers to Emmaus from Moses and the prophets and the Scriptures and reproach them for their slowness of heart. Once they came to see it, however, their hearts became burning within them.[22] And indeed, whoever meets God the Lord is overcome by rapture about life.

The difficulty, however, is that what is at stake is not only the very being of God but—within that—God's acts. The very being of God is being at work and joy[23] over all that is and that happens, over all that God does. Thus all thoughts of the creature's being taken up into the very being of God is foreign to the biblical doctrine of eternal life. The matter is quite the opposite. Salvation does not consist in the creature's being taken up in the very being of God, but in the fact that God pours out God's "very being" in and over God's creature. Therefore, God's concern is that God wants to express all of God's righteousness in existence and wants to endow all that exists with the luster of God's glory. That is the difficulty, the travail and the work of God. That is already the problem of creation; it is to an even greater degree the problem of atonement; it is, most of all, the problem of glorification. The entire apocalyptic process of history seems to be necessary to get matters *that* far. The living God wills the freedom and independence of the creature and in that God wishes to express God's own being—that is generous and good, that is beautiful and glorious. God wills humanness.

In this light, the problem of individuality caught between death and eternal life also comes into view. What remains of my personality, of my "I", in and after death? The light that falls on this question I would wish to typify as follows: God is the God of individualizing. God wills the relative autonomy of the creature outside and over against God's own being. God also wills the relative autonomy of the one creature outside and over against the other creature. In God's peace all life can flourish. Admittedly, in this regard we should at the same time have to consider the notion of community. In our present existence, typified as it is by sin and death, we never get quite that far. We merely attempt it. But we do have some preliminary forms of the community in the kingdom of glory: marriage for the body and song for consciousness. Just as the loneliness of the body is really overcome to some extent only in marriage and the loneliness of

---

22. See Luke 24:25–32.

23. "Joy" is a core motif in Van Ruler's theology. For cross-references to literature in Dutch, see Van Ruler's *Verzameld werk 5C*, 869, note 65.

thought to some extent only in song, so too eternal life is true community of true creatures over whom the fullness of God has been poured.

In this context the question whether we would recognize one another is a very depressing question. Recognition depends on remembering. And recognition is one of the most curious forms of consciousness, the one most deeply determined by guilt. And precisely consciousness is overcome in eternal life. Shall we recognize one another? We, together, shall but rejoice beyond words over all God's works. And in that we shall indeed recognize the *essence* of all things. For that is the song—now and in *saecula saeculorum*.[24] Thereafter we shall look upon one another and in that way recognize one another in Christ, just as we do it now already in the Lord's Supper, with the broken bread and poured wine.

So eternal life concerns *all* things. It does not concern only a few souls or a few people. It concerns the totality of all that exists. The entire riddle of reality is solved. Soul and body, person and community, church and state, mysticism and culture, history and nature, earth and cosmos—they will all share, each thing in its own manner, in eternal life and the luster of God's glory. Things are turned inside out; that is why the idea of judgement and verdict, sifting and separation, the crisis, dominates the foreground in the Christian future expectation. Everything that is hidden must be revealed, brought into the light. The books are opened, the books of God's counsel and of God's gospel, also the books of the dark heart and the silent cosmos. That is the true rapture of the last days: that we reach a place above this almost unbearable tension between inside and outside, between depth and surface, and that everything ends up in the light, that is, on the surface and the outside. The eschatological act of God is the act of *uncover*ing, of apocalypsis.

That also entails that in the end nothing substantially new is given to us. In the present we have already received everything, the full abundance of God's glory, only in the form of salvation [heil] and therefore of hiddenness. At the end this is given in another way, public, in the great lawsuit: *so* that God *and* the profoundly doomed existence are justified before the face of all creatures.

Scripture leads us, according to a dictum of H. Bavinck, in such an all-embracing description or rather indication of the kingdom of glory, as if there were no eternal death.[25] Of course, there is that. But it is the apex

---

24. *In saecula saeculorum*: In the ages of all ages.
25. Herman Bavinck (1854–1921), minister in the Christelijk Gereformeerde Kerk ("Christian Reformed Church"), professor of theology at the Theologische School te

of impossibility. And of the glory of God we should not say primarily that it embraces everything—at least, we should not say that in an undifferentiated way—but rather that it transcends everything, both the bliss of the elect and the misery of the lost. In the problem of eternal damnation, we are also fully cast on God *only*.

When we consider all this, what else is eternal life then but this life of mine that I live here and now, in its full visibility and palpability, redeemed from sin and death? Of another life that stands alongside or above or over against this spatio-temporal existence of mine I have, if I live strictly biblically, no knowledge. And as little of another life that may perhaps *replace* this spatio-temporal existence. I know of only *one* life and *one* reality. And of this: that these have been redeemed by the completed work of Jesus Christ. I have a Savior and *that* is how I stand in the world and in life. And his work is fully sufficient.

And in his work, seen from the angle of atonement, that which was done, really and truly *done*, in the guilt of sin, is really and truly *undone*, so that it has *not* been done. In the same way, in his work, seen from the angle of the resurrection of the flesh, that which has been undone, really and truly undone, in the destruction of death, is really and truly *done*, so that I who die and have died live in all eternity. The one—the resurrection of the flesh from death—is not stranger than the other—the atonement for the guilt of sin. They are both so utterly strange that both equally are totally impossible and can but be confessed in the light of the power and the strength that belong exclusively to God. When there has been atonement for my sin, then I have not done what I have done. And when my flesh rises [from the dead], then I—I who had become past tense in death!—get back my life, the one that I live in the present, completely, hundredfold—houses and brothers and sisters and children and lands.[26] The relationship between time and eternity in Christianity is precisely the opposite of what it is in Plato. With Plato, one gets back eternity, in the form of ideas, through anamnesis in time. In Christianity, one gets back time, in the form of salvation [heil], through the expectation of eternity. We have to study this reversal of things thoroughly if we are to confess to the article of faith: I believe in eternal life. This is an important moment

---

Kampen (1883–1902), and at the Vrije Universiteit te Amsterdam (1902–1921). The source in Bavinck's work could not be traced though Bavinck's oeuvre is available in searchable form online. Though Bavinck sometimes uses "eternal death", he never does so in the context indicated by Van Ruler.

26. See Matthew 19:29; Mark 10:30.

in the conversion that the gospel demands of our pagan hearts. The true knowledge of God and the true faith in eternal life cast us, in all our thinking about death, the hereafter and eternity, back into the present. In that and in that alone eternal life has been given to us. And this is eternal life, that they know Thee the only true God, and Jesus Christ whom Thou hast sent.[27]

Therefore, it is not only so that we die "in hope of eternal life."[28] We also live in it from day to day. We work and play, we marry and have children, in the hope of eternal life.

The article about eternal life ever again calls us to this zest for life. We are chased up from our bed, in which we nestle, the bed of fate and death, of acquiescence and melancholy. We must *arise* to life, just as God, the Lord, arises to battle. God does not give up and is not cast into despair. *Therefore* we must not give up either. The holiness of God forbids us every trace of contempt for life.

And what then of the hour of our death? Then too I shall love life beyond words and *only* life! Perhaps I am thankful when I die because I am tired. My deathbed is my bed of rest. But then too all the glory of God in life glows through my limbs. And I say: "Once, at the evening of my life, I, freed from care and struggle, shall bring You a higher, purer hymn of praise for each day *given me here*."[29]

And I know all about the terror of death. Or rather, I know absolutely nothing of it yet. For precisely that reason I know all about it. In the face of death, I can say freely: I know that I know nothing. That only a biblical Christian can say. Pagans and philosophers know much too much about it. That came about because they got God and the All entangled. The Bible, which proclaims eternal life, first made death fully problematic. And it preserves me, also in the face of death, in the same simplicity as that in which it makes me live. I place the trust of my life solely in God, also when flesh and heart perish. I am *preserved* in death, just as I am also preserved in life.

---

27. See John 17:3.

28. See Titus 1:2; 3:7.

29. This is a translation of the third couplet of hymn 280, "'k Wil u o God mijn dank betalen," from the *Psalmen en gezangen voor den eeredienst der Nederlandsche Hervormde Kerk in opdracht van de Algemeene Synode der Nederlandsche Hervormde Kerk opnieuw verzameld en bewerkt aan de Nederlandsche Hervormde Kerk aangeboden door de Algemeene Synode in het jaar onzes Heeren 1938* (Amsterdam, s.a. [1938]).

In the true knowledge of God there is not that much difference between life and death. In any case, they constantly change places. For instance, when I live I am in heaven far more than when I am dead: I celebrate the Lord's Supper and by the power of the Holy Spirit I am placed in heaven and eat and drink his true body and blood, yes, his who is truly God and truly human. And when I am dead, then I am on earth far more than when I live; then I lie in the grave and return to dust, dust to dust and ashes to ashes. That is merely one example. It reflects the Lordship of God, that God is Lord above life and death.

When I die, I must not let go of the life of the world and posterity. I have my children and my family and the generations that follow after me. That is a profound comfort. Life goes on and the world keeps turning. God's intention is reflected in *that* far more than in the destiny that I experience.

One would even be able to say: when I die, I have eternal life only and particularly in this reflection. It is the sign of history. Naturally, I do also have eternal life in other ways, for instance, sacramentally in the Lord's Supper, prophetically in the reading of Scripture at my [death] bed, mystically in the stirrings of my heart over the Lord and eschatologically in the intentions in God's heart. But I have it in the most visible and palpable way historically. History is the most closely related to the being of God.

But what happens to me in the meanwhile, while my children live on, work and play? Am I preserved in heaven and in the grave? Or does nothing whatsoever happen? The latter is also conceivable from a biblical perspective. Now, in death, I am most perceivably in touch with time. Now, when I have become entirely past tense. I have struggled all my life with the temporal form of my existence. I could never quite grasp it. [Consciousness of] guilt was the greatest drawback of my consciousness of time. And now, in death, I am in a complete tangle with it. Is it possible that I *have been*? Is it conceivable that a time will come that I will not be there? And can one still call that time, the time between the hour of my death and the day of Christ's parousia? The living God has kept us in time for years. God "held" us in guilt. God will also hold us in this "time".

Why God does that is not completely clear to us. If Christ has died for us, why do we still have to die? That is a question that concerns God rather than us. It is the theodicy question. Why does God allow this world to endure? Why does God need history? Here we find ourselves once more among the souls under the altar. It seems to me that there is an answer to these questions, provided that it is given piously. But it lies beyond the scope of this presentation to move over from death to history.

All that matters at this point is to be aware that in the hereafter, that is, in the situation of death, we remain caught up in some or other way in this problem of the historical process. And when we die, we must not primarily rid ourselves of all that is earthly—unless we are heartily tired of it—but we must far more fall into the hands of God and commend our spirit to God's hands.[30] God remains busy with the world. We can do that the more readily when we consider that the end of all God's ways is God's glory over everything and that, therefore, the article about eternal life calls us to pure joy in all circumstances, also in the gruesome situation of death.

---

30. See Psalm 31:6; Luke 23:46.

Relativizing Death and Life[1]
[1954]

"For to this end Christ died and lived again, that He might be Lord both of the dead and of the living." (Rom 14: 9, RSV)

THE WORD "(SO) THAT"[2] plays a large role in the biblical way of thinking. Reality is understood as the working of God. But God never does something in isolation or for the sake of that one thing. God ever again moves on to something else for the sake of which God had done the first thing.

Now this purposiveness also concerns Christ, his death and resurrection. "To this end" He died and returned to life, "so that" He should rule over both the dead and the living. Therefore, it is not about Him and his cross and resurrection in their nature as salvific facts, but about his being Lord in the present.[3]

On Him has been bestowed the name which is above every name (Phil 2:9). He is the Lord. We are now in this time and this dispensation. We live under the Lordship of Christ. *Grace* rules. It is the present of grace. The sacrifice is the great transformer through which the entire divine rule passes. We can no longer equate God with rational or moral

---

1. The inventory number of the Dutch text, "De relativering van dood en leven" is I,336. This meditation is included in Volume 5C of Van Ruler's *Verzameld werk* (2023), 871–73.

2. Translator's note: For the English "(so) that), Dutch has both "opdat" and "zodat". The former, used here, introduces final clauses; the latter resultative clauses.

3. One of the core themes in Van Ruler's theology is that the Christian faith indeed hinges on (Dutch: draait om) Christ, atonement and justification, but that it is about (Dutch: gaat om) something else: the redemption of creation and the coming of the kingdom of God on earth. In this regard, Van Ruler would also say that, for God, it is about (Dutch: gaat om) this world, this earthly, life, ordinary life, humaneness, sanctification and so forth. For cross-references to literature in Dutch, see Van Ruler's *Verzameld werk 5C*, 308, note 5.

fate. God is to be equated with Jesus Christ. Not the stars but Jesus Christ expresses how God is now.

Now Paul says something quite strange: He died and returned to life so that He may be Lord of both the dead and the living. That we live in the kingdom of Christ is not self-evident when we survey existence and world history. Certain contradictions are evident in it. We can surmount these only in faith.

But now this standing in the kingdom of Christ is extended to dying and being dead. He rules not only over the living but also over the dead. And those clearly as dead. They are, at least, not of the living. We must not erase this distinction. The dead are not the living; they are not in the land of the living; they do not walk in the light of life. We must respect this simple distinction. Nor must we turn "profound" and say that the living are perhaps dead after all and the dead living.

We have no need for this profundity. We know the Lord, the *kurios*.[4] He rules over both. Just as He can penetrate into the heart of the living with his rule, so He can penetrate into the graves of the dead. In both cases that surpasses our understanding.

But if we are "with Christ" in death, then that is not due to us (as if we were not really dead) but to his Lordship. He rules in the midst of his enemies, also in the midst of the enmity of death.[5] He is busy overcoming this enemy as well. And [He does] that with the soft force of grace: in the long run, death perishes as the walls of Jericho did.[6]

"If we live, we live to the Lord, and if we die, we die to the Lord"[7] That is to say, in every aspect of our existence there is this relationship-*to*. There is no real loneliness any more. We must also permanently leave off giving account of ourselves. We are there on the account-*of*. In our living, we have to grasp that firmly. But also in our dying. That too—our death!—we can no longer overlook. We do not have our dying in our hands. None of us dies to himself or herself—Paul says,[8] profoundly enough.

For that reason, it does not matter that much *in the kingdom of Christ* whether we are alive or dead.[9] The relationship towards the Lord,

---

4. Kurios (κύριος): Lord.
5. See 1 Corinthians 15:25f.
6. See Joshua 6:20.
7. See Romans 14:8.
8. See Romans 14:7.
9. See Romans 14:8.

the position of being placed under his rule, the passage of God's grace through life and death, are more important. This *one* orientation to the Lord relativizes the duality of life and death.

Round about it, outside the kingdom of Christ, thus in the first and the last of God's intentions, it does matter considerably. Originally and finally it matters that we be not in death but in life. But in Christ's kingdom of grace, that is in itself also the kingdom of hiddenness,[10] the first and the last have, so to speak, been suspended. Now there is still death—and furthermore disease as well as suffering.

And now: where the relativizing of the great opposition between life and death has taken place, more relativizing takes place. Should we eat meat or not? Should we drink wine or not? Should we observe certain days or not? If it actually does not matter whether we live or are dead then—Paul says in this context[11]—these oppositions do not really matter either. There must be room for them in the kingdom of Christ and in his congregation.

Some or other opposition constantly breaks loose in the church. The battle about it is justified only if the opposition is greater than that between life and death. That *may* be the case. Regarding a disputed point differing from the one that came up in Romans 14, Paul says: "If anyone should preach to you a gospel contrary to the one that we have preached, let him be accursed".[12] But then we have to *know* what we are about. In Christ's church there is room for many opinions. However, oppositions may come up that are greater than the one of life and death. Then there is much earnestness, struggle and suffering. Then we are tottering at the brink of the kingdom of Christ.

Doctrinal discipline's reach extends to beyond death.[13] It reaches into the place of perdition.

---

10. Elsewhere in his oeuvre Van Ruler regarded the *regnum Christi* (the kingdom of Christ) as a modality of the *regnum Dei* (the kingdom of God). For cross-references to literature in Dutch, see Van Ruler's *Verzameld werk 5C*, 716, note 19. On the hiddenness of God, see Van Ruler's *De vervulling van de wet*, 39, 58.

11. See Romans 14:15–23.

12. See Galatians 1:8–9. Van Ruler does not quote verbatim here.

13. Volume 5C of Van Ruler's *Verzameld werk* includes, besides the section on eschatology that is translated in this volume, also a section with 15 essays on "Confession and doctrinal discipline". For cross-references to literature in Dutch regarding Van Ruler's views on doctrinal discipline, see especially note 33 in his *Verzameld werk 5C*, 170.

Questions of Life and Death[1]
[1955]

AFTER THE FORTIETH YEAR of one's life, one contemplates, with body and soul, that there will come a moment when one dies. Before that not really: then one contemplates it at most cerebrally; it does not penetrate and does nothing to us. One lives towards life. Afterwards towards death.[2]

There are two reactions to that. On the one hand, the reaction of a great curiosity: death is a heavy curtain; of what comes after we know nothing from experience. Spiritism fascinates all people unless they are afraid of it. Of theologians they expect decisive answers from Holy Scripture, even to such an extent that we may think that theologians and preachers are of use only if there is a hereafter. But this curiosity is never satisfied even to the smallest extent.

On the other hand, the reaction of a deadly paralysis: is it all still worth the trouble at all? If, after all, it all comes to an end: my affairs, my home, my hobbies, my development? Never: my children—for they remain, push forward. Normally we do not allow this paralysis; at least we do not let it penetrate. We admonish ourselves. But it comes over us time and again nevertheless, in our silent and lonely moments. Therefore we have to come to terms with this matter! Because it sullies our experience of life radically!

---

1. The inventory number of the Dutch text, "Vragen van leven en dood" is I,350. These were notes for a presentation at a "congregation evening" in Kralingen on 16 February 1955 and in Beukbergen on 27 February 1958. It is included in Volume 5C of Van Ruler's *Verzameld werk* (2023), 874–76. Van Ruler himself added two notes to the text, here placed in square brackets as [1] and [2].

2. See the letter by Van Ruler addressed to "Miss Rijpkema," cited in full in the introduction to this volume.

Here I merely provide a few loose perspectives from which we can view life in the light (the shadow) of death, from which we can view death.

1. When we die, we fall into or are in the hands of God. That is why death is a radical boundary. We are no longer *in any way* in our own hands: no subject anymore, nothing but object. Also no longer in the hands of people, not even of the church: the problems of funeral services and funeral liturgy: the dome of the church over the dead as well, or the task of the minister—a brief pastoral visit to the bereaved?[3]

2. For that reason, we can also experience death as a form of love. It is the struggle of life: how do we ever get rid of ourselves, in full surrender to God, to the neighbor, to things? We never quite succeed. We constantly stand in our own way. But in death it happens, if we die in the fear of God. There we lose ourselves entirely, to God, in any case.

3. Thus we are *preserved in* death as well. In a twofold way: in the way of heaven (bliss) and in the way of the grave (being consumed). The way of the grave is also a form of preservation (therefore, from symbolic considerations, no cremation?): so we see what "preservation" is, how divine it is.

   This preservation is necessary! It takes place through the power of Christ's resurrection. *He* overcame death (*in his* resurrection; on that side of death; not in the raising of Lazarus, and so forth). This power works through in our death. We are not preserved through our nature: as if we at our core slip from the grasp of death (*that* is the objection to the doctrine of the immortality of the soul!)

   It is a preservation in death; death is more than dying (in one moment)[4] but is being in death. See the being *consumed* in the grave, see the separation of body and soul, grave and heaven; also in heaven we do not *hear*! "Being with Christ" is being in death! He has risen from death, but his power works in our death; that is a preliminary effect of his resurrection, of the solution to the problem in which creation has landed.

---

3. [1] To be the same object at birth.

4. Translator's note: At times, as is the case here, Van Ruler would use mathematical symbols such as > (is greater than) or = (is equal to) in his preparatory notes for an oral presentation.

4. An entirely new moment is added to this: God does not deal with individual people only but with the whole of God's created reality. Of that we are a small piece!

   Even if we were to be saved in the hereafter in our individuality, then the world would not yet be saved.

   Not merely the soul of the person but the total person, body and soul in their unity, is the object of salvation. And not only the entire person but the entire reality. We have to think not merely spiritually but also materially, not merely anthropologically but also cosmologically.

   There is a fundamental point here: not to experience the world in the image of a cycle (from which we escape in death) but in the image of a way. It goes somewhere. In the end, God shall do something radical and definite with God's world. The kingdom of glory.

   The basis of this expectation is [God's] revelation to Israel and in Jesus Christ: there God concerned Godself radically with humanity and the world—*for that reason* we have *hope* (and without this hope faith becomes empty!!).

   Much or everything is unknown, unimaginable and unthinkable. Holy Scripture speaks about it in images. Here we have to keep an entirely open mind. But with an ardent expectation.

5. This cosmic expectation places the relationship of life and death in a remarkable light. If it is true, then death can no longer give me the feeling that I shall at some stage leave this world forever.

   That already removes the paralyzing aspect from the certainty of death. Now, in my life, I am still busy in and with the world. But it is God's world and it too has a destination. It is not all purely vanity and transience! What I have as the most visible [token] is my descendants: therefore I have to accept my children positively and [with that] the *comfort* that they bring in the face of death!

6. But another weighty point has to be added. Up to now we have been thinking of the spiritual (the soul) and the material (the body), the cosmic aspects of being human. But now also the temporality of the human being, which is more that the fact that I have a beginning and an end. It is also that I am all that I have done and experienced between the beginning and the end. I am a *Zeit ausfüllendes Wesen*,[5]

---

5. The source of this description of being human as "a time-filling being" is not clear. Possibly this expression comes from van Ruler himself. According to a comment

a time-filling being, a piece of filled time (filled with action and eventuality).

Now Holy Scripture uses quite a number of words regarding the eschaton that indicate that what is at stake in the eschaton is this entire temporal, worldly reality. All of this comes to judgement (κρίσις), is revealed (ἀποκάλυψις), recapitulated (ἀνακεφαλαίωσις), consummated (τελείωσις), glorified (δοξάζω). "*I*" am glorified!

In the eschaton I find myself, that is, my whole life that I live here and now, again!! And I find there the entire temporal, worldly reality again: this is made public. I can never have God without having myself and God's world. Also and particularly not at the end.

That places me radically and solely just in the present and this world. It is precisely the eschatological expectation of the gospel that casts me back in it. *Then* it will *still* be about what I do and experience now. I shall rejoice with God about that in all eternity.[6]

Life, the present, is borne, willed, sanctified: borne by the sacrifice on Golgotha (so that existence before the face of God is possible)—willed by the sovereign pleasure of God (reality is God's play and my task)—sanctified by the Spirit to liturgy, the praiseful service.[7]

Therefore: the comfort in life is precisely the same as the comfort in death: that I am not my own.

---

from Jürgen Moltmann, a native German speaker would never put it this way.

6. [2] Not only judgement but also joy over the present moment!

7. The expression "praiseful service" (Dutch: "lofzeggende dienst" or "lofprijzende dienst") appears frequently in Van Ruler's writings. For cross-references to literature in Dutch, see his *Verzameld werk 5C*, 458, note 21.

Being Saved or Being Lost[1]

[1957]

WHEN PEOPLE REFLECT ON the future of human beings and the world, the hereafter, the last things, the following matter always comes up: Is there judgement, crisis, separation? Is there eternal perdition?

The Bible, at any rate, speaks clearly enough about this:

- We all have to be revealed before the judgement seat of Christ.[2]
- The sheep and the goats will be separated from one another.[3]
- And there is an outer darkness—there will be wailing there and gnashing of the teeth.[4]

However, I would now like to rationally elucidate, as much as is possible, what the Bible says by means of a few considerations: we do not believe purely on authority—we can also grasp that and why what is true is true.

My most important consideration is this: Only in this way can we hold on to the seriousness of life—and with that to humanness—in all its profundity.

- We live only *once*.

---

1. The inventory number of the Dutch text, "Behouden worden of verloren gaan" is I,442. These were notes for an address is Voorburg on 2 October 1957. This essay is included in Volume 5C of Van Ruler's *Verzameld werk* (2023), 879–882.

    Translator's note: The translation of the title is a makeshift. The Dutch "behouden worden" means "being kept safe / secure" (corresponding to the Latin "salvere"). Where "behouden" is translated as "saved" in the text, the Dutch is added in square brackets to avoid confusion.

2. See 2 Corinthians 5:10; also Romans 14:10.
3. See Matthew 25:32f.
4. See Matthew 8:12, 22:13, 25:30.

- This life—like all of history—has an eternal outcome: The books!⁵ The harvest!⁶
- A decision is taken in time; it remins binding for all eternity:⁷ the accent of eternity is placed on life in time.⁸

People have tried in all possible ways—quite understandably—to escape from this off-putting thought:

- The notion of conditional immortality and the annihilation of those who are lost.⁹
- The notion of reincarnation: one gets many chances and what went before continues to work itself out as a matter of necessity, until one gets to the point where one can be saved (from what?).
- The notion of a new offer of grace after death: as the tree falls, so it lies.

My opinion is: in the Christian doctrine we are not dealing with a somber, burdensome theory:

- This is, after all, what our situation as human beings is.
- Even if there were no hereafter: we would nevertheless, in all eternity, still have been there and that as saved [behouden] or lost: this life that I live here and now is either saved [behouden] or lost.
- And this fact is simply taken completely seriously and addressed openly in the Christian doctrine.

To my mind we have to be careful with the argument that it does not rhyme with God's love that there are sinners who are lost.¹⁰ For that does

---

5. See Revelations 20:12.

6. See Matthew 13:39; Revelations 14:15.

7. For cross-references to Van Ruler's use of the expression "remains taken for all eternity" (Dutch: "die geldt voor de eeuwigheid"), see the Dutch edition of Van Ruler's *Verzameld werk 5C*, 881, note 7.

8. In the expression "the accent of eternity is placed on ... time" Van Ruler implicitly refers to Søren Kierkegaard. A possible source is a Dutch translation of Kierkegaard's *Samlede Værker, Bind 10. Afsluttende uvidenskabelig Efterskrift, Andet Halvbind*, edited by A.B. Drachmann (Copenhagen, 1963), 237ff.

9. Van Ruler's source could be Herman Bavinck, *GD4*, 692. See his *Reformed Dogmatics Volume Four* (Grand Rapids: Baker Academic, 2008), 710.

10. Van Ruler's source could be Bavinck's *GD4*, 694v. See his *Reformed Dogmatics* 4, 712f.

sound humane. But in principle it amounts to the abolition of humanness if the almighty, divine love were in the long run to even out everything (water over sand) and to set everything to right. Then the freedom of human beings in their temporality would no longer be respected. All of being human is then exhausted in its being a wavelet in the sea of God's eternal love. We recognize full humanness only when we respect that human beings take decisions in time that remain binding for all eternity. Precisely then there has to be room for eternal perdition.

According to the Christian faith, matters do not proceed simply along two [parallel] tracks: a complete symmetry of being saved [behouden worden] and being lost as precisely equivalent possibilities.

Being saved [behouden worden] is the fundamental [one of the two]. That is the gift of the Son, of eternal life in Him, of grace. The preaching of the gospel goes out to each human being so that each can, in faith, be taken up into the community of salvation [heil] and be saved [behouden] in it.

It can, however, happen that a person stumbles over grace: that person does not want to live from grace but hardens herself or himself and rejects it—in this way that person *becomes* hardened and rejected by grace and is lost to and through grace.

We also have to think about becoming saved [behouden worden] (or being saved [behouden zijn]) through grace in the right way.

- What is central is the natural life of forgiveness.
    » I fully affirm myself although I am a sinner (N.B.!)![11]
    » Because God affirms me.
- But in Christ much more is surely given than merely the forgiveness of sin:
    » He and his work are God's atoning love as reality.
    » In Him the world and life are saved [behouden].
    » The fulness of salvation [heil], the entire kingdom of God, has been given in Him.
    » We share in it through faith.
    » Faith becomes incarnate in life.

---

11. For Van Ruler's views on self-affirmation, see the cross-references to literature in Dutch, see his *Verzameld werk 5C*, 881, note 11.

> In love we accept everything and fully experience this world as the kingdom of God.
- That is the way in which we *become* saved [behouden worden].
  > It is a form of *being* saved [behouden zijn].
  > This world and the life in it are not meaningless: it is praiseful service of God in God's kingdom.[12]
- We can, however, go against the grain of everything, persist in that and therefore not attain the peace: then we forgo bliss!

Now these are realities of being human and of the relationship of God and humanity,

- For long brought across through the images of the final judgement, a heaven and a hell, a place for those in bliss and those in misery.
- In the Old Testament we do not yet find that, but it quite clearly does operate in the New Testament.
- That is obviously a figurative representation of a reality we cannot imagine.
- Particularly important in it is the notion of the judgement of God— the eternal meaning of earthly life—that I myself am involved in it.

For this reason, I believe that we cannot abandon these images. The preaching of someone like Billy Graham[13] links up with them immediately and concentrates on them. That is the power of such preaching. That is also quite correct. What is at stake is "life in the abbreviation" (Van der Leeuw).[14]

We do have to consider that Holy Scripture often talks about the final end in such a way that it seems as if there were no *mors aeterna*, no

---

12. The expression "the praiseful service" (Dutch: "lofzeggende dienst" or "lofprijzende dienst") appears frequently in Van Ruler's writings. For cross-references to literature in Dutch, see his *Verzameld werk 5C*, 458, note 21.

13. William Franklin (Billy) Graham (1918–2018), American evangelist and author.

14. Gerardus van der Leeuw (1890–1950). Van Ruler's source is G. van der Leeuw, *Phänomenologie der Religion* (Tübingen 1933), 174: "Human life in its relationship to power is not primarily that of the individual but that of the community. […] Nor is it life in its variegated multiplicity, as we know it from newspapers or from modern novels. It is perhaps life in its simplified and abbreviated form, which, set apart from all distinctions of lifestyle, talent, temperament, and so on, is lived by all, that is, birth, marriage, death" (translation—DGL).

eternal death: the kingdom of peace in Isaiah 9; the banquet in Isaiah 35,[15] for instance.

I do not believe that these are based on currents of thought in which it is explicitly denied that there is an eternal death. It is simply that nothing is said about it.

In my opinion that is because the glory of God that arises over all of created reality at the end does not so much embrace all and everything but surpasses all and everything.

- It goes *beyond* the bliss of the saved [behoudenen] *and*
- the misery of the lost!

Both are also taken up in it.

Our vision regarding the final destiny of human beings gets lost at the horizon.

In any case: the darkness of the eternal perdition of the lost is indeed dark to us as well: it is not light to us; we can speak about it only with averted faces; but we must not deny it—for then all humanness collapses!

---

15. Van Ruler probably made a mistake in referring to Isaiah 35. It should be Isaiah 25:6–9.

Living in the Kingdom: Christ's Birth and Politics[1]

[1957]

IN THE GOSPELS JESUS is very soon, already at his birth, called "Lord" and "Savior".[2] These and similar words were derived from the political thought of the Roman world empire of the time. At least, they derived a distinctive coloring and tone from that. The emperor in Rome—and through him the state—was also experienced as "lord' and "savior". People expected authority and salvation [heil] from the political organization of the nations.

That was the arrogance of the gospel and of the earliest Christianity. By using these terms, they expressed nothing less than this momentous claim: "We know the *true* Lord and the authentic authority: we know the true Savior and the authentic salvation [heil]." Therefore Christianity in the first centuries was a revolutionary factor in political life. Until it came to the recognition of this Lord and Savior by the state in the fourth century.[3]

Since then, the enormous spiritual struggle to realize this recognition of Jesus Christ by the state in the political shaping of life as well washed this way and that way. That has been tested in a thousand ways. People have passed through many failures and disappointments. That is the rich and multi-colored history of Europe. But it did leave its stamp on life. And in our time, we see how other parts of the world too, among

---

1. The inventory number of the Dutch text, "Leven in het Koninkrijk Christus' geboorte en de politiek" is I,456. This essay is included in Volume 5C of Van Ruler's *Verzameld werk* (2023), 883–886.

2. See Luke 2:11.

3. Van Ruler refers to Emperor Constantine the Great.

others through the organization of the United Nations, begin to share in forms of life that have been acquired in this history.

JUSTICE AND LOVE

One can hardly say that this course of events went counter to the intention of the gospel. The New Testament itself understood the coming, person and work of Jesus Christ as the fulfilment of the Old Testament expectation. Jesus is indeed the Christ, the Messiah. And the Messiah is, in the sense of the Old Testament and when it comes to the core of the matter, the *king*. But what is at stake in kingship is not the king but the society of people around him. The king is the servant of God and the shepherd of his people.

That is God's intention according to the Old Testament: that there should be a community of the people in which the lines of justice and love have been drawn so that God's very being may be reflected in it. Human beings are, specifically also in their communality and the way in which their society is ordered, the image of God. To this end, the Lord God has called and established the people of Israel: that it would be image of God and in that sense also example[4] for other peoples. What it is about in the Old Testament is the brotherhood of all people[5] based on the recognition and praiseful service of the only and true God.

Now then, *that* is the act of God according to the New Testament: that, after all the failures in the history of the people of Israel, the true king has come at last, the king who will serve God faithfully and lead the people in truth. Now the kingdom of God on earth has come near and has arrived. Therefore "peace" has now been given on earth,[6] that is to say, a space in which life can flourish. That passes through the full acceptance of suffering, through sacrifice and death. But the cross is the tree of life.

Now, through the coming of Christ, new hope and new expectation have been born. Courage and hope for the earth.[7] That is why the

---

4. Translator's note: Here Van Ruler plays on the Dutch words "beeld" (image) and "voorbeeld" (example).

5. To describe the eschatological perspective on the kingdom of God more closely, Van Ruler uses, alternately, the "brotherhood of all people" or "the social ideal." For cross-references to literature in Dutch, see his *Verzameld werk 5C*, 447, note 57.

6. See Luke 2:14.

7. Van Ruler uses the phrase "confidence concerning the world" also in a broader

apostles go out into it. That is why the earliest Christians were the "third generation":[8] they no longer lived in the acquiescence of the Jews and no longer in the despair and presumption of the pagans: they lived in the kingdom. This new expectation is an essential element in the fulfilment. That everything has been fulfilled in Jesus Christ also and particularly entails that people again have expectations for *everything*.

DE-DEIFICATION OF THE STATE

This led to three consequences that are of the greatest importance for politics.

In the first place, the state has been de-deified by this preaching of the gospel. It has received a Lord. Jesus is the Lord of all lords and the king of all kings.[9] The state can no longer regard itself as the rounding-off and completion of all Being [zijn], as the fully conscious Spirit. It is no longer God on earth.

For the sake of this political statement, Christians allowed themselves to be thrown to the lions for three centuries. Through their unprecedented perseverance, they finally attained victory. From this the history of Europe was born.

It is evident that there is still a fundamental problem here. When it comes to dictatorship and the formation of an absolute state, this is not to be explained as the result of the malevolence of some who lust for power. It is inherent in the nature of the state and the needs of practical life. People unavoidably think that they can solve the problems of society in an absolute way in and through the state.

There is but one safeguard against this disastrous clouding of the mind: the Old and New Testament witness concerning God, the Christian faith in Jesus Christ.

This de-deification of the state—and this is the second point—has gained concrete expression in the fact that, through the preaching of the gospel, the church has come to stand *alongside* the state, so that the whole of life is lived within this fundamental *duality*. Throne and altar no longer sprout from one root, because in Christianity the altar came in from the

---

sense. For cross-references to literature in Dutch, see Van Ruler's *Verzameld werk* 5C, 936, note 18.

8. In the first centuries Christians were called a "tertium genus", a third generation after the Jews and pagans. See, for example Tertullian *Ad Nationes*, I.8 and I.20.

9. See Revelation 17:14, 19:16.

outside, from Israel.[10] That is why the church does not fall under the state, is not a component of the state, but stands fully alongside the state, on a level with an equivalent, albeit entirely different, divine authority. This duality of church and state has endowed European life with its specific tension and drama. Therefore it would be nothing short of a disaster if, in the future, this duality were to be abolished in some or other way.

With that, moreover, the third point is given. In Christ God gives us everything we need. In a sense God even forces things through.[11] *But*: God waits on us until we have assented to and accepted, also internally, the things that God has given. God does everything in the way of the Holy Spirit. That is to say, in the way of freedom. The current freedom is also politically anchored in the de-deification of the state and in the duality of church and state.

In our time, this presents us with an essential question. What is at stake in life is the good. But may we also impose the good, when we believe we know what it is, by force on other people? Democracy, as European form of life, says: "No." Instead, people should first see for themselves that the good is good; it has to be internally assented to and accepted. That is why the communists say, not entirely without reason, that democracy is essentially reactionary. Indeed, there is a retarding, obstructing element in it. We do not impose the absolute good on life with the absolute force of the absolute state. Instead, we wait until other people see it too. The things are enveloped in the secret of love.

This freedom—with all its enormous problems—is, moreover, an essential part of the fulfilment that has been given with the coming of Christ. The problems have not been solved by this coming. They have merely been posed in the correct way by it. The solution still lies before us: in the future, in history and in the last judgement. God and human beings are still busy with it.

---

10. For Van Ruler's views on throne and altar, see the cross-references to literature in Dutch in his *Verzameld werk 5C*, 886, note 19.

11. For cross-references to literature in Dutch, see the Dutch edition of the *Verzameld werk 5C*, 886, note 22.

Life after Death[1]
[1958]

I AM SLIGHTLY EMBARRASSED to be asked to speak at my first appearance [in this gathering]: makes an immodest impression—do not know exactly what is intended by the topic—do not know how things are done here and what is expected.

Life after death—that refers to what we usually call the intermediate state. It seems to me to be of great importance to keep this topic within the context of eschatology as a whole.

Else we are threatened with: individualizing, internalizing, churchifying of the hereafter: attention confined to the destiny of the individual souls and the community of souls. Alongside this, the attention should also be given to the body, the questions of state and culture, and the plants, animals and things.

Then it becomes quite clear that we can talk about it only in images and in the language of myth. But then that was already the case concerning "souls". All that matters is that we speak and think in the correct myths: that determines how we experience things. Where is my center of gravity: in the church or in the world?

We shall have to accept a realistic, endgeschichtlich eschatology: this world is God's world and God is holy and good—therefore it *cannot* be left to sin and suffering.

But we *expect* the future—not from within the void or the lack, but from within the abundance of the fulfilment, from what has been given

---

1. The inventory number of the Dutch text, "Het leven na de dood" is I,454. These were notes for a presentation on 3 January 1958 at the estate Dijnselburg in Zeist for a circle of Roman Catholic and Protestant intellectuals. Van Ruler kept a list of the members of this circle together with the manuscript. It is included in Volume 5C of Van Ruler's *Verzameld werk* (2023), 887–91.

to us in Christ. In view of that, it becomes self-evident that we should expect the future.

A few preliminary questions:

- Is it really true that we as believers, church and theologians may as well close up shop if there were no hereafter? If it were so that we live but once, would the will and the service of God not be equally important and urgent?

- Must creation not have an end, just as it had a beginning? There was a time when I was not yet there and God willed that I should be there—can we say: there will be a time when I shall not be there and God wills me [only] as having been there? Or do I become co-eternal with God? And what does that mean? And does it not become palpably problematic if I were to say that of the entire created world?

- Earlier on, people focused their attention on the soul, the spirit—at present, people say: "No, the totality of the person, body and soul"— I ask: "*Is* that how we are?" What am *I*: solely the totality of soul and body—not also a piece of filled time?[2] When "I" am saved, does that not mean that my life that I live here and now is saved—and that *this* life thus "returns" in the eschaton: *that* is what is judged, purified, consummated, brought under one head, glorified.[3] Humans are not only spiritual and material beings, but also temporal beings. Thus the eschaton casts us back into the present: the eschaton is about the present.

- In Christian thinking, can one separate eschatology and apocalyptic? Can we say that it is about God, the ἔσχατος, and about our meeting with God—and not about all sorts of ἔσχατα?[4] Is it not about what God does to God's world?

If, along these lines, we focus our attention on the destiny of the world (to which human beings belong), we also focus attention on the intermediate state as intermediate state: the destiny of the dead is tied up with God's as yet unfinished business with God's world.

---

2. Van Ruler could have derived the term "filled time" from Karl Barth. See his *KD*, *III/2*, 648; *KD*, *IV/2*, 476. It is an expression that Van Ruler uses frequently. For cross-references to literature in Dutch, see *Verzameld werk 5C*, 891, note 5.

3. Van Ruler frequently employs such a series of verbs to describe the eschaton. For cross-references to literature in Dutch, see his *Verzameld werk 5C*, 891, note 6.

4. Ἔσχατος: The last one; ἔσχατα: The last things.

That implies, at the least, that the bliss after death is a preliminary bliss: the definitive bliss becomes conceivable only when God's glory is seen in all reality.

That is also clear when we think of the body that is consumed in the grave. Could we say that this bliss in the intermediate state is bliss in death? Is death merely a moment, the moment of dying, through which we stride? Or is death a state into which we stride in the moment of dying?

Here the dual sense of "death" and "immortality" also has to be considered. The physical and the spiritual sense. Bavinck says: "Christ did not gain or disclose immortality in the philosophical sense, the sense of the continued existence of souls after death [the realization of that is given with being human and arises from it spontaneously]. On the contrary, both here and hereafter he again filled the life of humans, exhausted and emptied by sin, with the positive content of God's fellowship, with peace and joy and blessedness."[5]

That is why it does not matter that much either whether we are alive or dead: we live in the Lord and die in the Lord; in both cases we belong to the Lord.[6]

Eternal life is our share even now. Whoever believes in the Son *has* eternal life.[7] That is especially evident regarding love:[8] that God loves me—that I let myself be loved—that I love God—that I love everything and everyone [with[9]] God's love. This love is already eternal life; nothing about it has to change.

According to the reformed confession, I am, through the work of the Holy Spirit, already in heaven[10] in the present at the Lord's table, where I eat and drink his true body and blood,[11] yes, He who is true God

---

5. Herman Bavinck (1854–1921), minister in the Christelijk Gereformeerde Kerk ("Christian Reformed Church"), professor of theology at the Theologische School te Kampen (1883–1902), and at the Vrije Universiteit te Amsterdam (1902–1921). Van Ruler quoted Bavinck in the Dutch almost verbatim and added the text placed here in square brackets. The translation used here is by John Vriend. See Bavinck, *Reformed Dogmatic Volume Four* (Grand Rapids: Baker Academic, 2008), 616.

6. See Romans 14:7–8.

7. See John 5:24.

8. Translator' note: In this sentence Van Ruler uses as verb "beminnen" instead of "liefhebben" for "to love". In Dutch the former is generally more intimate and is all but restricted to interpersonal relationships. It is often used specifically of erotic love.

9. Van Ruler wrote "mij" (my). The context suggests that he meant "met" (with).

10. For cross-references in this regard, see Van Ruler's *Verzameld werk 5C*, 891, note 12.

11. This is a reference to the classic Reformed formulary for the Lord's Supper.

and true human being. Just as I am fully on earth only in dying: dust to dust and ashes to ashes.[12]

The power of Christ's resurrection works through in equal measure in the one and in the other. If I am in bliss now already in this way, how then can I be anything but in bliss after death? Is there a difference in essence here? Is there a difference in degree? Is bliss anything else but holiness, participation in the glory of God—as this is evident in God's commandment and God's work?

There is, I believe, no difference of opinion about the statement that the decision is taken in this life. After death there is no possibility of conversion, no offer of grace anymore.

There is indeed much contention about the question of how the decision is taken. Jesus is a complete Savior, who redeems me completely from sin (guilt, the power and the punishment of sin[13]) and completely gives me the right [recht] to eternal life and eternal life itself.

Therefore we do not see how there can be any place for a purgatory and how the living can, by means of prayers, alms, good works, indulgences, mass offerings, and so on, help to alleviate or shorten the punishments in purgatory.

The creatureliness of the dead in their bliss will have to be respected. They are not entering into God or into the void like a wave that recedes back into the sea.[14] According to Bavinck, they have their own space and time.[15] There is a multiplicity and variety of positions. One can posit a

---

12. This is a reference to words used at a funeral by the minister in the Reformed tradition.

13. See Bavinck, *Gereformeerde Dogmatiek Deel IV*, 230 (*Reformed Dogmatics 4*, 246).

14. For cross-references, see Van Ruler's *Verzameld werk 5C*, 891, note 16.

15. Bavinck writes: "For though there is certainly no progress like that on earth, and still less a possible change for good or ill, still genuinely existing souls cannot possibly be without activity unless one thinks of them as being in a coma. The dead remain finite and limited and can exist in no other than in space and time. Undoubtedly, on the other side of the grave the dimensions of space and the computations of time are very different from those on earth, where we measure by the mile and by the hour. Also, the souls who dwell there do not become eternal and omnipresent as God is; like the angels they must have a specific whereabouts (*ubi definitivum*) cannot be in two places at the same time, are always somewhere in a specific location, in paradise or heaven, and so on. Similarly, they are not elevated above all structured time, that is, above all succession of moments, inasmuch as they have a past they remember, a present in which they live, and a future toward which they are moving." See Bavinck, *Reformed Dogmatics 4*, 641–42 (as translated by John Vriend).

progressive development of bliss. The basic idea is also not that of rest but of active service: the holy labor of praise.

But how does that relate to the community of the catholic church? Is the latter not also catholic in that it exceeds the boundary of death? Is there not an active communion between the *ecclesia militans* and the *ecclesia triumphans*?[16]

At least—I would say—we celebrate this communion in the communal praise. We also have communion with the same Triune God and with the same benefits of the covenant of grace.

But is there no intercession from the blessed and may we not ask them for such intercession?

- How would we be able to ask the blessed in heaven? Via the angels? On the strength of the ubiquity of the blessed? Does God convey the content of our request?

- Does this asking not inevitably become praying? Should the boundary of being human and of death not be respected? In the *ecclesia militans* too we do not ask everyone for intercession—there too *human* rapport is limited.

- Further along the line of this invocation of the blessed lies the veneration of the saints. There matters are somewhat different. We should be glad about all that God in Christ-through-the-Spirit works in the lives of human beings. That obviously holds also regarding the living saints. But does it make sense to speak of veneration here? Are the charismata not for the entire congregation? And are we not called to the same sanctity? And do we not—in as much as we live in love—stand within this [sanctity]? Is there something vertical to sanctity—so that the saints stand "above" us?

- To return to the blessed and their intercessions: do they still have contact with and knowledge of earthly history? Is there anything more than a general intercession for the history of the church as one whole? In Holy Scripture there is no mention of intercession of the angels or the blessed for the living on earth.

---

16. *Ecclesia militans*: Militant church; *ecclesia triumphans*: triumphant church. For cross-references to Van Ruler's use of these terms, see the *Verzameld werk 5C*, 891, note 18.

The Parousia of Christ[1]
[1960]

OF THE LAST THINGS (the hour of our death—heaven—the last days—the kingdom of glory) we have no clear and complete knowledge.

- They have not happened yet and we have not experienced them.
- Our cognition is also clouded by sin and corruption.
- The last is what matters most—and that is a matter of the heart rather than of the mind.

Therefore, these cannot be thought or imagined either.

- This holds for the first things as well.
- And in essence for all things: we can but be and experience them.
  - » Childlike.
- We have to speak about them in images (myths).
  - » The time [of the last things] is hidden from us—the mode as well (television?).
  - » Holy Scripture speaks extremely soberly about them.
- But there are good and bad images: the good images are those that express a pure (= purified, converted) experience of life.

But we do speak about them on the basis of Holy Scripture.

- On the basis of God's self-revelation in Israel, in Christ.

---

1. The inventory number of the Dutch text, "De wederkomst van Christus" is I,580. These are notes for a presentation at a "congregation evening" in Delfshaven. The original consists of six handwritten pages. This essay is included in Volume 5C of Van Ruler's *Verzameld werk* (2023), 892–895.

- The God-man: God has become human in Jesus Christ.
- [He] has brought about salvation [heil], redemption on earth for humanity and the world.
- Therefore we do not have this expectation from out of a void, a lack, a yearning.
  » We do not expect from out of the fallen world.
  » But from out of the fulness, the abundance of what has been given to us.
  » In the present, we cannot encompass this fulness: it splashes over everything from all sides: that is the Christian future expectation, the *over*flowing pail.[2]

The parousia of Christ goes together with the resurrection of the flesh.

- That is the resurrection of the body (flesh and blood cannot inherit the kingdom).[3]
- Therefore of the entire person: that is the object of redemption.
  » We have an all-sufficient Savior.
- There is the unity of human nature in body and soul.
- *This* image is better than the images of the pagans and philosophers: the immortal soul—the dissolution of individuality in the All—nirvana—the transmigration of souls—the twilight of the gods—the eternal return.
- Not only corporeality, also temporality: I am also a piece of filled time:[4] that is redeemed and "returns".
- This redemption, also of the body, from death is given in Christ—yet it still has to become manifest: therefore we have to deal circumspectly with prayer healing (of *disease* only).

The parousia of Christ and the resurrection of the flesh also go together with the last judgement.

---

2. Elsewhere Van Ruler rejects the image of an overflowing pail in the doctrine of creation. See his *Verzameld werk 3*, 380.

3. See 1 Corinthians 15:50.

4. Van Ruler could have derived the term "filled time" from Karl Barth. See his *KD, III/2*, 648; *KD, IV/2*, 476. This is an expression that Van Ruler uses frequently. For cross-references to literature in Dutch, see his *Verzameld werk 5C*, 891, note 5.

- All that had been, had been done, had happened, returns.
  » In the parousia of Christ we find ourselves and the world once more.
- It comes in judgement: God calls us to account and asks us: What have you done with my world?
- It is: crisis—judgement—sifting—separation—purification—disclosure—making public—renewal—glorification—consummation.
- In this way everything is turned inside out (it precisely does *not* turn back into the abyss and the silence)—the world is swept clean of all injustice and violence and becomes habitable once more—all riddles are solved—it becomes evident that there is no injustice[5] at all in God—all tears (that we cried over ourselves and this world[6]) are wiped from the eyes—to see and love everything along with God—joy[7] over Being [het zijn], praise of God.

The God who is our judge was also our Savior.

- It becomes evident that we are able to exist before the face of God only through grace, the atoning work of Christ.
- Therefore the question is: Are we in Christ?: through faith—the sacrament—good works: Do we live our lives in Him (through imputation, incorporation, imitation)?
- But this should once more and definitely be stated: on Golgotha, in preaching, in our conscience, a judgement is passed as well—but there is still much toing and froing. That is why the faithful too come before the judgement seat: then it is *entirely* definite *and entirely* public.

At the same time, the Son returns the kingdom to the Father.[8]

- Then we are redeemed and can exist before God's face by ourselves: God then takes pleasure in us.

---

5. See Deuteronomy 32:4; Psalm 92:16; II Chronicles 19:7; Zephaniah 3:5.
6. See Revelations 21:4.
7. "Joy" is a core motif in Van Ruler's theology. For cross-references to literature in Dutch, see Van Ruler's *Verzameld werk 5C*, 869, note 65.
8. The thesis that the Son returns the kingdom to the Father in the eschaton and that the incarnation is then cancelled is discussed in more detail in an essay entitled "Theologie van het apostolaat" ("Theology of the Apostolate" in Van Ruler's *Verzameld werk 5C*, 721–48. This essay is not included in this volume.

- Then all that remains is: the Triune God and created reality.
  » Christ lays off the flesh; He is no longer our Mediator.
- Because it is not about Christ but about the kingdom that is established in Him and in his work.
- And the kingdom—we are that, before the face of God, according to God's will.
- Therefore the whole of created reality is the object of salvation.
- Not all people—there are those who are lost forever.
- But certainly the human race as such.
- And that on earth and not purely in heaven, eternity, the spiritual, the invisible: also in the visible, material reality.
- A new heaven and a new earth in which righteousness dwells: the social ideal, the *co*-existence of humanity.[9]
- That passes along the way of ruin (that is how enormous the problem of iniquity is)—but it *is* the *same* earth.

The core of everything we are to receive we have already received.

- Love—that never perishes; nothing about that changes.
- This is eternal life, that they know Thee the only true God, and Jesus Christ whom Thou hast sent.[10]
- Therefore also joy and praise: faith is enthusiasm about Being [zijn].[11]
- The Christian future expectation cast us fully back into the present: God has not yet come that far and if God has, God is still concerned with the things of the present.
- So we hold the present to be "full" (it is filled with God's glory) and we also hold on to it [the fulness] *in* the present.[12]

---

9. To describe the eschatological perspective on the kingdom of God more closely, Van Ruler uses, alternately, the "brotherhood of all people" or "the social ideal." For cross-references to literature in Dutch, see t the *Verzameld werk* 5C, 447, note 57.

10. See John 17:3.

11. Van Ruler derives the expression "enthusiasm for being" from J.H. Gunning Jr. The source is probably J.H. Gunning Jr., *Het kruis de waarheid voor wetenschap en kerk* (Amsterdam, s.a. [1882]), 12f.

12. Translator's note: Here Van Ruler plays on the Dutch "vol houden" (regard as full) and "volhouden" (persevere"). The wordplay could not be fully maintained in English.

- This hope purifies: we experience Being [het zijn] as that which will be shown to be.

Therefore the parousia of Christ is in a certain sense already there in the present.

- On the day of Pentecost the glorified Lord returned in the Spirit.
- In each sermon the Lord comes to us.
- In the liturgy and the Lord's Supper He is with us.
- In the purification of the heart, in the sanctification of life, the Lord enters into communion with us.
- In our activity in the world, the Lord wishes to be with us up to the end of the age.

But: it is for now in the coils of death.

- We are preserved in that by virtue of the resurrection of Christ.
- Also *in* death (in the grave and in heaven).
- Death is the last enemy that is conquered.[13]

---

13. See 1 Corinthians 15:26.

Eschatological Notices[1]
[1961]

I

ONE CAN SAY THAT, in general, the concept "future", the orientation to it and the expectation of it, are specifically biblical-Christian notions. At least, if they are adequately grasped, that is, when they are understood, first, as relating to humanity and the world as a whole and thus not to individual human beings, and, secondly, as what it is really about, what matters to God and what should matter to us.

Of course, people in all religions and all philosophical systems have had a notion of the future. That comes along with the daily experience of life: ever again there is a new day. The beyond of death is also experienced as lying *ahead* of us.

But all of this is not yet an eschatology in the true sense of the word. That emerges only when the two above-mentioned stipulations appear: the future of the world as a whole is what it is about and *that* is what is really at stake. This world is not a cycle (*from* which there is a way only for the *individual*). This world itself is a way. At least, it follows a way. It is going somewhere. That to which we are going is worth the trouble, is good. Therefore, too, the world is a unity. And an irreversible unity at that. We

---

[1] The inventory number of the Dutch text, "Eschatologische notities" is I,623. This was based on a paper for the fifth congress of the Christelijke Vereniging van Natuur- en Geneeskundigen ("Christian Society for Natural and Medial Scientists") in Oosterbeek, 27–28 October 1961. It was previously published under the title "Bijbel en natuurwetenschap over de toekoms" ("Bible and natural science on the future") in *Geloof en Wetenschap* 60 (1962), 33–53, but later also as "Eschatological Notices" in the volume *Theologisch Werk 1*, that Van Ruler himself compiled. It is included in Volume 5C of Van Ruler's *Verzameld werk* (2023), 896–915.

as humans are, in our thoughts and actions, taken up in this unity: we can have a conception of this irreversible, meaningful unity and we should act responsibly from within this unity. That is the life that has been given to us. Our being human is taken up in that.

This stringent conception of the future is a specifically biblical-Christian one. In the Parsee religion we find some parallels. The historical thought of some Greek authors reaches out in this direction now and then. But it came to full unfolding and realization only in Israel. There God is experienced as the One who elects and calls. God does not merely elect and call one single person (Abraham) but this single person together with his seed. God wants to be surrounded by a people. With that [people] God establishes God's covenant. God also gives God's law. Moreover, God has something in mind with this people and, following through on that, with God's human world of humanity, even with God's world as such. God performs acts in history. Through these, history is constituted. History is the totality of the acts of God.[2] People are called to interweave their acts in this and to accomplish the work of God on earth.

All of this is concentrated in the one great act of God of sending God's Son and in the work accomplished by Christ. In that the kingdom of God (*the* eschaton par excellence) is established on earth. Time is now fulfilled. That is, time has now become full, life has its meaning, history has gained its eschaton, there is redemption—not *from* time, of the individual, but *of* time. The whole of created reality is—in principle—redeemed.[3] The apostles saw this lightning flash of God's act in history; they derived confidence concerning the world from it.[4] For that reason, they went to all the peoples of the earth—proclaiming, teaching, baptizing, exercising discipline. The church has accepted and taken over all these realities and realizations. It marches with the peoples to the

---

2. Van Ruler often describes the dance of God's acts (Dutch: reidans). See also the Greek term *perichoresis*. For cross-references, for example to a volume of meditations for Advent with the title *Reidans*, see the Dutch edition of the *Verzameld werk 5C*, 173, note 63.

3. For Van Ruler's views on the salvation of the whole of time, see the cross-references to literature in Dutch in the *Verzameld werk 5C*, 911, note 3.

4. For Van Ruler's use of the expression "confidence concerning the world" (Dutch: "moed voor de wereld"), see the cross-references to literature in Dutch in the *Verzameld werk 5C*, 912, note 4. Van Ruler also published a volume of morning devotions on the book Zachariah under the title *Heb moed voor de wereld* ("Have confidence concerning the world," 1953).

eschaton that is now present, fulfilled and veiled, and will once, at a later time, be unveiled, made public.

This is the first and fundamental meaning of the Bible and Christian faith regarding the questions about the future: it constitutes überhaupt the concept "future". As soon as the suppositions of Christian faith fall away, this concept "future" is also in danger of falling away.

II

If someone were to ask what precisely we are to understand by this future-in-the-strict-sense, what we can think and imagine regarding it, we stand at a loss. What are these: The parousia of Christ? The last of days? The final judgement? The resurrection of the flesh? Eternal life? The new heaven and earth? The kingdom of glory?

To these questions we can but answer: "I don't know that precisely. Here I am no longer speaking quite exactly, in discursive concepts. I speak in images." Now that occurs more frequently. The core of our existence we can express only in images. Not only Christians are confronted by this inevitability. But all people who think through these things more deeply. We do not mount a better scientific defense when we go on about "the twilight of the gods", "the return of all things", "the brotherhood (!) of people," "nirvana,"[5] "the return into the All-One,"[6] "the absolute void," These too are images. They are beautiful and gripping. The theologian constantly keeps sifting through all the pictures [plaatjes].[7] The one image is better than the other image to express what we have to say when our thoughts are guided by the witness of the prophets and the apostles. Some images are definitely bad, false, untrue. They have to be rejected. Other images are definitely good; they are true. We have to cling to them.

Does the Bible not provide clarity? Yes, the Bible helps greatly in our sorting through the pictures. It places the correct pictures [plaatjes] in our hands. But these, too, are mere pictures [plaatjes]. The prophets and

---

5. For Van Ruler's view on nirvana, see the cross-references to literature in Dutch in his *Verzameld werk 5C*, 912, note 5.

6. For Van Ruler's views on the "All-One", see the cross-references to literature in Dutch in the *Verzameld werk 5C*, 9121, note 6.

7. Editor's note: Van Ruler often describes the task of a systematic theologian as one of playing with, sifting through or sorting out images. The Dutch term that he uses ("plaatjes") has the connotations of pictures, off-prints, templates, graphic metaphors and images, but also slides for a slide-projector. For cross-references to literature in Dutch see the *Verzameld werk 5C*, 912, note 7.

apostles were not systematic theologians, much less scientific prognosticators. They stood in the reality of revelation and of Christ. In this way they stood in the reality of life and the world. They bore witness to what they saw. But they did that in figurative words and concepts. One has to be a poet rather than a scholar to understand what they were saying.

Nor can we take biblical passages such as the Book of Revelations as a detailed prognosis either of what things will happen at the end or of what things await us before the end, in history (of the church and the world). They are, rather, kaleidoscopes; the colored pieces of glass in the kaleidoscope are the ingredients of both the historical process and the eschaton. Time and again the kaleidoscope is given one turn and then the pieces of glass appear in a new configuration before the astonished eyes of the beholder. From this we can in no way deduce what will happen at a specific moment, not even the date of the parousia.

We as Christians feel even less embarrassed about this impossibility of forming an image of the eschatological expectation when we become aware that precisely the same configuration crops up in communism. So we do not know precisely how to express what we understand by eternal life and the kingdom of glory. But would communists[8] dare to state that they have a clear vision of what their eschaton, the classless and especially stateless society would look like? In my opinion all communists will at some time be assailed by challenges to their faith similar to those with which all thoughtful Christians constantly have to grapple.

III

This comparison of Christianity and communism brings me to my next point. We may be seduced into simply forgoing an eschatology because it is so utterly unimaginable and seems impossible. But then we must consider that we do not merely lose eschatology. But also history. That we see very clearly in the case of communists. If they were to abandon their dream of the eschatological kingdom, of the classless and stateless society, then they would also have to abandon their claim that they see and are the absolute meaning [zin] of the historical process. Along with that they would also lose their activity. They become as inert as the West without any faith.

---

8. For Van Ruler's view on communism, see the cross-references in *Verzameld werk* 5C, 912, note 8 *et passim*.

In other words: the future and history, the eschatological and the historical, determine each other reciprocally. Without eschaton there is no history. The eschaton is the pulling point [trekpunt] that keeps history in motion and draws a line through it.[9] It also gives history the character of unity and irreversibility without which history would cease to be history.

We can also safely aver that not only eschatology, the concept "future" in the strict sense of the word, is a specifically biblical-Christian notion. The same would have to be said about the concept "history". That too comes from Israel and is an apostolic heritage of Christian Europe.

Before we leave this notion of "history" behind, we do have to consider it again a few times. We should consider how intimately this notion is interwoven with that of humanness. Is it not essential to the being human of humans that they, in their context, have to act responsibly within the directed, moving, irreversible, meaningful and knowable unity of world history? If that is no longer essential to the person, if it should even be a completely untenable claim, what then remains of the person? An absurd wad of freedom? A fully determined piece of nature or cosmos? A fluorescence of the void? A fragment of God? One can go pick and choose to understand oneself. But we all have, in my opinion, the feeling that we lose the aroma and essence of humanness if the history that surrounds the human person falls away.

And history falls away if eschatology, the unimaginable future-in-the-full-sense-of-the-word falls away.

We can also indicate this correlation of eschaton and history in the opposite sense. If the eschaton falls away, then the pulling force of history falls away, then history also falls away. In a correlative way, the eschaton is necessary for history. But history is in an equally correlative way necessary for the eschaton as well. The eschaton is the eschaton of history, the end, the summary, the consummation of it. Had there been no history, then there could be no eschaton. But to that I shall return in another context. I mention it here merely to indicate that the correlation of history and eschaton is truly reciprocal, an authentic *cor*relation.

At the same time, the clinging to this correlation (with all the mental anguish that comes along with the unimaginability of the one pole) clearly entails a choice of faith. That, however, is not purely a matter of

---

9. Van Ruler frequently describes the eschaton as the "pulling point" (Dutch: trekpunt) of history. For cross-references to literature in Dutch, see the *Verzameld werk 5C*, 912, note 9.

religion and worship in which things are foisted on us that are added to the data of ordinary life and experienced reality. Faith, religion and worship are never—if they are genuine—such separate things. This choice of faith concerns purely and only the data of ordinary life[10] and experienced reality. In clinging to the correlation of eschatology and history, we are saying: "We believe that that which we are and have here and now and with which we are busy is actual history, that the world and life are worthwhile, that there is meaning in that, that at least we will, affirm and accept that, that we are fully prepared to be there—and that with joy."

This faith is, as far as I can see, confessed in this world only by the Christian church (if it is at least still a little biblical) and further by the communists, but by the latter only in a highly heretical and, moreover, bourgeois form.

The rest of humanity does not yet believe it or no longer (in the West) does so. They depart to one of the other images. Especially the shares in the image of nirvana are currently trading at a high: God is a projection, but the world and the self are also projections. We have to de-project, retract all projection. Then not only God falls away; the world and the self also fall away. In principle then ascetics are the images of authentic humanity: they have already ventured as far as is possible along this desert way of de-projection. Hitler and his followers wanted to foist another figure on us, that of the heroes who promptly cast themselves into the abyss of the twilight of the gods. Of course, we also have the possibility of the mystics who want only one thing: back into the All-One. And that of the people who continue to sit on the merry-go-round of the eternal return of all things.

Amid this turbulent cacophony, the Bible calls us to the staunch[11] choice of faith: we do not de-project, do not cast ourselves into the abyss, do not hanker back, do not continually turn around. We do but one thing: we accept ourselves, the present, the world, the deed, and we trust that all of that is good.

But we have to be thoroughly aware that here almost nothing (except perhaps the strange fact that we are there and that the world is there)

---

10. For Van Ruler's emphasis on ordinary life, see the cross-references to literature in Dutch in his *Verzameld werk 5C*, 912, note 13.

11. Van Ruler uses the Dutch term "stoer" (here translated as "staunch", also "sturdy") frequently in his work. For cross-references to literature in Dutch, see his *Verzameld werk 5C*, 912, note 15.

is self-evident. We make a choice. We believe. The background of all is theological in nature.

This background works through to the foreground in a decisive way. We can barely imagine what effects it would have for both science and politics (both as engagements of humanity with the world) if one of the other images were really to dominate [our] minds in general. Is the Christian-theistic conviction not an absolute condition for a meaningful and somewhat tolerable engagement with the world?

IV

At the same time, the Christian choice of faith is not a random statement, a leap. There is a biblical-Christian expectation for the future (of the world) based on the self-revelation of God.

With this train of thought we are, of course, in danger of simply shifting the problem a little further backward. For is the self-revelation of God not simply another random statement, a leap? An expectation for the future does *follow* from it. So this does have a ground. But is the ground itself not a leap?

In my view we can at this point never get any further with rational arguments. The prophets and apostles, the psalmists and evangelists, claim that God revealed Godself in a special way to Israel and in Christ. In this revelation God made Godself known. God has given Godself. The prophets and apostles (and so on) were there to proclaim this in the world, so that we too—along with them—can have communion with the living God who communicated Godself in God's revelation. People can but be obedient or disobedient to this proclamation. They cannot, at least not to the very end, argue or prove *that* there is indeed revelation here and that the revelation is *authentic* revelation. They can in no way present arguments as to why this revelation was granted in particular to the one people of Israel and in the one person Jesus Christ.

But *if* it is indeed true that God revealed Godself to Israel and in Jesus Christ and that God's revelation was in accordance with what is claimed about it, then, following from that, the choice of faith for the correlation between history and eschaton has become perfectly self-evident.

The very idea that God made Godself known and gave Godself in a special revelation already leads to this [conclusion]. After all, it follows from, or rather, it consists in (among other things), the fact that God, the eternal Creator, cares about humanity, takes trouble with the world, intervenes and acts in the historical process. If we consider this rationally, there is something as fantastic about this as, for instance, about the idea of the kingdom of glory. Rationally seen, it is really too crazy to be allowed to run loose. Although it does have to be kept in mind that the simple existence of the world and humanity confronts us with something similar. If we consider it deeply, it is practically unavoidable to use words for it such as "self-revelation of the ground of Being" [zijn].

Alongside the "that" stands the "what" of God's revelation to Israel and in Jesus Christ. On the one hand, there is the pole of God's grace and holiness. On the other hand, there is God's intention of the kingdom for humanity and the world. If God is really like this, it is unavoidable that there has to be a future and that in the future history has to be redeemed. In his book *De verwachting van het koninkrijk Gods* ["The expectation of the kingdom of God"], G.J. Heering formulated this connection beautifully in the following syllogism: 1. God is good and holy—that stands firm on the basis of the gospel; 2. This world is God's world—that is a fundamental truth of the entire Bible and one of the core affirmations of the Christian faith; 3. For that reason it is utterly impossible that the world should remain as it is now, so full of sin and so full of suffering.[12] Seen from the heart of the gospel, eschatology is absolutely necessary, and then an eschatology so envisaged that nothing of history is abandoned.

This ground of the correlation of history and eschatology in the self-revelation of God also entails that we as Christians do not have an eschatological expectation out of poverty, because of the emptiness of life, but precisely out of abundance. What we have gained through Israel, in Christ, is *so* much, is to such an extent the fullness, that it is over-full; it is not to be contained within any of the forms of earthly, temporal life. The best [of it] we still only hold in the form of a paltry piece of bread and a mouthful of wine in the sacrament. We have received the germ of eternal joy. Were we to bring that to full realization, the walls of our hearts would burst. Therefore there is such a mass that we have to reserve for the hereafter and eternal life. But that does not mean that we have nothing now. On the contrary, we already have everything now, the full salvation of the totality of being. That is also what makes us stand, precisely in view of and from the eschaton, so completely in the present of history. We do

---

12. Gerrit Jan Heering (1879–1955), professor at the Remonstrants Seminarium in Leiden (1917–1949). For the source of this syllogism, see G.J. Heering, *De verwachting van het koninkrijk Gods*, Arnhem 1952, 204f.

indeed stand there particularly or in the first instance, sacramentally, that is, ecclesially. But in the discipline of the church, in the sanctification of life as service to God and to the world as theater of God's glory, we do stand in the present of history—and not only ecclesially. We also stand in it as "of the world" or rather as worldly. And then still in this very same fullness and abundance.

Between brackets: Both these tensions (1. to be ecclesial and worldly and in the present, and 2. To have fullness in the present and still also in eternal life) are examples of how little of the bourgeois there is in Christianity regarding the correlation of history and the eschaton. By way of contrast, communism has not the vaguest notion of these tensions and therefore experiences the world and being human in a much too shallow and narrow way. It has traded the church for the political party and has shriveled the eschaton to a piece of history that can be reached only through a revolution.

V

With some of this we have also said that from a biblical-Christian perspective it is all about and concerning this world, not merely historically but also eschatologically. It is God's world. There is no other world (at least not for human beings; for angels that is another matter). It is not a good thing to speak about this world as "merely this world" and then to act as if there is some completely different world that is not earthly and not temporal. That inevitably leaves the suggestion that the other world is much better. And that we really belong there because we come from there and shall thus return there, that we should in any case be far better off in it; that we should therefore live vertically, in the direction of the other world. When this idea is concentrated in a Christian way, we soon say: in the direction of the being of God.

These are all suggestions that have indeed for long played a role in Christian thinking. But in my opinion, they should be purged [from it]. They do not come from the Bible, also not from the New Testament. They do not fit into the fundamental structure of the Christian faith. This fundamental structure is eschatological in nature. That is to say, in the Christian faith we do not live vertically but horizontally;[13] we do not go upward

---

13. For this emphasis on the horizontal, see the cross-references to literature in Dutch in his *Verzameld werk* 5C, 913, note 24.
Editor's note: See also the essay on "Vertical and Horizontal" in Van Ruler's *This*

but forward, we are not oriented to the being of God but to the will of God. In the eschaton too we find not only God (or, as contemporary theology loves to say, Christ), but also ourselves and the world. The kingdom of God is not Godself (Ruusbroec)[14] but we are it. We would have to erase the truth of creation completely if we were to deny these statements. After all, the truth of creation implies that the world is not from us, nor from the devil, nor is it simply there. Instead, it is God's world—and God does not give up what is God's.

The words that are used in the Bible to indicate the eschaton also point in this direction. I am thinking of words such as *anakephalaiōsis* (recapitulation, bringing under one head, literally "summarizing")—*apokalupsis* (revelation, uncovering)—*crisis* (judgement, verdict)—*teleiōsis* (fulfilment)—*sunteleia* (consummation).[15] What is summarized, uncovered, judged, perfected, consummated, glorified? To that there is but one answer: that which we are and do here and now, in the historical process. When I arrive in eternity, then *I* would be interested in only one thing: I would then at last wish to see the eternal things, if need be (for want of the eternal ideas of Plato) nothing but God. But *God* would then still be interested only in the temporal things. In the judgement, God would ask me: "Old man, what have you done with my world?"[16] Here a clear contrast between Platonic and Christian thought is evident. In Plato's thought, eternity returns in time in the form of *anamnesis*, and that is the only glory of time. In Christian thought, time returns in eternity in the form of salvation [heil], and that is (for us, at least) the only glory of eternity. We—that is to say, this filled time[17] that we are—we are saved! For that reason, all the tears will be wiped from our eyes, namely, those

---

Earthly Life Matters: The Promise of Arnold A. van Ruler for Ecotheology, edited by Ernst M. Conradie and translated by Douglas G. Lawrie (Eugene: Pickwick, 2023), 253–58, where he emphasizes both orientations.

14. Jan van Ruusbroec (1293–1381), Dutch priest, mystic and hermit. Van Ruler refers to a citation in Jan van Ruusbroec, *Werken, Deel 1*, Tielt 19442, 122.

15. For a similar series of verbs to describe the eschaton, see the cross-references to literature in Dutch in Van Ruler's *Verzameld werk 5C*, 913, note 26.

16. On the contrast between Christian and Platonic thinking, see the cross-references to literature in Dutch in Van Ruler's *Verzameld werk 5C*, 913, 29.

17. Van Ruler could have derived the term "filled time" from Karl Barth. See his *KD, III/2*, 648; *KD, IV/2*, 476. It is an expression that Van Ruler uses frequently. For cross-references to literature in Dutch, see his *Verzameld werk 5C*, 891, note 5.

that we have cried in and about time: it *was* all glory (also the suffering? Also sin?)[18]

So we also take all of history with us into the eschaton. A peripheral problem is that of the intermediate time. What happens to me after death and before the last of days? The pedant in me says: "That is no problem, because the 'after' and the 'before' are false prepositions. What matters is eternity. There all the distinctions of time fall away." See just how sly and sharp-witted a pedant can be! But he also messes up by erasing everything in this way. The poet in me says: "There is, nevertheless, a problem. Dying I do on my own and this is about the world. That has still not been saved for everyone to see. How then would I be completely saved?" The theologian in me enters the conversation and says: "Let me table a new picture [plaatje]. In the interim, I am, for the time being, preserved in heaven (and in the grave). That is, after all, where Christ too is. With Him our lives have long been hidden in God. It is, however, a matter of preserving, storing, hiding: it is not yet the essential. That arrives with the last of days. Then the soul is united with the bones again, the human being with humanity, humanity with the world. But in the meanwhile (the theologian says), you must draw no false conclusions from the heavenly interim as if there were, after all, a verticality in existence, history and salvation [heil]."

This eschatological horizontality—which the Christian faith taught me—further entails that I retain a measureless interest in the world. It is said of Abraham Kuyper that on his deathbed he spoke and thought more about the future of the anti-revolutionary party than about his soul and heaven. If that is true, it is a sign of the man's piety.[19] In doing thus, he at least showed an abiding interest in the world.

Here a wide vista suddenly opens before us. The world goes its course. The newspapers report on it. More than the Bible does. The Bible holds up—as we have said—maximally kaleidoscopic images of it to our view. The newspaper is more exact. For that reason, I would place the newspaper next to the Bible and read both. Do I do that only as a person

18. See Revelations 21:4.

19. Abraham Kuyper (1837–1920), prominent Dutch pastor, theologian, journalist and politician. He was a central figure in the *Doleantie*, that led to a schism in the Dutch Reformed Church (Nederlands Hervormde Kerk) that took place in 1886. He established the Vrije Universiteit te Amsterdam and was professor there from 1880 to 1901. He was a long-standing member of Parliament and also served as the Dutch Prime Minister (1901–1905). It is not clear what Van Ruler's source is or whether this story about Kuyper's death bed is indeed an accurate portrayal.

or also as a theologian and a servant of the Word? It is not unimaginable that I would, now and then, take the newspaper with me to the pulpit. What it is all about, then, is that the historical reality, as it is reported in the newspaper, is to be illuminated in the prophecy from [the perspective] the Word. In doing so we do not generally fare that well. Most of the time, we are too sadly lacking in the Spirit for that. But would it not be better if people from diverse sciences—historians, psychologists, sociologists, statisticians, and so on—were to read the newspaper? To that I would wish to answer with a resounding "Yes". But so as not to embroil myself in too much discussion, I say: "At least these people should also read the newspaper and make their contribution; they must not expect all that much from theologians and servants of the Word. These too merely make a contribution." From time to time, an authentic, charismatic prophet does arise. Such a person simply sees through the entire historical process and knows which way it should go and how, in view of this, one should act. But just as we should not, on account of healing through prayer, leave the surgeon aside, so we should not, for the sake of charismatic prophecy, leave statistics aside. Not that these will cure the world. But they too may help.

In brief: they all belong [in the conversation]. Such a conversation between natural scientists and medical practitioners on the one hand and theologians on the other is also useful. It would have been great if we were all gifted with a bit of charisma. But let us not imagine that we have the world completely in our grip. Christ is still in the throes of death (Pascal).[20] Or let me sing an octave lower: Do not expect that theologians can tell how the future will go and how the last things will play out. If you expect that of them, they will say: "You must not bother us. We are busy playing around with [various] charts [kaarten]."

VI

I have just placed one of my most important trumps on the table: in history and in the eschaton it is about and concerns this world.

We do, however, have to delve somewhat deeper into that. Because some objections against it are commonly raised.

---

20. See Blaise Pascal, *Pensées de Pascal. Texte de l'Édition Brunschvicg* (Paris 1925), 214.

In the first place there is the objection of the catastrophic. Is the eschaton in the biblical, Christian world of imagery not a catastrophe that overtakes the world? And does this catastrophe not mean ruin [ondergang], the end, death for the world? How can one then still stress so strongly that both in history and in the eschaton it is about and concerning this world? To that it has to be replied that we should not stress only the catastrophe but in equal measure the continuity that marks all catastrophes. The boat goes through the great rapids but it goes right through them. How great the rapids of the eschaton are we can barely imagine. We have to use words such as "ruin" [ondergang], "end" and "death". Do we also have to use a word like "nothing", "the void"? Does the world fall back into nothing eschatologically, just as it was created out of nothing? One can argue about that. But not about the fact that, *if* we say that it returns to nothing, we must also say it is carried through the void. That is the power of the Creator and the Savior. That is why we as Christians stand with such a sunny disposition in the world: we are safeguarded in this power. It is, however, not only the power of God but also the loyalty of God. God does unimaginable new things but in all the novelty of God's acts God is also loyal to all the old things—those that were also from God. The new earth is not another earth but this earth renewed. All that is catastrophic does not take away the least bit of this identity.

In the second place there is the matter of inside or outside time. There it becomes quite palpable that we theologians are playing with pictures [plaatjes]. Immanuel Kant already indicated how antinomic our thought becomes when it comes to questions about the beginning and the end of the world.[21] But in the meanwhile, it is of crucial meaning to our experience of life and to our life practice which pictures [plaatjes] we shelve as less good and which we prefer as being the most accurate. Does the eschaton take place inside or outside time? Is it the end of time? Is the meaning [zin] of history realized within the scope of history or is that impossible? And if we say, no, not within the scope of history but outside time, at least in the radical ending of time, must we not then take [the following] two consequences as part of the deal: 1) That there is something tragic about the whole matter, one could almost say something tragicomic: the meaning [zin] of history is realized outside history! Every reasonable person would surely look at this a little crestfallen. 2)

---

21. See a passage from Kant's *Critique of Pure Reason*, A426/B454-A433/B461. Van Ruler read Kant's *Kritik der reinen Vernunft* in German while still in the gymnasium in Apeldoorn.

That the eschaton entails that we are in a sense lifted above our creatureliness, because [we are lifted] above our temporality. Our Roman Catholic fellow Christians do not fear this as much. They are much taken by this verticality, by this elevation, by the orientation to the being of God. But as Reformed Christians we have to ask ourselves with some care whether, in these speculations of ours, we remain adequately within the scope of the Bible.[22] How we judge at this point is of no small importance for the discussion between Christianity and communism and for a Christian assessment of communism. Communism holds the view that the eschaton is realizable in time. Should we as Christians not also hold to this? Have we not made it too comfortable for ourselves by reclining in a dualism of history and eschaton, of time and eternity?

In the third place, there is the matter of time and the times. If we do not place the eschaton in this dualistic way outside and in opposition to time but—in some or other way—in time, then it opens the way for the idea that each day in time has something to it that is a prefiguration of the last of days. Then we longer simply content ourselves with the longing for the last of days—that easily introduces something romantic and idealistic into the Christian eschatological expectation and threatens to turn it into its opposite. The last of days, the eschaton, cast us radically back into the present: there it is already prefigured. In the present, in each new day, in the future we are busy with this world—some only in the mode of preaching, the liturgy, the sacraments, others in the mode of politics, science, culture. There is sanctification in that. And all sanctification is a form of glorification. In heaven and in the kingdom of glory we receive nothing that is qualitatively and essentially different from what we already have, namely, sanctity, sanctification, which is also a sanctification of the earth. It is at most modally something different, namely, not so hidden and therefore no longer so broken by the implications of sin.

So we find here—and that comes in the fourth place—two elements that have to be underlined again. On the one hand, that the human deed is incorporated and taken up [in this]. God is at work. Particularly with regard to the eschaton we are used to saying: "The kingdom does not come through our efforts, but solely from God, perpendicularly from above." That is one-sided. We must in the same breath say this of history. We lose hold of the essence of history if we do not hold on to this: that God is at

---

22. Van Ruler often criticizes the distinction between the natural and the supernatural, together with the notion of "elevation" associated with that. For cross-references to literature in Dutch, see his *Verzameld werk 5C*, 191, note 2.

work (in the tumult of the nations and in the tumult of our hearts). But then it is still one-sided to accentuate only that God is at work. But then in the mode of the Spirit. Therefore with the incorporation (in election and rejection) of humanity. We are also at work. For instance, in science and politics. Must we say that of history only? Must we not also say that of the eschaton? Is it permissible to consider that a nuclear destruction of the world may be understood theologically from the perspective of the human aspect of God's eschatological wrath? I am merely asking.

On the other hand, within the previous train of thought there is also the element of evolution. We are currently busy synthesizing the Christian notion of creation and the modern notion of evolution with each other. Should we not attempt something similar regarding the Christian notion of the eschaton? The eschatological way of thinking has from old had evolutionary aspects. That is one of the things that enabled the young church to win the day. The fatalism and pessimism of the Hellenistic experience of life was breached. The realization dawned that the world will finally land on its feet. Also the realization that everything happens in the sphere of freedom, both on God's side and on the side of humanity. Therefore also the realization that there is advance, change, movement, progress in the historical process. All these are arch-Christian notions. Biblical yeast works in them. Should we not take them up again in the present time? Of course: there is also the incarnation of Satan, the concentration of evil, hence the element of catastrophe. But we have already said: it passes through that! Also these heights and depths of the Christian eschatological expectation put no obstacle in the way of despairing of the notion of evolution.[23] On the contrary. Furthermore, we must not take this notion in an excessively bourgeois way but in a Christian-catholic way. Particularly when we think of evolution in its hominizing phase (Teilhard de Chardin).[24]

Not that we grasp everything in this way. With this theological system of coordinates we do not have reality, just as it happens, entirely

---

23. Translator's note: The sentence seems to contain too many negations. By leaving out "of despairing" the sentence makes better sense.

24. Marie Joseph Pierre Teilhard de Chardin (1881–1955), Roman Catholic (Jesuit) priest, geologist and palaeontologist. He strove to integrate scientific insights with his faith. This led to conflict with Roman Catholic authorities. In his book *The Phenomenon of Man* (New York: Harper Colophon, 1975), Teilhard identified various evolutionary phases and regarded the phenomenon of man (the noosphere) as the center of the evolutionary process. For references to Teilhard in Van Ruler's oeuvre, see his *Verzameld werk 5C*, 914, note 34.

in our grip either. But my question is: "Are these not the perspective in which we must stand in this reality: in limitless expectation—strictly in the present—entirely prepared to act—in the feeling that each day is better?"

VII

To this system of coordinates we do have to add a new and extremely important element. From a biblical-Christian perspective we cannot rest content with a gaze at history and the eschaton, at the correlative relationship between these two, and at the position of the human being within this whole. All of these are indeed important. Also in themselves. Also before the face of God. In them the counsel of God is realized and served. In them the image of God is displayed. A destination for the human person is also contained in them: to be a moment in the network of the generations and in the historical process.

But to that has to be added that the central concern of God—as we know God from special revelation—is the social life of people with one another, not only on the small scale, from person to person, but also on the large scale. The most typical aspect of the new earth is that righteousness dwells in it. So God does not call only Abraham, as solitary individual; in calling him, God makes a start with his posterity. Clearly, God does not want only persons; God wants a people. God does not only want communion of a person with God—as reflection? as realization? as scope of it?—also the communion of people with one another. For this reason, God gives God's law. The prophets stand guard over this community and society, so that they may be the right community and society and that thereby the glory of God on earth may be realized. The Messianic expectation is in its core the expectation of the true king, around whom finally the true community of human beings will be realized. When the New Testament says, "Jesus is the Christ; the Messiah has come", then that basically says, "The true king has come."[25] The gospel is a political matter of the first order. Because the community around the true king, around the Messiah, is not to be found only in the church. We can find it there too. But Christ and his sacrifice on Golgotha does not only have ecclesial import; it also has worldly import.

---

25. Van Ruler frequently makes this point in his writings. For cross-references to literature in Dutch see his *Verzameld werk 5C*, 914, note 40.

I do not wish to enter into any debate about the questions concerning theocracy.[26] This bears on the core of the political shaping of this fundamental idea of the gospel. But this fundamental idea itself—which is a fundamental reality (Jesus is the lord of lords and the king of kings[27]—cannot be denied.

This [idea], however, entails that we should, along biblical-Christian lines, pay limitless attention to the social ideal[28] and for everything that can be done to realize it. And not merely for reasons of Christian neighborly love. Obviously that as well. The neighbor is a basic given, both in existence and in salvation [heil]. For its [salvation's] sake too the social ideal occupies such a central position in our attention. Indeed, the eschatological is abundantly represented here: in the realm of glory we do not only *not* lose the world and the self; we do not lose the neighbor either. But I hold the view that we risk seeing the matter too superficially if we, as Christians, are interested in the social ideal only from [motives of] neighborly love. We should also be interested in it from God's love. Because—in biblical and Christian perspective—God is so interested in it. God seems to seeks God's greatest glory in this: that society should be shaped in such a way that God's love and righteousness radiates from it.

It is difficult to say what the social ideal would look like in concreto. It would be ever different in each situation. But here, in my view, we cannot argue exclusively from special revelation, the law of Moses and the gospel of Christ. The data of the historical process and of human reason also play a role. And beneath it all we are in search of natural law—however dynamically we conceive of it.

Here too special revelation, the church and her prophecy, theology, merely make contributions. The state, culture and the other sciences should make no less important contributions when it comes to the question: What is the social ideal?

But in the meanwhile, the perspective of the social ideal is an extremely important moment in thinking about the future in history and eschatology. Now we can no longer scatter in all directions. We have been put on a leash. We have been confined in a corset. Let us busy ourselves

---

26. Van Ruler's views on theocracy may be found in Volumes 6A and 6B of his *Verzameld werk*.

27. See Revelations 17:14, 19:16.

28. To describe the eschatological perspective on the kingdom of God more closely, Van Ruler uses, alternately, the "brotherhood of all people" or "the social ideal." For cross-references to literature in Dutch, see his *Verzameld werk 5C*, 447, note 57.

with working towards the social ideal! Then we are busy with the future in history and the eschaton, that being our allotted share.

Not that we should lock ourselves up completely in the social ideal. That, again, is the bourgeois mode of the communists. There is *more*. That lies all around it. There is nature and the universe. There is the heart and its solitude. God is there in all eternity. There is also the church. We have to keep all of these in mind when we are busy with the social ideal. But we would not be permitted to escape into any of these other things. The society of human beings is the heart of history and the eschaton.

VIII

How far can we go in our work towards the social ideal? In answering this question, I gladly point to a few ideas from A.G.M. van Melsen.[29] He proposes that modern natural science and technology have given human beings a completely new place in the world. The world has, so to speak, become fluid in their hands. Now at last mountains can be moved, just as Jesus said they could by faith. The plight of the world can be tackled resolutely, *caritas* can be realized on a scale [hitherto] unthought of. We are, so to speak, busy with self-saving. Before, we had to fight against superstition as a form of faith. Currently we have to fight against little faith as a form of faith.

It seems to me that this is not speaking too presumptuously. To be sure, this view of the matter will still leave certain problems. I am thinking, for instance, of the problem of sin. Is there only the *neediness* of humanity and the world? Is there not guilt as well?[30] And how can we locate that within the image of humanity and the world that we are inevitably inclined to develop on the basis of modern science and technique? I am also thinking of a problem that is closely related to this. Can human beings, who not only do sinful deeds but are themselves sinners, save themselves from "being-sinners"? Can science by itself see to the moral development of humans, of which they, amid their own enormous

---

29. Andreas Gerardus Maria van Melsen (1912–1994), Dutch chemist and Roman Catholic philosopher. The source that Van Ruler uses is A.G.M. van Melsen, *Natuurwetenschap en techniek: Een wijsgerige bezinning*, Utrecht/Antwerpen 1960, 300ff.

30. The understanding of sin as guilt and of reconciliation as atonement for guilt are core motifs in Van Ruler's theology that are expressed throughout his oeuvre. In this regard, he gives preference to Anselm's understanding of atonement as satisfaction. For cross-references to literature in Dutch, see Van Ruler's *Verzameld werk 5C*, 127, note 28.

development, have such a crying need? That automatically brings us to a third question. Do we really dare to take the words "self-saving" on our lips when we look at what modern science and technology has brought us? Are we not inclined, rather, to use the term "self-destruction"? What has happened to piety? What to trust in God? What to surrendering to God's grace?

Undoubtedly there is this side to the matter as well. Therefore it cannot possibly be the purport of the conception sketched above that science and technology is the alpha and the omega, the one and all. *Alongside* it, *around* it, *beneath* it, there must also be ethics and politics, philosophy and theology, revelation and salvation. It is God who saves and has reality in God's hand.

But does that mean that we cannot speak of "self-saving" in any way whatsoever? And that as Christians we should face the development of the modern world only in a deprecating and hesitant way?

To find answers to these questions we should also consider a few other things.

The most fundamental in this regard is that human beings—according to the biblical witness—have received an enormously powerful and important position from Godself. This holds in particular for the salvific process: there they, proceeding from themselves, through the Holy Spirit, have to affirm, accept, embrace and appropriate—in a word, believe—if they are to share in salvation [heil]. They can also refuse faith. That determines their eternal bliss. So in the life struggle and the heart of each person a decision is taken that is of eternal importance. That is then also a divine decision (election and rejection)—only: in the form of a purely human decision.

It does not, however, hold only for the salvific process. It holds for the historical process as well. The human being is the image of God and God's fellow worker.[31] All the work of God (history is that too) also wants to take shape in the work of human beings. Then the work that human beings do *is* also the work of God. Therefore human beings are also called to account for it. That further implies that both the work of God and the work of human beings also have, in an essential way, this profane, worldly character. Together they are busy with the whole of created reality. Their work is not purely religious or solely ecclesial in nature.

---

31. Van Ruler often emphasizes the notion that humans are God's co-workers. For cross-references to literature in Dutch, see his *Verzameld Werk 5C*, 915, note 51.

In this view on God, humanity and world, science and technology find their place in a quite organic manner. Historically they have, after all, to a considerable extent grown from it. It is not merely God the Creator who is active in the historical development of science and technology This development played off and is playing off within the Christianized culture that is co-determined by the gospel and the Bible. It is God the Savior who is at work in that as well. It is also realization, effect of salvation. And all the while the human being—as image, as counterpart, as partner, as fellow worker—is involved in it. Salvation, which is the work of divine grace, assumes across the board the form of self-saving. The preaching of the gospel does not help if the person does not accept it in faith. Already the sacrament is entirely a twofold work of the Triune God on the one hand and of the believing and confessing person on the other hand. Rebirth is a way in which the human person is touched by God *so that* the person's will is freed and begins to will. Sanctification is a conscious and active walking of the person in the good works that have been prepared in Christ. The more we pass over from the circle of the church and religion into the circle of history and culture, the more this human manifestation [gestalte] of the divine work comes to the fore.

Does not the scientific unlocking of created reality manifest a colossal unveiling, unfolding and revelation? Is that not also the purpose: that not only God would know the secrets of the atom but that this divine knowledge would be mirrored in human consciousness? Should we not also say that knowledge is indeed power and that this position of power of human beings in the midst of reality belongs in essence to their being image of God? After all, God is the Almighty and this omnipotence of God surely does not reside *only* in God's powerlessness (of Christ on the cross)? And if it is necessary in science and technology to speak of power and revelation in this way, can we then avoid speaking of salvation as well? That might not be salvation from guilt. It is also not salvation from death. But between guilt and death there lies an endless terrain of distress, corruption, disease, injustice, violence, suffering, and the like. Human beings engage with that, armed with science and technology. In their modern form, they are highly effective instruments. Much of the distress (and so on) can be solved and cancelled by them. And would that not be self-saving? This term cannot possibly be meant in the sense that it stands as an antithesis to salvation through God. On the contrary, it *is* the divine salvation in the mode of salvation by human beings.

In view of these considerations we, as Christian-religious people, can, to my mind, but position ourselves entirely positively within the development of the modern world, both regarding nuclear fission and regarding space travel and also regarding everything in between them, these too being at work towards realizing the social ideal.

We do have to keep these things within their context. Modern science and technology[32] have a milieu and background. We cannot adopt them in themselves, apart from all the rest. People are more than scholars and engineers. They are human beings. They have a heart. They also have a conscience. There is mysticism and ethics. There is also politics. And, in particular, there is history. And in history [there is] religion, revelation, Christianizing. Woe is the community and humanity when science and technology are abstracted and isolated from this context, when they are absolutized! Then science and technology can indeed result only in the self-destruction of the human race.

Therefore all depends on it that the basic idea of Christian theism *remains* the perimeter fencing of modern Western culture and *becomes* that of the coming world culture.[33] The church and Christendom are the bearers and representative of this theism. This theism itself is still to a considerable extent the unconscious background to the Western experience of life and consciousness of the world. The bearers of it should, through an unprejudiced and open attitude, make it possible for this to remain the case. They would most definitely forsake their high, divine calling in the modern era if, regarding science and technology, they were merely to lift an admonitory finger and merely to voice the doom prophecies of "presumptuous rebellion against God" and "self-destruction." These doom prophecies could be accurate were science and technology to be isolated and absolutized. They should, however, rather be integrated into a more encompassing context of divine and human being and life. It is precisely to *this* that the church and Christendom have been called.

The church and Christendom cannot even rest content that theism is and becomes an *un*conscious background. Surely it befits human dignity that whatever is factually the background should also, in as far as possible, be made conscious to the last detail. But how will modern culture ever be able to recognize its theistic background, if in theism,

---

32. For Van Ruler's views on science and technology, see the cross-references to literature in Dutch in his *Verzameld werk 5C*, 915, note 54.

33. For Van Ruler's views on the cultural influence of Christianity spreading from the West, see the cross-references in his *Verzameld werk 5C*, 915, note 55.

as represented by the church and Christendom, there is no room for its greatest achievements, namely science and technology? And these, moreover, taken utterly seriously (as I have attempted to do by using the term "self-salvation").

IX

That brings me to the final point: the position of Europe (and America) in the future of the world. Is it all done with us? Should we withdraw into our shell, the shell of our guilt (towards other races)? Are we becoming, at least in Europe, an old-age home for those who while away their last years of life?

Obviously such a thing as the "decline of the West" is possible.[34] Specifically, also from a Christian-theological perspective. God is not wedded to the white race—as God is indeed to some extent to Israel. Asia Minor and North Africa can provide an example of what God can do with Europe. That we shall then note in due course.

But in any case, we should not reject ourselves. For *then* we are in any case rejected by God.

There is, moreover, not that much reason yet to reject ourselves. Modern science and technology are products of the West. All the peoples of Asia and Africa jostle to pump from Europe in order to slake their thirst for these products. Together with that, they imbibe a complete *Seinsverständnis* [understanding of being]. The colony as [mark of] political status has been all but stripped away. But the real colonization continues and will continue in this century and the coming one on an as yet unknown scale. It is not to be hoped that Asia and Africa will become copies of Europe. The kingdom of God may acquire its own form there too, as it did among us. But all signs indicate that Europe will retain an enormous importance in the near future.

That becomes the more evident when we consider the matter not only according to the extent of the space but also according to the length of time. Then we can say with certainty that the European phase in the history of the kingdom of God is an element in the process of world history that cannot be renounced. The gospel has by and large acquired a cultural form [gestalte] and the culture a more or less evangelical form [gestalte].

---

34. This is probably a reference to Oswald Spengler's *The Decline of the West*. See Spengler, *Untergang des Abendlandes: Umrisse einer Morphologie der Weltgeschichte* (München, 1919).

We have received freedom as a political form of society. Among us, it led to an enormous revolution concerning the position of the human being in the world through science and technology.

Why all of this in Europe? That nobody knows, just as nobody can answer the question why precisely Israel was chosen. But there is—whatever the contingencies and facts—but one world-historical process. And in that Europe simply *is* a moment that cannot be cancelled.

This insight regarding the position of Europe does not completely remove the veil that covers the future of the world. But it does provide a glance into this future. What we then see makes us think: let us above all be and remain ourselves; let us continue working with unflagging diligence. We are obviously not the purpose of the historical process, yet we are certainly an important phase. About that we can be glad.

In the meanwhile, it is quite certain that the work of mission should be continued with full force. The kingdom of God wants to be established in Asia and Africa as well. For that reason, the church there should also be built up. Because the world-historical process is also and by no means least the process of Christianization. The future too is replete with mission work.

But then the church and Christendom must not renounce their true theistic and salvific substance, as is commonly done nowadays. Theologians and Christians in our time are so inclined to stand all agog, gaping open-mouthed at the modern world, and trotting along ever so bravely in the circus of current conceptions derived from philosophies and views of life that they barely still get around to representing openly and forcefully what has been entrusted to them. If it continues in this way and the church does not rediscover itself and revelation, [the church] is without doubt done for. How the historical process would then develop further can in no way be overviewed.

Van Ruler included the following bibliography at the end of this essay (retained according to the original style):

- G.C. Berkouwer, *De wederkomst van Christus, Deel 1*, Kampen 1961.
- Emil Brunner, *Das Ewige als Zukunft und Gegenwart*, Zürich 1953.
- Rudolf Bultmann, *Geschichte und Eschatologie*, Tübingen 1958.
- Erich Fülling, *Geschichte als Offenbarung. Studien zur Frage Historismus und Glaube von Herder bis Troeltsch*, Berlin 1956.
- G.J. Heering, *De verwachting van het Koninkrijk Gods*, Arnhem 1952.

- A.E. Loen, 'De geschiedenis', in: *Nederlands Theologisch Tijdschrift* 15 (1960–1961), 353–365.
- Karl Löwith, *Weltgeschichte und Heilsgeschehen. Die theologischen Voraussetzungen der Geschichtsphilosophie*, Stuttgart 1953.
- A.G.M. van Melsen, *Natuurwetenschap en techniek. Een wijsgerige bezinning*, Utrecht/Antwerpen 1960.
- A.G.M. van Melsen, 'Geloof en wetenschap', in: *Streven* 15/1–2 (november 1960).
- Reinhold Niebuhr, *Beyond Tragedy. Essays on the Christian Interpretation of History*, New York 1946.
- Hans Urs von Balthasar, *Theologie der Geschichte. Ein Grundriß*, Einsiedeln 1950.
- R. Wittram, *Das Interesse an der Geschichte*, Göttingen 1958.

Limits to Eschatologizing
[1967]

I

Over the past decades, we have seen a progressive eschatologizing[2] of theology and the Christian faith playing itself out. Over the last years, even at an increased tempo. That does not mean only, not even primarily, that more attention [is being paid] to the last locus in dogmatics. People used to speak derisively about such attention as old-fashioned fundamentalism. One is far more refined oneself.[3]

Suddenly people want a complete eschatologizing of the entire theological system or, more simply put, of the [very] concept of theology. People want to think purely eschatologically and then also to live [that way]. The one does it in this way, the other in a quite different way. But it all goes under the banner of "eschatologically."

What lies behind it? To deal with this question fairly, we would have to give many answers. Here I mention two that, in my opinion, leap to the eye. In the first place, people think that they can construct for theology as a science a bomb-proof shelter against historical criticism and philosophy. In the second place, people acquire in this way sufficient elbow room for the church and Christians to cooperate with non-Christians in the things that are going on in the world on the basis of common humanity or at least mere "critical solidarity". There are, however, limits to such

---

1. The inventory number of the Dutch text, "Grenzen van de eschatologisering" is I,707. It is included in Volume 5C of Van Ruler's *Verzameld werk* (2023), 916–33.

2. Editor's note: The rather ugly term eschatologizing (Dutch: eschatologisering) is a neologism in Dutch. The argument of the essay suggests that Van Ruler employed this term to some extent derisively.

3. Editor's note: Van Ruler's sarcasm should be noted here.

eschatologizing. That is to say, there are data, realities, points of view, that we can and may not lose sight of and that resist complete eschatologizing. The intention of this contribution resides solely in the indicating of some of these boundaries.

Before starting, it should be noted that we leave aside completely the question of the intermediate state (what is happening with our dead?).[4] We proceed as if the only question is that of history (society, culture, existence) and the eschaton. Not that [the intermediate state] is not an important matter. Pastorally it is of immeasurably great importance in view of both the dying person and the relatives. The more one approaches one's own dying hour, the more the interest [in this] grows in one's own heart as well. But even purely theoretically it is surely beneath the dignity of thought not to pose the question about the destiny of the dead. At least we should not allow ourselves to be silenced in this respect by theologians appealing to the Bible ("no immortal soul", and so on).

II

I have already hinted before at the many forms of eschatologizing that we find. Let me mention a few examples. It is an old-fashioned idea that is still worth considering that there are norms and values, that these have validity, have not yet been realized but have to be realized, that the center of gravity of the active life lies in them, and that existence (which has to realize the values) and Being [zijn] (in which the values have to be realized) are in this sense eschatological by nature. Another form of eschatologizing resides in the mystique of the self. There is self-consciousness. The subject of this consciousness coincides with its object. [In self-consciousness] one gathers together all things from their dispersion in multiplicity and gather them up into a unity. One reaches the point of identity. Is this self-identical self not also identical to eternity, to God? Is it not, in its identity, absolute? As mysterious as the norm and the self is the "now." Is the now not always also to some extent the *nunc aeternum*?[5] Does it not, in its incomparability and its ungraspable actuality (it can but be lived,

---

4. This theme is addressed in other essays included in this volume. See, e.g. "I believe in eternal life" and "Life after Death."

5. *Nunc aeternum*: Eternal now, the dimension of eternity that is present in a single moment in the here and now. This is a classic term used in mystical and philosophical circles. For Van Ruler's views in this regard see the cross-references in his *Verzameld werk 5C*, 815, note 32.

not thought), rise above time? Does it not stand in an essential contrast to the past and the future? Does it not touch on God, the Eschatos? Is it not the *confinium*[6] between the relative and the absolute?

These old-fashioned considerations are currently mixed together. Then a cocktail emerges that is presented as brand new. The ingredients, however, have long been known. The cocktail is called: eternity here and now, the absolute moment (je und je), the unconditional nature of existence that is always my existence, the decision character of active existence. We are permanently standing in the *Entscheidung* [decision]. In the process, we never know exactly whether that is a decision that *I* take and that therefore contains an element of choice, or whether it is actually a decision that—in that I am present—befalls me, thus one that I myself am, in which case it contains no element of decision but is completely predestinarian in nature, edging towards the fatalistic. Sometimes a dash from the flask of the apostolic gospel is added to it. Then predestination assumes the shape of the apostolic kerygma. From the outside, through another person, perhaps through the tradition, which was perhaps inaugurated and legitimated by the man Jesus of Nazareth as God's eschatological act, I am told that my sins have been forgiven, that I am thus liberated from my past and that the future is once more open before me, and that that is salvation [heil]—purely eschatological.[7]

Others ask what Jesus and the apostles had to do with it and whether the problem of sin and forgiveness should really play such a major role. Let us pay attention to the structure of time! There is not only the past and the present. There is also the future! What water is to fish, the future is to faith: it is its element. Yes: it is its product. Faith is: to have a future and to create a future. The future is an existential, one may even say *the* existential, of existence in time. It even seems to have something salvific in itself. That is: "the principle of hope."[8] A saved life is life in pure hope. Those who take it entirely radically, take it in a decompositorial sense: there is no structure to it anymore, they no longer see the fixed points, there is no concrete content to the hope, it does not have any grounding in the present or the past, there are only some lines—as in a modern drawing—that all run over the edge of the page and refer to something, not, it is hoped, to nothing, but to God or to identity or to the entire freedom

---

6. *Confinium*: Boundary, boundary line, boundary region.

7. Editor's note: Van Ruler's sarcasm should again be noted here.

8. This is an implicit reference to Ernst Bloch, *Das Prinzip Hoffnung* (Frankfurt am Main, 1959).

of everything. Is Jesus not the quiet voice that ever again whispers in our ears this pure, almost desperate hope for the realm of identity? As long as there is life, there is hope. We can equally well say the converse: hope is precisely what vivifies.

III

I would not want to deny that there are elements of truth in all these forms of eschatologizing. There is something of the striptease about all of them. The formed and clothed life is stripped (that is the eschatologizing) to its pure nakedness (the norm, the self, the now, the future, the principle of hope). That is not very decent. For better or for worse, creation and culture wear clothes. But is the bare body not also a reality? And do we not now and then undress—for instance to take a shower or to have sex? There could be something essential about these forms of eschatologizing.

But do we have to undress to get to eschatology? Is the eschaton not far rather precisely being dressed, being "clothed over"? The Christian-European tradition (Augustine—Hegel) has always grasped that well. It has always brought the matter of the eschaton into relationship with the matter of history. In that respect, Jewish apocalyptic has preceded it. In my opinion, the apostolic gospel (act of God in history + sending out to the peoples of the earth) has given its sanction to that. Regarding the word "history", we should remain entirely sober and not get ourselves drunk on profound distinctions such as those between *Geschichte* and *Historie*, *Geschichte* and *Geschichtsbild*, *Geschichte* and *Geschichtlichkeit*. All of these distinctions may be there. They do also mean something. They do give rise to enough difficult questions. But we should not treat these questions as an alibi for the real question. The real question runs as follows: What is the relationship between, on the one hand, the world-historical process that plays out in all of chaotic reality and, on the other hand, the eschaton? Only by posing this question do we arrive at the true and authentic eschatology. Therefore this question is an enormous and powerful limitation to all the subtle eschatologizings that I have paraded above. Those who slip away from the historical process, no longer eschatologize honestly. That is, they have cut the heart from the eschaton.

To the real question a twofold answer has to be given. On the one hand, the eschaton is the pulling point [trekpunt] of history.[9] If there

---

9. Van Ruler frequently describes the eschaton as the "pulling point" (Dutch:

were no eschaton, there would also be no history. After all, the eschaton is by definition that to which everything moves, that in which everything issues, let us say, the "purpose". That purpose does not, in the fashion of entelechy[10] (the oak is present in its germ in the acorn), reside in the created reality as such. It has been added to it.

On the one hand, from God's side. *Gubernatio*, as an aspect of *providentia*[11] in its distinctness from *creatio*, contains, among other things, the element that the Creator has been kind enough not merely to call things into existence but to give them a destination as well, one to which God then also leads them (that too is an aspect of *gubernatio*). Those who believe (in the Creator and the Creator's goodness and thus also in reality and its goodness) cannot but hold the view that the cat will finally land on its feet.

On the other hand, this purpose is also added to it from the side of human beings. That is implicit in the inestimable seventeenth-century theolegoumenon of the *foedus operum* (*pluralis*):[12] human beings have to do a whole lot of things (the historical process), then, according to God's promise (*foedus*! Not *creatio*!) everything will turn out for the best.

But how this purpose came to be there is not the most important thing in this context. It is more important that it is there. It gives direction and meaning to what happens in time in the form of eventualities and human acts. It also provides coherence and even joining-as-a-unity of all the multiform and contradictory contents of time. It further provides a strict irreversibility to the historical process. Nothing is left lying. Nothing is left behind. Nothing is dropped. Everything is taken up in the summation. The eschaton is an *anakephalaiosis*, a sum, a consummation.[13] All of these are determinations that are of constitutive meaning for the concept history. Therefore: without eschaton, no history. If there were no

---

trekpunt) of history. For cross-references to literature in Dutch, see the *Verzameld werk 5C*, 912, note 9.

10. Entelechy: The Greek term ἐντέλεχεια was introduced by Aristotle in *De Anima* II.1, 412a9. Its meaning in Aristotle is debatable. Van Ruler uses it to describe a goal that is immanent in a particular reality—like the oak is present in germ in the acorn.

11. In the Reformed tradition a distinction is made between three aspects of God's providence (*providentia*), namely *conservatio* (conservation), *gubernatio* (governance) and *concursus* (accompaniment) or *cooperatio* (cooperation).

12. *Foedus operum*: Covenant of works.

13. Such phrases are frequently found in Van Ruler's writings, including elsewhere in this volume. For cross-references to literature in Dutch, see Van Ruler's *Verzameld werk 5C*, 930, note 13.

eschaton, there would be only senseless whirling of leaves in the autumn storm or—still worse—the perforce eternally identical revolving of the wheel of nature and the universe. The eschaton makes history what it is and keeps it in motion.

The converse, however, holds to exactly the same extent: no eschaton without history. The eschaton is by definition the eschaton of history.[14] History is the totality of all the ingredients of the eschaton.[15] If there were no history, it would have been impossible even for God to have arrived at a true eschaton. God could at most have called an entirely new reality into existence. Without history the eschaton is impossible for God, just as without the eschaton history is impossible for human beings. This correlation of eschaton and history is a true correlation: both the relationships presuppose and determine each other—and fully to boot, by definition. Here we stand before a boundary to all eschatologizing that may not be transgressed: those who eschatologize in such a way that the reality of the world-historical process falls away, no longer eschatologize. What they actually do is not so easy to state. But in any case, they eschatologize eschatology to death. There is never only the eschaton; there is always *eo ipso* history.

IV

To this correlation of eschaton and history we must cling steadfastly—not only from the logical considerations mentioned above but also from humane and social ones. The concept of history and the idea of humanness are especially closely related to each other. After all, the core of being human resides in that human beings are responsible, acting creatures in the community and (NB) in the pilgrimage of humanity. Each contributes a stone to the building of society. Each sweeps her or his little street clean as part of the great highway across which the human race proceeds. The historical is an essential component of the humane, the one that makes all the others cohere. As soon as the historical falls away, the mystical, ethical, social, cultural and cosmic components fall apart in a hopeless

---

14. The observation that there is no eschaton without history is frequently found in Van Ruler's writings, also elsewhere in this volume. For cross-references to literature in Dutch, see Van Ruler's *Verzameld werk* 5C, 930, note 14.

15. Editor's note: Van Ruler may have meant the opposite of what he actually wrote: Everything that ever occurred in history forms part of the eschaton. Or: The totality of history provides the ingredients of the eschaton.

fluttering. That is why full humanness was not found even by the Stoa. There people still remained a fragment of the rational universe. What being human is, was uncovered only in Israel, because Israel discovered history.[16] With a faulty stress one would be able to say: human beings are not eschatological beings but historical beings. But the stress is faulty because this contrast, as we have said, is no contrast. In any case, if one simply continues eschatologizing, one defaces being human. Mostly one then hops over from a Christian to a gnostic anthropology.

The twofold reference to the community and to the historical process brings another aspect of the matter to the fore. In our humane considerations, the social should also play a large role. In the historical-eschatological train of thought of biblical and Christian thinking, the social ideal is not, to be sure, the only aspect but [it is] definitely a completely unique, essential and perhaps even *the* central aspect.[17] The way in which people live together with one another and in which their society is organized is the most sensitive, even the holiest matter imaginable from a biblical-Christian perspective. *That* is what it is about. That is the ultimate image of God. In that the lines of justice, love and joy have to be etched. Therefore the eschaton is not only *anakephalaiosis* but also crisis, judgement, verdict.[18] The accent on the aspect of judgement, retribution,[19] vengeance in the eschatological expectation implies that it is about justice and, consequently, that [justice] is established on earth. The earth really has to be swept clean of all injustice and violence.

That is a new limit that has to be set for eschatologizing. This eschatologizing, imbued by the gnostic as it is, constantly tends to spiritualize, internalize, render invisible. I do not say: to individualize. In general people are precisely deeply opposed to that. This individualizing they generally ascribe to traditional eschatology. But they themselves come— in a protracted conversation I had with J. Moltmann,[20] that was even

---

16. The observation that it is Israel that discovered a sense of history is frequently found in Van Ruler's writings. For cross-references to literature in Dutch, see Van Ruler's *Verzameld werk 5C*, 930, note 17.

17. To describe the eschatological perspective on the kingdom of God more closely, Van Ruler uses, alternately, the "brotherhood of all people" or "the social ideal." For cross-references to literature in Dutch, see Van Ruler's *Verzameld werk 5C*, 447, note 57.

18. For cross-references to literature in Dutch, see again Van Ruler's *Verzameld werk 5C*, 930, note 14.

19. For Van Ruler's view on retribution, see the cross-references to literature in Dutch in his *Verzameld werk 5C*, 930, note 20.

20. Jürgen Moltmann (1926–2024), German Reformed theologian, based at the

the conclusion—no further than the purely spontaneous ("authentic") "brotherhood of all people." Does one remain true to the social ideal in this way? Is it only a matter of people living together (thus as individuals after all)? Is it not also a matter of the structuring of their society? Are there no institutions? Is it not at bottom about justice? Do no authorities, do no authoritative bodies remain? Is there no power? Does life lose its gravity eschatologically? Is that not a dissipation? Is the typical-historical (the objective Spirit) merely a crust that falls away eschatologically? Said in the opposite way: we cannot possibly eschatologize to such an extent that we surrender the social and the political to shaping according to individual inventiveness because they are, after all, merely external, [part of the] world that passes away. Then we escape the real danger, what it is all about (and that never entirely succeeds): the shaping of society (up to and including the state and the united "nations") from the eschaton, the kingdom of God.

V

If we want to spread our wings still further from here, we touch on the neuralgic spot of this matter. That resides in the relationship between creation and eschaton. For now, I leave aside the question that immediately arises: *whether* the eschaton has a plus with respect to the proton and, if it does, *in what way* it does so.[21] We shall, without any doubt, have to give a positive answer to this question in some or other way. Precisely in that plus—however it is understood—lies the content of the historical process. If the eschaton were purely a return to the proton, history falls away as without content. But then again, creation should not, in our theological concept, be buried under and disappear beneath history. In the eschaton not only the historical process comes to the fore. Created reality, redeemed and completed, also comes to the fore. The main point here is: all of this has been! We ourselves are reality (the thing aspect dominates) and actuality (the act aspect dominates). At least, let us hope

Eberhard Karls Universität in Tübingen (1967–1994). On the relationship between Van Ruler and Moltmann, see Dirk van Keulen's introduction above.

Editor's note: It is not entirely clear from the text whether Van Ruler and Moltmann agreed or disagreed in this conversation. Later in this essay he indicates where he disagrees with Moltmann.

21. Van Ruler frequently raises the question whether there is a plus in eschaton in relation to the proton. For cross-references to literature in Dutch, see his *Verzameld werk 5C*, 931, note 23.

(and believe), that we are there and that the world is there. It could all be a bad dream of an evil spirit, that does not exist.[22]

But if we take things in a biblical and Christian way, that is not the case. The awareness of reality is the first basic choice of faith. Is that perhaps the eschaton itself: the having-been-there of everything? Having been is, after all, a mode of being? Would we be able to call it the eschatological mode [of being]? Surely all the water in the sea of eternity cannot wash away the fact that the temporary reality—if it had been real in its time—really had been? Surely that is and remains an "eternal fact"?

We would be able to shade this in and give it some depth by remarking that that the having-been-there of everything is a remaining of everything in the memory of God. God might always think back on this with joy. Yes, in this God might exceed the bounds of thinking and pass over into willing. Then everything that has been would, in all eternity, be willed by God in the eternal kingdom as what has been there, just as God in God's eternal counsel willed all as what should be. The troubling question then remains whether, in all this, we ourselves shall be present in any way. Departing from the idea of Paul that we now know in part but that we ourselves will then be able to know (active) as we have been known (passive),[23] we may even cast the question in the following form: Are we fully present now? Are we not in some or other way absent (as pure objectivum walking in the counsel of God)? Must it not then happen at some time that we ourselves are fully present and is that not the eschaton? In any case: if created reality is there, if it is anything whatsoever, then both the that and the what of it cannot be assessed from a Christian perspective as anything but anticipation of the eschaton. Therefore we may never go *so* far in our eschatologizing as to design an eschatological theology and to imagine that we can put it in the place of, for instance, a creation theology. We are, if we think as Christians, never rid of the first article about God the Father and our creation. Creation, too, is a limit to eschatologizing.

---

22. On Van Ruler's use of the expression "bad dream", see the cross-references to literature in Dutch in his *Verzameld werk 5C*, 931, note 24.

23. See 1 Corinthians 13:12.

VI

From an Old Testament perspective, we may be able to content ourselves with the previous [items]: creation, history, the social ideal, humanness. From a New Testament perspective, in any case, we cannot content ourselves with that. The core of the apostolic gospel is that the Savior has come and salvation (not merely atonement—that would be too narrow) has been achieved. It is not without good reason that we can speak about the gospel as "realized eschatology". We have to guard against speaking as if the anticipation of the eschaton first sets in with the incarnation, the resurrection and the outpouring of the Holy Spirit. Were we to do that in the strict sense, then our talk becomes Marcionistic. We have already said that creation is no less anticipation. But creation is not solely a matter of soteriology. It is a matter of ontology.

That means, in the first place (new limit!), that we cannot, on the basis of a complete soteriologization of thought (*the* dangerous disease of contemporary theology!),[24] proceed to a total eschatologizing of thought, in which we suffer from the world and existence to such an extent that we do but one thing, namely, to long for salvation. But, on the other hand, it also means that the granted salvation is a reality, a distinct reality of history, historical *factum* plus mediation and appropriation in the tradition, that we have to respect to the highest degree in our theological reflection. We cannot possibly stake everything on the one card of the eschaton. The Son of God in human flesh is there as well! The Holy Spirit who has been poured out over all flesh and who dwells in all bodiliness no less so! It is impossible to see why theology has to be eschatologically structured and cannot as readily be structured christologically and pneumatologically. Salvation [heil] is surely history? This history is surely more than a field filled solely with signs, promises, references? There are not even words of God only; there are also acts of God. There is the entire reality of salvation [heil] that fans out in a series of mysteries, "glories of grace" (M.J. Scheeben[25]), all of which can be preached and confessed, celebrated and lived.

---

24. Van Ruler frequently criticizes a tendency to soteriologize theology. He insists that one should not offer soteriological answers to ontological questions. For cross-references to literature in Dutch, see his *Verzameld werk 5C*, 931, note 26.

25. Matthias Joseph Scheeben (1835–1888), German Roman-Catholic theologian, professor of dogmatics in Cologne. Van Ruler refers in a general way to his *Die Herrlichkeiten der göttlichen Gnade*, nach P. Eusebius Nierenberg, S.J., frei bearbeitet von M.Jos. Scheeben (Freiburg im Breisgau, 1862).

This is the central point in Christian eschatology: we do not hope and expect because of the poverty and lack of the present, but solely and only because of the wealth and abundance of it. The salvation [heil] that has been given to us is the basis of the certainty concerning salvation [heil] that shall be given to us. More strongly put: the salvation [heil] that has been given to us and that we possess in all fulness and reality is so abundant that it splashes over the edges of all forms of present existence. It cannot be contained within any form, *therefore* it can, in the end, only be expected. This state of affairs also entails that a huge degree of continuity is typical of Christian eschatology. Love simply "remains". It is not eliminated. Nor is it changed. We already have the eschatological reality of love. We live from it. We even live in it. Those who trade in love completely for hope as the sole category of Christian existence betray the gospel. Similar things can be said of eternal life. That too has been given to us, we who believe in the Son. At the least, we share in eternal life. But we can also say that we already live it. Surely eternal life is life here and now, redeemed from sin and death, from perdition in all its forms?

Meanwhile this soteriological idea also collapses, precisely as soteriological idea. That we have been redeemed from perdition in really all its forms will still have to become apparent at some stage. It will have to become visible, material reality. Gruesome reverse of this truth: evil will still at some stage have to be cut out of created reality to the bone. The same in its broadest contours: The Savior has indeed come and salvation has also taken place, but the world (God's good and beautiful creation) is still not saved. In that the Jews are correct.

We do not, indeed, have to turn all this into a huge task. There is not only the reality of the salvation [heil] in Christ and then—with a giant leap—the eschaton. There are also the mediation and the appropriation,[26] the manifold work of the Spirit,[27] the tradition of salvation [heil] through the centuries and hearts, the passage of the apostolic Word, the Christianization of the nations. All of this is no less essential within the reality of salvation than the incarnation or the sacrifice of atonement or the rising of Jesus from the dead. For instance, Christianized Europe is a counter-image of the people of Israel.

---

26. Van Ruler offered a course on the theme of appropriation. The notes are included in his *Verzameld werk 4B*, 312–74.

27. Van Ruler wrote extensively on the multiple aspects of the work of the Holy Spirit. See the cluster of essays included in his *Verzameld werk 4A*, 285–490.

VII

In view of all the considerations that we have dealt with up to now, we have to, on the one hand, set a limit to all absolute eschatologizing, but we have to, in equal measure, argue for the necessity of the idea of the eschaton. Before we proceed from here, we have to insert an intermediate comment. The eschaton is indispensable, yes, unavoidable, but it is also radically unimaginable and unthinkable. We do not find ourselves in the eschaton but in that which is summed up and criticized in the eschaton. Even if we [were to] existentialize the eschaton radically, so that we do indeed find ourselves in the eschaton, then, precisely then, we would encounter the unimaginability, the *Unverfügbarkeit*,[28] yes, the ineffability of existence and thus of the eschaton.

But it is better not to existentialize so radically. It is safer to mythologize somewhat.[29] Existence itself, the fact that we are there, is, after all, the first myth. Therefore we need not be astonished at the unimaginability and unthinkability of the eschaton. A myth is a story. Mythologizing is telling a story. The story is always malleable and rich in images.

Who is to say what the eschaton is? Answer: Look around you at the abundance of realities of Being [zijn] and salvation that exist and happen. This abundance supplies an unlimited source of images with which to express the eschaton. One image is, to be sure, better than another. Some images are definitely bad and can only be rejected. Other images are definitely good and need to be retained in preference to others. Among the first group I would class, for instance, the myths of the eternal return of all things and of nirvana,[30] among the second group those of the resurrection of the flesh and the final judgement. Systematic theology consists in the sorting of the pictures [plaatjes].[31] Some are placed on the left, others on the right. About the group in the middle, further discussion is necessary. We are dealing with symbols of faith, not with scientific concepts (although we can also ask about them whether they too are perhaps "merely" images, symbols, myths). That is how matters stand not only in

---

28. *Unverfügbarkeit*: The state of not being at our disposal / in our hands.

29. For Van Ruler's view on mythological language, see the cross-reference to literature in Dutch in his *Verzameld werk 5C*, 931, note 30.

30. For Van Ruler's views on nirvana, see the cross-reference to literature in Dutch in his *Verzameld werk 5C*, 931, note 31.

31. Van Ruler frequently describes the task of theology as sorting through templates. For cross-reference to literature in Dutch, see his *Verzameld werk 5C*, 931, note 31.

eschatology but in all of systematic theology, not only in Christianity but in each religion, not only in religion but in all the deeper and fundamental experiencing and thinking through of realities and problems. Is even skepsis not a myth?

We have to be thoroughly aware of this symbolic character of eschatological teachings. This confers on it an element of the incomplete, just as precisely eschatology itself renders the system of doctrine *and* reality incomplete. In this, too, the eschaton corresponds to creation. The world as creation implies that the world is not a gaping hole, an empty space, but rather that it is—towards the Creator—an open reality. Does this marginal comment also indicate a limit to eschatologizing? The limit would then reside in our capacity of thinking and imagining. We should not think that we can expound the eschaton in the finest detail. Is eschatologizing then still a fit tool to cast a bombproof bastion of concrete for theology as science? Are we not running into a blind alley in doing so? Are we not slinking away into an *asylum ignorantiae*?[32] Better than this flight into eschatology is the frank admission of the mythological character of *all* theological discourse, with the additional comment that all people who live and think more deeply find themselves in [the realm of] theology and end there. Without a set of myths, a person dies spiritually.

VIII

Having said this, we may proceed. Let us rejoice in the mythological possibilities and impossibilities! How should we speak about the eschaton? A tempting possibility is to speak about the eschaton as only a disclosure. The reality of the fulfilment is there. We can find it in the Messiah and the Pneuma. We can find it, more broadly, in the duality of the given salvation [heil] and the created being. We can conceptualize this fulfilment as veiling, although this category, when applied to creation, has a particular objectionable side to it. Then the eschaton would be nothing but the unveiling, the apocalypsis, of this veiling of the fulfilment. It would then amount only to this: that which has always, in all plerophory, already been true and real would then be fully publicly apparent. To this we do have to add: excusez du peu![33] Is this unveiling not a momentous event?

---

32. *Asylum ignorantiae*: Asylum of ignorance.

33. *Excusez du peu!*: That is not nothing! Literally, "Pardon the little," but said to indicate that it is not that "little" after all.

Does it not have the force of a nuclear explosion? Can we in full seriousness append to it the qualification "nothing but"?

In the above we have already referred to two other possibilities. We have pointed to the great importance of the image of crisis, the judgement, the final verdict as indication of the eschaton. We have also pointed to the no less important image of the *anakephalaiosis*, the summation, the consummation. In the eschaton there is not only analysis but in equal measure synthesis. We have already warned against the image of the spiritualization of everything. It is remarkable that currently P. Teilhard de Chardin, in his imposing conception of a "hyper-physics" in which he sees nature and history as [involved in] the one process of evolution, finally—even beyond the noösphere—points in this direction.[34] Behind it lies, no doubt, the old idea of the lifting, the elevation to the higher order of grace that has played such a great role in the tradition of Christianity. It seems to me that we would have to reject[35] this idea in all its forms if we wish to and can maintain of creation that it is purely good and is not, from God's side, in any way a *verbum abbreviatum*, a word not fully enunciated.[36]

Matters stand differently concerning the word glorification. Even seen from the perspective of the pure creation through the binoculars of the *foedus operum*, we might find the ultimate destination of everything in that created reality should become fully (which is to say, especially, actually) image of God, glory of God. The hamartiological and soteriological problems that have intruded have brought it about that we can conceive of this glorification as the final redemption from all guilt, from all sin, from all suffering. Death is the enemy that is the very last to be truly conquered. Mostly we, in our helplessness, end up by muttering the word consummation, *synteleia*. What precisely we express by it we never know. At least we express by it that there is movement, progression,

34. Marie Joseph Pierre Teilhard de Chardin (1881–1955), Roman Catholic (Jesuit) priest, geologist and palaeontologist. He strove to integrate scientific insights with his faith. This led to conflict with Roman Catholic authorities. In his book *The Phenomenon of Man* (New York: Harper Colophon, 1975), Teilhard identified various evolutionary phases and regarded the phenomenon of man (the noosphere) as the center of the evolutionary process. For references to Teilhard in Van Ruler's oeuvre, see his *Verzameld werk 5C*, 914, note 34.

35. Van Ruler frequently criticizes the distinction between the natural and the supernatural and the associated concept of elevation. For cross-references to literature in Dutch, see his *Verzameld werk 5C*, 191, note 2.

36. For cross-references on Van Ruler's use of the term *verbum abbreviatum*, see his *Verzameld werk 5C*, 931, note 37.

progress and completion in the Trinitarian work of God (perhaps also in God's Trinitarian being?[37]). In no event is the consummation termination. Rather the opposite. But how are we to express that? Is there a continuation of the created and redeemed existence in the eschaton? Or should we replace the word continuation by the word repetition? Or is that not correct either and we should rather speak of return? Then the temporal reality would return in eternity (in the form of salvation [heil]) just as in Platonism eternity (in the form of anamnesis) returns in time.[38]

It should be stressed with great emphasis, against J. Moltmann in particular, that the eschaton is in no way a *creatio ex nihilo*.[39] It might indeed be so that as much divine power is needed for the eschaton as act of God as for the *creatio ex nihilo* as act of God. But the nature and structure, as well as the content, of the one act of God [i.e. creation], are totally different from those of God's other act [i.e. consummation]. The eschaton is not *ex nihilo*. It is *ex creatura, ex culpa, ex salute*![40] Therefore the *kainê ktisis* is in no way a *nova creatio* (the Anabaptist view of the sixteenth century and the docetic one of the second century) but exclusively a *recreatio*.[41] The question as to which myth one tells at this point is of decisive importance for everything that one says further, not only in eschatology, not only in the other loci of dogmatics, but also in cultural theory, politics and philosophy (of history). There is a radical novelty in God's eschatological acts, but this novelty is radically united with God's radical loyalty to all that God had ever said and done.

The focus of the Christian eschatological expectation, in my view, then resides in the article about the resurrection of the flesh.[42] That that is somewhat different from the immortality of the soul we have now all

---

37. For Van Ruler's view on the inner-Trinitarian mysticism, see the cross-references to literature in Dutch in his *Verzameld werk 5C*, 931, note 37.

38. For Van Ruler's critique of the Platonic notion of eternity, see the cross-references to literature in Dutch in his *Verzameld werk 5C*, 931, note 39.

39. Van Ruler's implied references include Jürgen Moltmann, *Theologie der Hoffnung: Untersuchungen zur Begründung und zu den Konsequenzen einer christlichen Eschatologie* (München, 1964). On *creatio ex nihilo*, see p. 27 and on *nova creatio ex nihilo*, see p. 278.

40. *Ex creatura*: From creation; *ex culpa*: from guilt; *ex salute*: from salvation [heil].

41. Van Ruler very frequently resists the common translation of II Corinthians 5:17 where the Greek words καινὴ κτίσις are translated as *nova creatura* (Vulgate) or as new creation or new creature. For cross-references to literature in Dutch, see his *Verzameld werk 5C*, 931, note 42.

42. For Van Ruler's views on the hope for the resurrection of the dead, see the cross-references to literature in Dutch in his *Verzameld werk 5C*, 931, note 43.

come to know. But it is childish to fight about the question whether the word "flesh" here is faulty and should be replaced by "body" or "from death" or perhaps "from the dead". The problem is immeasurably greater! I arise from death! What am I? More than merely my soul! But also more than my unity and totality of soul and body! I am also and especially this piece of time filled[43] with destiny and deed! As such I arise—at least, if I am there and am saved. About this radical positivity and problematic of the Christian eschatological expectation we can trouble our heads endlessly. We are truly dealing with the eschaton, without eschatologizing everything without limit, only when we do this.

IX

With that, moreover, a limit has been placed on the edifying form of a radical eschatologizing of everything. In this way one does not seek it in the human self but in God's Self.

Then one says—extremely piously and at the same time extremely bashfully in the face of all sciences—that it is not about the eschata but about the Eschatos! God is our eschaton! At most, one adds to this: our communion with God (away world!) is our eschaton. Or, somewhat more dubiously, our destination is *in* God, in God's Trinitarian life. Is the Eschatos God? Or God in Christ? Or Christ Himself? That does of course make a significant difference. One then speaks in either a Trinitarian or a mediatorial or a Christomonistic way about the eschaton. But in my view the one is as radically incorrect as the other is. Can we, as Christians, speak about God a-cosmically, that is about God-without-God's-world? In the doctrine about the being of God and the one about God's counsel we shall, in view of the character of creation as free and a luxury[44]—thus for the sake of our lives—be compelled to do so. But in the doctrine of the eschaton that is surely not possible under any circumstances. Where would *we* then be left? Do we perhaps supplement the Trinity to [make it] a Quadernity? And can we be without the world? Does redemption consist in it that we are freed from the world? Or is the escape route that

---

43. Van Ruler could have derived the term "filled time" from Karl Barth. See his *KD*, III/2, 648; *KD*, IV/2, 476. This is an expression that Van Ruler uses frequently. For cross-references to literature in Dutch, see his *Verzameld werk 5C*, 891, note 5.

44. Editor's note: Elsewhere Van Ruler maintains that God did not create under the influence of any internal or external constraints or compulsions. It was simply God's pleasure to create—a luxury rather than a necessity.

Dorothee Sölle shows us perhaps one we can follow? This escape route apparently involves that God, through the process of the world, of history and especially of consciousness, arrives at God's identity and is thus saved.[45] Is that still a Christian thought?

Should we not persist in the more naive and simpler myth (all the rest are also myths!) that the eschaton is an act of the Triune God to and with God's created, fallen, atoned and redeemed reality? Then it is not purely about the future of Jesus Christ or about God as our future (the inverse of the idea of our futurity as God). It is not even purely about our future. The eschaton is more than a mode or perspective of existence. Even more than the final realization of the social ideal. It is about all of created reality, about all that is and happens, about its salvation, which in this case [implies] its glorification.[46] We cannot think crudely enough about these things. Nor can I see how we can distinguish so clearly between eschatology and apocalyptic and keep the former free of the latter. The apocalyptic coarsening is a necessary limitation of the eschatological refining. In other words, we look forward to the redemption of reality as a totality. At a first glance, one is inclined to say that it is more than and considerably different from the resolution of all problems of thought (though we should not think too lightly of that); it is redemption from the problems of reality, liberation from all suffering, from all injustice, from all sin, from death. All tears will be wiped from our eyes.

But then again, the distinction between the resolution for thought and redemption for reality becomes somewhat hazy. The tears that are wiped from our eyes are surely not the tears that we find ourselves crying in the eschaton but those that we have cried in the historical process.[47] We arrive in the eschaton with them. These are then wiped from our

---

45. Dorothee Sölle (1929–2003), German theologian, taught systematic theology at Union Theological Seminary in New York (1975–1987). At the time that Van Ruler wrote this, Sölle was regarded as an exponent of the theology of the death of God. Van Ruler's formulation indicates that this was his interpretation of Sölle's book *Stellvertretung: Ein Kapitel Theologie nach dem Tode Gottes* (Berlin 1965), especially sections III.7 "Christi Identifikation mit Gott" and III.8 "Christi Abhängigkeit von Gott."

46. One of the core themes in Van Ruler's theology is that the Christian faith indeed hinges on (Dutch: draait om) Christ, atonement and justification, but that it is about (Dutch: gaat om) something else: the redemption of creation and the coming of the kingdom of God on earth. In this regard, Van Ruler would also say that God's concern is with (Dutch: gaat om) this world, this earthly, life, ordinary life, humanness [humaniteit], sanctification and so forth. For cross-references to literature in Dutch, see Van Ruler's *Verzameld werk 5C*, 308, note 5.

47. See Revelations 21:4.

eyes. Does that also entail that in the eschaton all the negatives of the historical process are transformed into positive things? Is the entire historical process shown in the eschaton to be nothing but a *pulcherrimum carmen*[48] about which we can in all eternity but say amen and hallelujah with a gliding voice (Augustine)?[49] Is it perhaps merely a matter of a new view that we get of it through God's unveiling of God's mysteries, of the new insight in which *pistis* passes over into *gnosis*?[50] Is nothing negative done away with? Is the negativity merely transformed into positivity? Is and was the atonement as *expiatio* not after all an undoing of what had been done, even if we can venture, in a severely restricted way, to speak of a "felix culpa mea"?[51] How do we ever overcome the scars of time—the scars of suffering and guilt—in the eschaton? And then the eschatological scar of the eternal perdition of those who had rejected and are rejected! Or is the *apokatastasis pantōn* (without the supposition—as in Origen—of the pre-existent fall and the return of the pure spirits!) perhaps more humane?[52] Is it humane that nothing that had happened in time would finally be taken seriously in the eschaton? Is the double predestination, understood as *praedestinatio gemina* (not as *praedestinatio dialectica*),[53] not an irrevocable limit to the total eschatologizing of all theological thought?

X

A final limit still has to be signaled. It is theoretically and especially practically of no lesser importance than the previous limits. On the contrary!

---

48. *Pulcherrimum carmen*: Most beautiful song.

49. It is not clear where Van Ruler gets this reference from. Possible sources include Augustine's *Sermo* 236.3 or Sermo 362,28.

50. *Pistis*: Faith; *gnosis*: knowledge.

51. *Felix culpa*: Happy fault. For cross-references to Van Ruler's use of this term, see the Dutch edition of Van Ruler's *Verzameld werk 5C*, 857, note 83. The expression is derived from the "Exultet" (the hymn formerly sung to the Easter candle as symbol of the risen Christ during the Easter eve celebration). It contains the line: "O felix culpa, quae talem ac tantum meruit habere Redemptorem!" (O happy fault that deserved to have a Redeemer of such quality and greatness.") It is cited by, among others, Thomas Aquinas, *Summa theologiae, III*, q.1, a.3, ad 3.

52. *Apokatastasis pantōn* (ἀποκατάστασις πάντων): The restoration of all things. For Van Ruler's views in this regard, see the cross-references to literature in Dutch in his *Verzameld werk 5C*, 932, note 53.

53. For Van Ruler's views on double predestination, see the cross-references to literature in Dutch in his *Verzameld werk 5C*, 932, note 54.

We start with the simple question: is the eschaton purely God's act? We have already previously touched on the inverse of this ubiquitous idea. It resides in the idea that the eschaton is solely act of God to the extent that it is the true and only act of God and that created reality (this is then in any case mostly forgotten) and history merely constitute the field of God's promises and references to the true and only act, the eschaton. As against this we posit that there are not merely words of God in history and the entire reality but also acts. We may even understand all that is and happens as act of God, as dance of God's acts.[54]

Then the question arises: what do we do with it? Do we merely *hope*, on the basis of what God has done, for what God shall do? Or do we also believe and confess God's acts in history? Do these too not have a meaning in themselves? Just one step more and we have passed over from hope via faith to love. We can also start to love God's acts and, with that, all that has been called into being by them, that is, in essence, all of existing reality. Then we live in love. That is truly a form of or dimension in Christian existence that differs from hope and expectation.

In love there is by nature more of an impulse to act than in hope. That leads us to the real question that has to be posed here. Do we also do it ourselves? Is—the maximum score—the eschaton also our act? Is our act at least incorporated in it? Is our activity—that is the very minimum—at least marked by it?

In what preceded, we have argued that there is a very great deal of anticipation of the eschaton, from creation to the indwelling of the Holy Spirit. As the eschaton is the consummation of the historical process, so the historical process is the anticipation of the eschaton. Should we not now say—in order to remain on the Christian track—that our entire active existence is anticipation? It can of course also be regarded from entirely different perspectives. For instance, as the implementing of the creation mandate or as the carrying out of the divine doom regarding the human race or as the realizing of the salvation [heil]-in-Christ through the Spirit. But the perspective of the anticipation of the eschaton may surely not be left out. Hope purifies our existence of unrighteousness. The expectation is an impulse to and a positive power in our acting. The kingdom is the vision, the dream, the model, the pattern according to

---

54. Van Ruler often describes the dance of God's acts (Dutch: reidans). See also the Greek term *perichoresis*. For cross-references, for example to a volume of meditations for Advent with the title *Reidans*, see the Dutch edition of the *Verzameld werk 5C*, 173, note 63.

which we try to act. All of existence is streamlined by it. We too are building the kingdom of God. At least, we contribute to the building. At the very least, we are building in view of the kingdom. Does God ever do anything without the mediation of God's creatures? All of that together amounts to sanctification. This is also a limit to eschatologizing. Being that, it requires a few more comments.

In the first place, we have to consider that the eschaton entails that created reality passes through ruin [ondergang] and the end, in a certain sense even through the void. The world passes away. It even perishes. Compared to this Christian expectation of the ruin [ondergang] of the world, every revolution is child's play. The most [intensely] revolutionary mentality still shows up as bourgeois compared to the eschatological expectation of Christian faith. This consideration should restrain us from suddenly stepping over from the eschatologizing of theology into the revolutionary mentality of politics. Those who see nothing but the revolution from the perspective of the eschaton are victims of a massive illusion.

In the second place, it has to be noted that the eschatological expectation is not only greater than the revolutionary mentality ruin [ondergang] is greater than revolution); it is also smaller. Christian-ethical acting is totally distorted when it is described—appealing to the eschaton—as consisting mainly in the shooting of smaller or larger holes in what exists. Some go so far in this that they wish to turn all of Being [zijn] into one large hole, thinking the eschatological salvation [heil] would consist in this. Christianity and Buddhism then amount to roughly the same thing. Salvation is then the abolition of what exists and even of existence as such. As against this, the Christian future expectation is again far more bourgeois. It holds that reality, created and occurring, reality does indeed pass through ruin [ondergang], but that also means that *it*—reality created and occuring!—passes right through it and really passes right *through* it, and therefore also comes to the fore once more, having been saved. No crumb of good reality falls to the floor, saving only the adopted human nature of the Son of God[55] and the church as the body of Christ![56]

---

55. Elsewhere Van Ruler defends the thesis that the Son return the kingdom to the Father in the eschaton so that the incarnation and the indwelling of the Spirit are cancelled in the eschaton. For cross-references to literature in Dutch, see Van Ruler's *Verzameld werk Deel 5C*, 745, note 73.

56. Van Ruler regarded the incarnation, the indwelling of the Spirit, the ascension, heaven, the church, the New Testament apostolate, theocracy, and so forth as an intermezzo. This is closely related to his view that special revelation, the incarnation, the

For that reason, a [mode of] acting determined by the eschaton cannot possibly consist only in simply smashing up the whole caboodle in the fashion of hooligans.

In the third place, it has to be emphasized that, for these reasons, the Christian-eschatological expectation also has nothing to do with a romantic or idealistic escape from given reality into [a world of] dreams. On the contrary: the eschaton casts us back entirely and solely into the present. That is where our place is. That is where our task is. If we do not remain there and do so actively, no eschaton is possible. In other words, the eschaton is no escape from time[57] but an accent on time.[58] We may, however, say: the sole real accent on time. Who can still take the present seriously while lacking any eschatological expectation? The reproach of betrayal of life that has sometimes been directed at the Christian future expectation has no foundation. But then we must, on the other hand, not provide any occasion for this reproach. We should let the ethical work in the present (right into the political: the theocratic shaping of life[59]) set a true limit to the eschatologizing of thought.

In the fourth place, it can be concluded that this ethical work in the present, departing from and in view of the eschaton, can be defined as a synthesis of breaking down and building up, of preserving and destroying, of revolutionary attitude and conservatism. Carefully considered, we have really to do but one thing in sanctification: to retrieve creation from beneath sin! Sin is the only real evil that there is.[60] Evil is not[61] inherent in what exists and in existence as such. Creation is in no way alienation, neither for God nor for the true self of human beings. Therefore it is in no way—for instance, because it is finite—to be overcome. The sole alienation that there is resides in sin. One could wish that Christians would

---

church, the offices of the church, and so forth are God's emergency measures. For cross-references to literature in Dutch, see Van Ruler's *Verzameld werk 5C*, 176, note 89.

57. For Van Ruler's view on escapism (escaping from time), see the cross-references to literature in Dutch in Van Ruler's *Verzameld werk 5C*, 332, note 59.

58. On Van Ruler's view that the eschaton is no escape from time but an accent on time, see the cross-references to literature in Dutch in his *Verzameld werk 5C*, 490, note 48.

59. Van Ruler's views on a theocratic shaping of life are found in his *Verzameld werk 6A*.

60. For Van Ruler's views on sin, see the two texts included in *This Earthly Life Matters*, 211–22.

61. In the original published version of this text the negative is missing but this seems to be a printing error. Van Ruler's theology clearly suggests such a negative.

drum this fundamental statement, this primary axiom, well and truly into their heads and hearts. Then they would once more become immune to the innumerably many gnostic bacilli that are polluting the atmosphere of our modern European culture (currently particularly departing from Marx, with his Hegelian background).

In the fifth place, I call to mind the brilliant remark of Jodocus van Loderstein that it is sickly-sweet sentimentality to believe that the eschatological bliss, in its nature and essence, differs even a tiny bit from actual sanctity.[62] At most it differs from it in degree. But in content these two are identical. What we expect eschatologically is nothing but that to which we have been called now already: to experience creation once more, fully and exclusively, as that which it is, namely, as creation, as glory of God, holy up to its finest detail and up to its crudest externality. That is also why traditional orthodoxy has always seen the doctrine of sanctification and the doctrine of glorification as extensions of each other and in essence brought them under one heading. To take these two apart or even oppose them to each other (our sanctification is not a big thing. But the glorification that is coming—*that* is it!) is perhaps the most dangerous eschatologizing imaginable.

XI

Conclusion: not only the eschaton or (more bourgeois) the future is important; the past and the present (also the past!) are precisely equally important. We should love the entire historical process and all that exists. That we should then also process in our hearts and lives and think through in our theory. In our reflection—this means—we should, among others things, strive for a philosophy of history[63] and an all-embracing ontology. It also means that in dogmatics (in as much as we do not convert that into a universal philosophy of revelation[64]) we should devote as much love and attention to all the other loci as we do to the locus of the *novissisimus*. We can then with a clear conscious place eschatology at the end as the last locus. There is not the least reason to make of eschatology

---

62. Jodocus van Lodenstein (1620–1677), Reformed pastor known for his ascetic lifestyle and mysticism.

63. For Van Ruler's views on a philosophy of history, see the cross references to literature in Dutch in his *Verzameld werk 5C*, 933, note 65.

64. Van Ruler is probably alluding to Herman Bavinck's Stone lectures in 1908, published as *The Philosophy of Revelation* (London: Longmans, Green & Co., 1909).

the first or the most important locus or to turn it into the function, exponent or quality, of the entire dogmatic system. That is to say, one can and must do that as well. But precisely the same can and must be done with every other locus. Those who are not willing to do so render the matter of theology top heavy and cause it to tumble over.

The Christian Future Expectation[1]
[1967]

HUMANITY HAS ALWAYS AND everywhere had some awareness of the future. There are three givens that have constantly led to that. In the first place, the self-evident expectation that another day will come tomorrow and also the day after and that I still have quite a number of years lying ahead of me. In the second place, the vague uncertainty regarding the hereafter. What will happen to me when I am dead? I have after all been here, have I not? That is a reality that cannot be erased. Would I then be completely missing in death? In the third place, people have always asked themselves where the world will end up—and your own tribe, your own people, humanity as a whole.

But regarding the more precise details of the expectation for the future, the human race is divided in a scary way, to the very bottom. Millions of people think of nirvana, in which consciousness and the will are doused and reality is to all intents and purposes abolished.[2] Other millions feel themselves in their individuation to be drops from the ocean and expect a final, blissful return of the drops into the ocean of the All-One, of God.[3] A totally different expectation slumbers in the idea of the twilight of the gods, in which everything that is, up to and including the gods, collapses and goes under. That is the feeling of ruin [ondergang] to

---

1. The inventory number of the Dutch text, "Christelijke toekomstverwachting" is I,717A. This was originally a morning devotion for AVRO-radio on 20 July 1967. It is included in Volume 5C of Van Ruler's *Verzameld werk* (2023), 934–37.

2. For Van Ruler's view on nirvana, see the cross-references to literature in Dutch in his *Verzameld werk 5C*, 936, note 4.

3. For Van Ruler's view on the "All-one" and his rejection of any notion of a return into God, see the cross-references to literature in Dutch in his *Verzameld werk 5C*, 936, note 4.

which everything is heading. This expectation, in turn, easily switches to a completely different one. It is that of the eternal return of all things in an eternal cycle of what is in essence always the same. If one restricts this idea to individual people, one arrives at the image of reincarnation: a person is caught up in the wheel of births, must see how this fate can be made fruitful by rising higher with each incarnation, in order to escape at last from this awful wheel.

In contemporary Europe mainly two forms of future expectation can be found. On the other side of the Iron Curtain, people live from the grandiose myth of the stateless and classless society as the result of the historical process. On this side of the Iron Curtain, people have abandoned Christianity far more radically than the communists have. Here people live, when it comes to the future—as far as the public tone of life is concerned—either in skepticism or in nihilism. In skepticism people say: We know nothing about where things are going and whether they go anywhere. Nor can we know anything; we may as well leave this question aside. In nihilism people say: Existence *now* is already absurd in itself. One should not reflect on [the possibility] that it could still have a future as well. That would merely raise the absurdity to another level.

Humanity is terribly plagued in its thinking and feeling by all these possibilities. For one's own part, one can obviously stand only in one's own spiritual place. For many of us this place is determined by Israel and the New Testament.

Carefully considered, the true and full future expectation, the eschatological awareness of things, fully broke through only in Israel. That was due to a multitude of things. Israel believed in the unity of the human race. Israel also discovered history as a coherent, irreversible and purposeful process of free divine and responsible human acts.[4] Israel stood up for the social ideal,[5] the right way for people to live together with others and for the right structuring of their society. Israel also assessed bodiliness and materiality entirely positively. It believed with heart and soul that the entire world reality is God's creation and that God is not only free but also wise and good. For that reason, it also stood up for the individual person. A person is more than manure on the field of the

---

4. For cross-references to literature in Dutch on Israel's "discovery" of history, see Van Ruler's *Verzameld werk* 5C, 936, note 9.

5. To describe the eschatological perspective on the kingdom of God more closely, Van Ruler uses, alternately, the "brotherhood of all people" or "the social ideal." For cross-references to literature in Dutch, see his *Verzameld werk* 5C, 447, note 57.

future.⁶ Bodily resurrection, resurrection from the dead, resurrection of the flesh, is a future expectation that lies fully within the perspective of the Old Testament. And then the enormous matter of good and evil and of justice. God is, according to the prophetic-Israelite faith, not only free and wise and good. God is also holy. And this world is God's world. For that reason, it can never remain as it is now. It must and shall at some time be redeemed. The snow plough of God's judgement shall pass over the earth. Good and evil shall be torn asunder. The world shall be swept clean of all injustice and violence. Righteousness shall triumph. That which it is about in everything, that is the kingdom of God!⁷

The New Testament directly links up with this. It adds a few important things to it. It says that the Messiah has come. It also says that in Him the kingdom of God has in principle been established on earth. It says further that in the Messiah, who is also the Mediator, the full salvation [heil] of the atonement for guilt and of eternal life has been given, so that we may already live in the salvation [heil] now. [This entails that] the future is no longer purely future. It has, in a certain sense, already become present tense, even past tense. In any case: the salvation [heil] in Christ is the ground of the Christian future expectation. Those who know, believe and confess God in Christ—in as much as they do so truly—can no longer doubt that their own existence and that the world will come into their own.

In particular, we should here also think of the central datum of the New Testament. Jesus has been raised and has risen from the dead. In that the kingdom of God, the final future of the world, has broken through and appeared, almost already in full visibility, in any case in full bodiliness.

Christ is, however, not only the secure ground for the certainty of the Christian future expectation. What we have received in and through

---

6. The German communist Eugen Leviné (1883-1919) was arrested and condemned to death after the fall of the Bavarian Radenrepubliek. Before his execution on 5 June 1919 he said that "he wishes to be nothing but manure on the field of history." See Ger Harmsen, "Een afscheid, maar niet van de dialectiek," in *Afscheid van de dialectiek? Rondom het afscheid van Ger Harmsen als hoogleraar* (Nijmegen, 1988), 79.

7. One of the core themes in Van Ruler's theology is that the Christian faith indeed hinges on (Dutch: draait om) Christ, atonement and justification, but that it is about (Dutch: gaat om) something else: the redemption of creation and the coming of the kingdom of God on earth. In this regard, Van Ruler would also say that, for God, it is about (Dutch: gaat om) this world, this earthly, life, ordinary life, humaneness, sanctification and so forth. For cross-references to literature in Dutch, see Van Ruler's *Verzameld werk 5C*, 308, note 5.

Him is also, according to the Christian conception, the content of the eternal future. We have eternal life. We live in love. Joy is the core of the Christian existence.[8] The Spirit sanctifies our bodies. All of that remains. Paul says that explicitly of love: love remains in all eternity.[9] But we can also say that of other things: holiness, joy and eternal life.

Are we therefore awaiting nothing new? In a certain sense we have to say: No, not really. For what is essential we know already. We already have it. But, on the other hand, the parousia of Christ, the last judgement, the great unveiling, the full transfiguration and glorification, the glorification of everything, are such colossal events that the mind boggles at them. To gain some understanding of that, we might, for instance, imagine but this one: what a remarkable, unimaginable experience would it be to me that I should arise from my death on the last day!

Therefore: on the one hand, we already have everything; on the other hand, we have not the faintest idea of what we shall be. We know only one thing with certainty: there is every reason to entertain unlimited confidence concerning the world and concerning ourselves.[10] That we can do in only one way: by persevering bravely and merrily in the present. Because the Christian future expectation stringently casts us back into that, into the present, into the eternal life of every day. That is what will finally be saved.

---

8. "Joy" is a core theme in the theology of Van Ruler. For cross-references to literature in Dutch, see Van Ruler's *Verzameld werk 5C*, 869, note 65.

9. See 1 Corinthians 13:8.

10. See the title of Van Ruler's book *Heb moed voor de wereld* ("Take courage/heart for the world") (Nijkerk: Callenbach, no date). This was a series of morning devotions from the book Zachariah. Van Ruler also uses the expression for the task of the apostles. For cross-references to literature in Dutch, see Van Ruler's *Verzameld werk 5C*, 936, note 18.

Biblical Future Expectations in Earthly Perspective[1]

[1968]

I

The notion that God (or Christ) is our Eschatos does indeed seem to be an easy solution to many problems, but it leads us—from a Christian perspective—on false trails.

ONE MIGHT ARRIVE AT the idea that what it is about is not at all the eschata, nor even the eschaton, but rather the Eschatos. This pronouncement

---

1. The inventory number of the Dutch text, "Bijbelse toekomstverwachting en aards perspectief" is I,731. This was a lecture in a course for continued theological education for pastors in Hydepark (Doorn) on 12 November 1968. It is included in Volume 5C of Van Ruler's *Verzameld werk* (2023), 938–96, based on an original hand-written document of 29 pages. The essay was first published in Van Ruler's posthumous volume *Theologisch werk II* (Nijkerk: G.F. Callenbach, 1971), 220–40. This published text deviates from the original in several significant ways. It is not clear who was responsible for these changes. Some were probably made by Van Ruler himself, some stylistic changes were probably made by his widow, Ms J.A. Van Ruler-Hamelink. There may also be changes that were made by the publisher. This is not clarified in the introduction to this volume—which only includes a biographic sketch in honor of Van Ruler who died on 15 December 1970.
   Editor's note: The published version in Volume 5C of Van Ruler's *Verzameld werk* follows the hand-written text but indicates in endnotes where the published version in *Theologisch werk II* deviates from the original. In this translation, the same policy has been followed, except that minor changes that do not significantly affect the translation are not indicated. In all other cases, footnotes refer to additions or alterations, indicating that these appear in *Theologisch werk II*.

even sounds pious when one first hears it. One can also trot it out in the modern age shaped by science. At least, that is how it appears.[2]

There could then still be some difference of opinion concerning the question as to how we should indicate our Eschatos more precisely. Is it God as such? Is God the Eschatos of our existence? Is God also the Eschatos of the world? "Existence" is narrow enough to allow us to suspect that there is some meaning in the thesis that God is its Eschatos. When it comes to the cosmos, matters are considerably more difficult. It is much too malleable and ontic. Those who remain true to the cosmos cannot be satisfied with the Eschatos.[3] They look for eschata as well.

Or should we not think of God as such but of God-in-Christ, therefore of Christ, in whom the covenant between God and humanity and, along with that, Godself and humanity itself, is realized? Is He the Eschatos, the Eschatos who appeared in time but also the Eschatos who puts an end to time and history?

But we can leave this question aside.[4] What it is about now is the thesis: no eschata, no eschaton, only the Eschatos. This thesis does not merely sound pious. It also seems extremely welcome. It suggests to us a comfortable solution to quite a number of problems. Does not all talk of eschata as eschata of the temporal-spatial reality of the cosmos have something so mythological about it that it is simply intolerable to modern people? Let it be noted here that in general these modern people, when it comes to the future of the cosmos, do not see beyond their scientific noses and those noses do not go very far.

But talk about the eschaton is also beset by considerable objections. There remains in it something not only unimaginable but actually something unthinkable. Being [zijn], the fact that there is something and not nothing,[5] existence, the reality that I am there—there is some-

---

2. In *Theologisch werk II* this paragraph was revised to read: "In the last instance it is all about God only; God or God's presence is our Eschatos, the final destination of everyone and everything. One can also trot it out in the modern age shaped by science. At least, that is how it appears. For then one no longer says anything about visible and palpable reality, that with which science and technology busy themselves and about which they want to have the last word."

3. *Theologisch werk II* inserted here: "Nor with one single eschaton."

4. *Theologisch werk II* inserted here: "Nor does it make that much difference whether we say 'God' or 'Christ' in this context. For with 'Christ' we surely also mean 'God' in as much as God enters fully into God's covenant relationship with human beings."

5. For cross-references to literature in Dutch on this observation, see Van Ruler's *Verzameld werk 5C*, 953, note 8.

thing unthinkable about that as well. It can never be fully captured in thought. Regarding existence, it would appear as if in self-consciousness the subject and the object coincide fully, but that is, nevertheless, not entirely true. Regarding Being [zijn], we can indeed fully think the "being so." But does not a residue remain beyond thought, namely, the thatness and particularly the thisness, the *haeceitas*?[6] But however unthinkable it may be, we are there, we live, we also experience the world. Existence and the cosmos have that advantage over the eschaton. [The latter] in all its unthinkability we can but expect.

Are we not saved from all these problems if we say: "But it is not about the eschata at all; that is not even what it concerns; it is solely about and concerning the Eschatos"? Then we would be rid of the problem of the relationship between the biblical future expectation and the earthly perspective. The former would be only an expectation of *God*, of the Eschatos,[7] and the latter we could[8] leave to be what it is.

The problem that constitutes the topic of our discussion would then disappear. One feels immediately that that would be all too easy. The biblical future expectation is without doubt not directed so exclusively at God that the earthly perspective would no longer add anything to it.[9] As soon as we no longer have any place for perspectives for the earth in the system of our eschatological pronouncements, something has to be amiss.

Moreover, we can ask ourselves whether the eschatological pronouncements that are conceptualized on the basis of the idea that it is about the Eschatos are not perhaps beset, though perhaps not by the objections regarding the mythological, unimaginable and unthinkable, by the no less weighty objection that they are to an extent platitudinous. They become, on the one hand, self-evident. Obviously, God is the Eschatos of humanity and the world! On the other hand, they become exaggerated. When we are dealing with God, we lose our bearings.[10]

---

6. *Haeceitas*: That-ness, a medieval term coined by Duns Scotus.
7. *Theologisch werk II* inserted here: "of God's entirely new presence."
8. *Theologisch werk II* inserted here: "theologically, confessionally."
9. *Theologisch werk II* inserted here: "It is indeed directed at God, perhaps even at God's being and at the contemplation of that, but at least also, surely, at God [as manifested] in God's acts. And what is the object of God's acting but God's created reality?
10. *Theologisch werk II* inserted here: "In both instances we are really saying nothing. The self-evident needs hardly be said and the ineffable can hardly be said."

For that reason, we would have to introduce some distinctions. God is the Eschatos of humanity and the world, of existence and the cosmos. That means that God is their ground and boundary. It does not in any way mean more than that. It does not mean that God is their origin and their purpose.[11]

But even the terms "ground" and "boundary" have to be treated with care. Is God that dry? Should we not say that God is not so much the boundary of reality but that there is a boundary between God and reality? And is the reason for that not that we should not find the ground of reality so heedlessly in God? [Does it not lie, rather,] on the one hand, in God's sovereign pleasure and therefore in God's decree, God's counsel, in which will takes the lead and thought is present as an accompaniment, and, on the other hand, in God's act, the act of creation? The counsel and the act come in between, between created reality and God. They constitute the irrevocable and non-transgressable boundary. This boundary, this finis, is, moreover, merely a boundary, not a goal.

[12]The human being and the world are not fragments of God.[13] Nor are they [emanations] from God.[14] And therefore also not [aimed] towards God.[15] The biblical future expectation does not in any way imply that we shall finally be taken up into God in the way that a drop that flies up returns again into the ocean. There are layers in ontology that cannot be undone.

We cannot even (or, rather not at all) say that we shall finally be taken up into Christ. The major objection, alongside many other objections, against this idea resides in the implication that we would then have to replace ontology by soteriology or dissolve the former into the latter. The concept of the Mediator would dominate all thinking.

---

11. *Theologisch werk II* inserted here: "Creation is not an emanation from the very deing of God. Therefore the eschaton is not a flowing back into it."

12. *Theologisch werk II* inserted here: "Those who abandon these theses—which imply, among other things, the transcendence and the 'theistic' independence of God—can no longer experience either the world in its reality and worldliness or themselves in their individuality and humanity."

13. For cross-references to literature in Dutch on this phrase, see Van Ruler's *Verzameld werk 5C*, 953, note 20.

14. *Theologisch werk II* inserts here: "At least, not from God's being."

15. *Theologisch werk II* inserts here: "even if it be to God's honor."

II

The idea that the eschaton is a *nova creatio* that appeared in the resurrection of Christ, is a misconception from the outset.[16]

But perhaps there is a completely different way out of the difficulties of our topic. [That appears] if we interpret the biblical future expectation in the sense of a *nova creatio*. Then it would not primarily be God who is the Eschatos; a new *act* of God would be the eschaton. At the end, God calls a new world into being. All our expectations for the future should be directed at that.

In the Christian context, one cannot avoid adding to that: And this eschaton has already appeared in history, namely, in Jesus Christ, particularly in his resurrection. The old aeon has come to an end in that and something of the new aeon has broken through. The resurrection is the great beacon of light in the field of history. It is a signal of the eternal future which causes all sorts of other elements in history, at least in the history of Israel, to radiate the same light by way of reflection.

But that would then also be the only importance of history: this series of references to the future. There is no epiphany; there is only the promise. Christian theology is solely a theology of hope.[17]

It is remarkable how one-sidedly people concentrate on the resurrection of Jesus in this train of thought. [The resurrection] is undoubtedly of central salvific meaning. But surely one can hardly take this christological center to be the entire christological circle. He arose bodily, even if it were—of course—in a glorified bodiliness. This human nature he adopted from the Virgin Mary. The [phrase] "*ex Maria*"[18] is then decisive. It is not "*per Mariam*."[19] The Son of God did not pass through Mary with a human nature newly created by God in heaven. That is how people in the second and sixteenth century understood the gospel as message of the

---

16. Van Ruler very frequently resists the common translation of II Corinthians 5:17 where the Greek words καινὴ κτίσις are translated as *nova creatura* (Vulgate) or as new creation or new creature. For cross-references to literature in Dutch, see his *Verzameld werk 5C*, 931, note 42.

17. Van Ruler hints at Jürgen Moltmann's *Theology of Hope*. See *Theologie der Hoffnung: Untersuchungen zur Begründung und zu den Konsequenzen einer christlichen Eschatologie* (München, 1964).

18. *Ex Maria*: From Mary.

19. *Per Mariam*: Through Mary.

nova creatio. That reflected a somewhat more profound thinking through of the matter than that delivered by the current theology of hope.[20]

But from a biblical perspective it seems that everything pleads for "ex Maria." If we hold on to that, it follows that salvation links up with creation. There is indeed novelty, *novitas*. That is the element of truth in the idea of the *nova creatio*. The question, however, is how we should understand the novelty. Does the new creation come in the place of the old one ontologically? Is the replacement so permanent and so complete? Is the old creation, the old created reality that we are and have here and now, pensioned off? Does something completely different come in its place?

Or should we rather say: "No, the new is precisely the old, only radically renewed, completely liberated from all forms of corruption? That, precisely, is what is fantastic about the gospel! To call forth another world from nothing is child's play compared to calling this world into renewed existence from the abyss of sin and guilt,[21] from eternal perdition.[22]

Naturally, in salvation a divine force similar to the one in creation is necessary. For that reason, the resurrection, the eschaton, rebirth, can be compared to the *creatio*. But that should not seduce us into thinking that it is in each case the same divine action regarding content. Regarding content, it is never real *creatio*, *creatio ex nihilo*. Even the *conservatio*, the first element in the *providentia*,[23] is no *creatio continua*[24] but a *creatio*

---

20. *Theologisch Werk II* inserts here: "– even though in this way one brushes by the heresy of docetism so closely as to virtually fall into it."

21. The understanding of sin as guilt and of reconciliation as atonement for guilt are core motifs in Van Ruler's theology that are expressed throughout his oeuvre. In this regard, he gives preference to Anselm's understanding of atonement as satisfaction. For cross-references to literature in Dutch, see Van Ruler's *Verzameld werk 5C*, 170, note 28.

22. *Theologisch werk II* inserts here: "in such a way that it—this lost world—can exist again. The eternal perdition of guilt is another, completely different reality, at least a completely different situation, from 'the' nothing from which creation was called forth. Regarding the 'linking up' of salvation with creation we should, therefore, not form notions that are too trivial and superficial. On the one hand, creation does not merely supply a few starting points with which salvation can link up: created reality in its totality is the object of and, in this sense, encompassed by salvation. On the other hand, salvation is, at least in the last instance, exhausted in being solely and exclusively the salvation of creation, albeit along many byroads and thus with the addition of elements that are in principle new."

23. In the Reformed tradition three aspects of God's *providentia* (providence) are typically distinguished, namely, *conservatio* (conservation), *gubernatio* (governance in history), and *concursus* (accompaniment) or *cooperatio* (cooperation).

24. *Theologisch werk II* inserts here: ", created being is not ever again called forth from nothing."

continuata.²⁵ In [the matter of] salvation it still more important that we should synthesize the novelty of all God's acts with God's eternal faithfulness to everything that God had done.

When we consider the matter carefully, we have to come to the conclusion that it is illusory to think that only the *Christusereignis* is anticipation of the eschaton, realized eschatology. Creation itself, everything that is, is already anticipation. The world is—as regards the content—the eschaton.²⁶

What then is the eschaton? At least it comprises creation and salvation. Does the novelty of the eschaton reside only in the fact that it would then become evident that all has been saved, has already for long been saved? If that were so, I would say: excusez du peu!²⁷ After all, the "becoming evident" is by no means such a small matter. Salvation is an unimaginably great thing. But then the becoming evident of salvation is also something momentous.²⁸

Or should we say that the eschaton also comprises this, that created reality is finally saved? If that were to imply that it is now only "reconciled" and would then be "saved", I would be inclined to distance myself somewhat from this thesis. Regarding the Son, we can more rightly speak of our salvation.²⁹ Regarding the Spirit, we would then speak of sanctification and glorification. That would then be the eschatological categories par excellence. In the eschaton it is not primarily salvation that takes place.³⁰ Nevertheless, it would also be saying too little to mention only

---

25. *Theologisch werk II* inserts here: ", a preserving of that which has been called forth from sinking back into nothing."

26. *Theologisch werk II* inserts here: "The eschatologizing of theology is a good thing. At least, it is a legitimate possibility and even a necessity. But if we are to engage in it with Christian consistency of thought, we may not let anything that was and happened slip away. The God who acts eschatologically does not deal in such a messy and wasteful way with God's creatures."

27. *Excusez du peu!*: That is not nothing! Literally, "Pardon the little", but said to indicate that it is not that "little" after all.

28. *Theologisch werk II* inserts here: "For this reason, we can by no means say that the eschaton is 'merely' the unveiling of the salvation that had been veiled up to then."

29. *Theologisch Werk II* inserts here: "Even though it is so that atonement, in all the meanings of the word, is an essential moment, indeed, the core of this salvation."

Translator's note: In speaking of "all the meanings of the word", Van Ruler may be considering that the Dutch "verzoening" is used for both "atonement" and "reconciliation."

30. *Theologisch Werk II* inserts here: That has already, in all abundance, taken place in the work of the Son in the flesh."

the becoming evident of salvation. It is about sanctifying and glorifying—*sanctificatio, transfiguratio, glorificatio*.

Seen in this way, we have to launch a direct assault on the formulation of the theme. It creates the impression that there are two [things]: the biblical future expectation and the earthly perspective. This dualism is a crease that has been ironed so thoroughly into our Christian thinking that it would not be easy to iron it out again. But it skews everything fundamentally. After all, it is, also and particularly in the biblical future expectation, solely and only about an earthly perspective.[31] The earth and earthly life are created reality. They have been saved from perdition. For that reason, they fall within the perspective of future expectation. In other words, there is not the least need to search for a spot for the earthly perspective within the biblical future expectation. For this expectation is exclusively a perspective for the totality of earthly life.

III

The eschaton and history (all of history! Not only that of Israel, Jesus the Christ and Christianization) stand in a strictly correlative relationship.

Some of this we can best capture in the statement that there is a strictly correlative relationship between the eschaton and history. In a true correlation the one component is as essential to the other as the other is to it. There is a complete reciprocity to it. So it is in our case: without eschaton no history, but also, without history no eschaton. We can also, somewhat more graphically, state it in this way: the eschaton relates to history as the pulling force relates to the ingredients.

The eschaton is the pulling point that makes history. It is more that the boundary of history. Even more than its purpose. It is the summation,

---

31. *Theologisch werk II* inserts here: "What sort of other perspective could it really be? Is—in the Christian view—a non-earthly perspective, for instance, a perspective for the soul, the spirit, the individual self, God, conceivable?"

One of the core themes in Van Ruler's theology is that the Christian faith indeed hinges on (Dutch: draait om) Christ, atonement and justification, but that it is about (Dutch: gaat om) something else: the redemption of creation and the coming of the kingdom of God on earth. In this regard, Van Ruler would also say that, for God, it is about (Dutch: gaat om) this world, this earthly, life, ordinary life, humaneness, sanctification and so forth. For cross-references to literature in Dutch, see Van Ruler's *Verzameld werk 5C*, 308, note 5.

the recapitulation and the consummation, the "completion" (συντέλεια) of history [that makes it] a unity.

It is only through this that history becomes fully history: its unity, the relatedness of its parts to one another, becomes visible. The pulling force also bring movement into it. The harvest has to ripen. All individuals have to be born. All possibilities have to be tried out. The eschaton is the *pleroma*.[32] Therefore it requires multiplicity. That is why history goes ahead. This movement is also irreversible. History owes that to the eschaton as well. It is moving somewhere. History is not a wheel that revolves, not a snake that coils itself, not a labyrinth in which one ever again retraces one's steps.[33] We are on our way to the eschaton.[34] When we reflect on this thoroughly, we are ever again inclined to go for the maximum and to say: "We see the meaning [zin] of history. It resides in the eschaton as the kingdom of glory."

All of this can be said only hypothetically: only if there is an eschaton, is there history as a unity in a meaningful, irreversibly directed movement. The Bible has a future expectation, knows of an eschaton, preaches the kingdom of God. For that reason, the Bible also knows of history. The eschaton is, so to speak, exhausted in being the pulling force of history. Someone who lives eschatologically lives historically. The eschaton casts a person fully back into the present as a moment in time.

That is why the opposite in the correlative relationship also holds. The eschaton is indispensable for history. But history is equally indispensable for the eschaton. History is the totality of the ingredients from which the eschaton is constituted. If there were no history, even God would not have been able to call a true eschaton into existence. God would at most have been able to proceed to a *nova creatio*.

One does have to realize fully what is at stake in all this. In my view, nothing less than the fulness of humanity is at stake. What is the human being? What is the humanity of the human being? Surely this, that human beings are thinking and willing, and particularly, acting beings, that they are responsible for their deeds, that they act together with

32. *Theologisch werk II* inserts here: "the fulness of all realized possibilities."

33. *Theologisch werk II* inserts here: "It does often present itself to us in these ways. There is also much in history that can hardly be experienced in any other way. But if we are entirely dominated by these nightmares, we lose the consciousness of and the reality of history."

34. In *Theologisch werk II* this sentence was replaced by: "We are on our way. Where to but to the eschaton? In some or other way we cannot stand within history—as true history—and let it be what it is."

their neighbors, yes, within the larger whole of the community and thus socially, that their actions are incorporated in a meaningful way in the pilgrimage of humanity. Human beings are more than a piece of nature. More than a radiation from the void. More than a product of fate. More than a moment in the divine reason. More than a wad of absurd Being [zijn]. That is to say, one can obviously understand being human in those ways as well. But all Christianized Europeans immediately sense that full humanness is not grasped in such ways.

That is grasped only when we see human beings as standing in history. And history is grasped only when we see it as standing in the correlative relationship with the eschaton. And the eschaton is grasped only when we see it in its relatedness to the whole of created reality, when we are, therefore, also prepared to speak of the eschata. About the eschaton and the eschata we can speak only mythically, in supple images.[35] We have to be fully aware of what the consequences will be if we give up the myth of the eschaton. In principle we then give up humanness.

Israel had discovered all of this. In dogmatics we capture this fact in the concept of special revelation. In Jesus Christ all of this is confirmed. He keeps the future open and thereby keeps history in motion. According to old dogmatics, the *praedictio rerum futurum* is an aspect of his *munus propheticum*.[36] With Doroteé Sölle this old motif returns. She even stakes everything on this card. She changes her tone, however, because she sees Jesus the Christ as also keeping open the future of God, who died.[37] That, in my opinion, is too much of a good thing.

We also have to consider that Israel and especially its Messiah knew of more than history and the eschaton. The Messiah of Israel is also the Mediator of the new covenant. That is a covenant in his blood. What is at stake in that is guilt and the atonement for guilt. Only in this way can Jesus keep open the future effectively. In that all things seem to come to a halt for a moment. People fix their concentration completely on the

---

35. For Van Ruler's view on mythological language, see the cross-references to literature in Dutch in his *Verzameld werk 5C*, 955, note 69.

36. *Praedictio rerum futurarum*: Proclamation of future things; munus propheticum: prophetic office. Van Ruler's source is probably Heinrich Heppe, *Die Dogmatik der evangelisch-reformirten Kirche* (Elberfeld, 1861), 324. Second edition (Neukirchen, Kreis Moers 1935), 357.

37. Dorothee Sölle (1929-2003), German theologian, taught systematic theology at Union Theological Seminary in New York (1975-1987). Van Ruler's source is Dorothee Sölle, *Stellvertretung: Ein Kapitel Theologie nach dem "Tode Gottes"* (Berlin, 1965), esp. 175-84.

mystery of guilt *and* on the mystery of the atonement. Western orthodoxy has often been mesmerized by this to such an extent that it forgot about history and the kingdom, in other words, what it is about in the sacrifice of atonement.[38]

But all of *that* is not the only one-sidedness. People proceed in an equally one-sided way when they see the eschaton as standing in a correlative relationship only to the history of Israel, of Jesus the Christ and of Christianization. The eschaton is not only the eschaton of salvation [heil]. It is the eschaton of all of history, yes, of created reality, of Being (zijn] as such.

Also without sin there would have been history and the eschaton would have manifested a plus in relation to the proton. That is the incomparable meaning of the barely biblical theologoumenon of the "covenant of works". Of course, there is not only the *foedus operum*.[39] Therefore there is not only history, human actions, dynamics. There is also *creatio*, that is, Being [zijn], a static substratum, authentic reality. That too look forward to the eschatological transfiguration and glorification. But the *foedus operum* adds some things to it. It includes human beings, the action of human beings, even their works in the plural and the promises that pertain to them.

Proceeding from the truth of the *creatio* and the *foedus operum*, we can, from a Christian, theological perspective, get a mental grip on the whole of history, the entire cultural process and all of cosmic reality. The earthly has then been fully incorporated into the biblical future expectation. In the end, it is not about salvation [heil], about Israel, about Jesus the Christ, about the church, about Christianization. In the end, it is about the world, specifically as kingdom of God—however much the church and the covenant of grace are irreplaceable means to this end.[40]

---

38. *Theologisch werk II* inserts here: "Currently it is even inclined to forget that this atonement for guilt is at most the core of salvation. All it retains from the gospel is the atonement, mostly even only in the sense of *reconciliatio*. In this way, it loses the abundance of the total salvation in the work of the Mediator."

39. *Foedus operum*: Covenant of works.

40. One of the core tenets in Van Ruler's theology is that special revelation, the election of Abraham and of Israel, the incarnation, the covenant, the suffering of Jesus, atonement, justification, the church, the offices of the church and so forth, are not ends in themselves but only means. For cross-references to literature in Dutch see his *Verzameld werk 5C*, 191, note 13.

IV

Is sin (evil) also taken up in the eschaton in some or other way?

When our topic is tackled in this broad way, we are definitely faced by a daunting problem. There are not only history and created reality, perhaps the history of created reality. There is also sin, evil in its manifold forms and gradations. There is the guilt of sin.[41] There is the power of sin. There is suffering of unimaginable extent and depth. There are the demons, or, to put it less mythically, there is heathendom.

Are all of these also anticipations of the eschaton? Are they also integrated in the kingdom of glory? They are, after all, also [part of] reality! Can we maintain the strict correlation between eschaton and history at this point?

This is already an enormous problem in protology. There we ask if and how sin appears in God's decision. We are not dealing with that now. But a Yahwist or a Calvinist does feel the need to say that there is, in some or other way, a decision concerning sin in God's counsel (no matter how infralapsarian the decision may perforce be taken to be) rather than to say that there is an idea of evil in the very being of God,.

But that we have to leave aside for now. We are not now enquiring protologically but eschatologically. Then all will be light, be eternal light, light from light and darkness.[42] What does the Yahwistic clause "and from darkness" mean? Does the earthly darkness contribute to the eternal light? Does this darkness itself turn out to be light? Or is it transformed into light?

Or do we land up in theosophical, gnostic speculations in this way? Do we go beyond the Christian? Does the gospel amount to this, that God has, in Christ, condemned sin and radically abolished it? Is that all that can and may be said about evil from a Christian perspective? That depends entirely on how we conceptualize atonement. One could, for instance conceptualize it dramatically.[43] Then evil has been expelled from

---

41. On guilt, see note 21 above.

42. Van Ruler is hinting at the final lines in Hymn 131 of *Psalmen en gezangen voor den Eeredienst der Nederlandsche Hervormde Kerk, in opdracht van de Algemeene Synode der Nederlandsche Hervormde Kerk opnieuw verzameld en bewerkt, aan de Nederlandsche Hervormde Kerk aangeboden door de Algemeene Synode in het jaar onzes Heeren 1938*, Amsterdam s.a. [1938].

43. *Theologisch werk II* inserts here: "This is what happens—as far as I know, for the first time in history—in Karl Barth's theology." Elsewhere Van Ruler briefly explains

the world entirely by [the atonement].[44] That, however, seems to me to be hardly tenable without entering into the sphere of the idea of the *nova creatio*. One could also conceptualize atonement more in the sense of the *satisfactio vicaria*.[45] Then one exercises a far greater ἐποχή[46] regarding the reality of evil.[47]

Evangelically speaking, what happens to the demons? They are cast out.[48] They are overthrown and made powerless. Where are they then? Where is there überhaupt a place for evil eschatologically? The demons are also cast down. They are made into a footstool for the feet on which people can rest.[49] That seems a useful function. In this way they are positively linked in. Origen thought that the demons could also be baptized.[50] That, however, does go a little too far.

The question of what is to happen to the demons stands alongside the question of what is to happen to sin. The guilt of it has been atoned for. Is it done away with in this way? It is at least obliterated. But another image concerning this matter is that it is covered. It is borne. Up to the end of the earth, up to the last judgement. Thus [it is] not just quickly disposed of. In other words, the guilt is not simply gone.[51]

But the guilt [itself] is not identical to what has been guiltily done. Is the guiltiness merely the wrong intentions of the deeds? What has been guiltily done is at any rate fully a reality. And is all reality not created reality and therefore good reality? Is it not anticipation of the eschaton just as the whole of created reality is? Would it then not be integrated? Is the negative of history to be transmuted into something positive?

---

why he classified Barth's doctrine of reconciliation as "dramatic." See a preliminary study on the doctrine of atonement in the Van Ruler archive, inventory number V,6, IV.

44. *Theologisch Werk II* inserts here: "It has even been unmasked in its a priori nothingness. Did it ever have any reality?"

45. *Satisfactio vicaria*: Vicarious satisfaction / substitution.

46. Ἐποχή: Withholding (of an opinion or view), reserve.

47. *Theologisch werk II* inserts here: "Sin is then at its very least the guilt of human beings, a reality in history (in the past!) and thus in the eminent sense of the word reality that happens and functions."

48. See John 12:31.

49. See Psalm 110:1; Luke 20:43; Act 2:34-35; I Cor 15:25; Heb 1:13, 10:1.

50. The idea that demons can be baptized cannot be found in the writings of Origen. It is not clear where Van Ruler derived this idea from. Origen did consider the possibility that the devil and his angels could return to God anew in a cycle of worlds that follow after our contemporary world.

51. *Theologisch werk II* inserts here: "It is covered over in the end."

Or must we go even further and say similar things about guilt as well? It would be possible to speak of *felix culpa*.[52] The *felicitas*, the blessed fertility of the *culpa*, could then be found in the fact that in guilt people experience and live through what is deepest in the creaturely situation, in the *condition humaine*. Or, alternatively, in the fact that guilt leads to the highest, or perhaps also to the deepest in God, namely, God's grace. Or, alternatively, in the fact that people become fireproof[53] through the experience of the confession of guilt and the proclamation of grace, both of these being intrinsically terrifying, and pass over from the *posse non peccare* to the *non posse peccare*.[54] In any case: in this or that way guilt too would be integrated as a moment in the eternal song of praise of the kingdom of glory.

It may be noted in passing that such an integration of evil into the eschaton does not per se have to imply an ἀποκατάστασις πάντων.[55] Evil is something rather different from evildoers, the reality from the realizers. Eternal perdition must be kept open as a possibility in the biblical future expectation. Humanness as a whole depends on that. Human beings are human beings if in their lifetimes a decision is taken that holds for all eternity.[56] When the accent of eternity is no longer placed on time, time becomes worthless.

---

52. *Felix culpa*: Happy fault. For cross-references to Van Ruler's use of this term, see the Dutch edition of Van Ruler's *Verzameld werk* 5C, 857, note 83. The expression is derived from the "Exultet" (the hymn formerly sung to the Easter candle as symbol of the risen Christ during the Easter eve celebration). It contains the line: "O felix culpa, quae talem ac tantum meruit habere Redemptorem!" (O happy fault that deserved to have a Redeemer of such quality and greatness.") It is cited by, among others, Thomas Aquinas, *Summa theologiae*, III, q.1, a.3, ad 3.

53. For Van Ruler's use of the term "fireproof" (against sin), see the references to Dutch literature in his *Verzameld werk* 5C, 957, note 100.

54. *Non posse peccare*: Not possible to sin. Augustine contrasts this expression with *posse non peccare* (the possibility not to sin) that applied in paradise. See Augustine, *De correptione et gratia*, XIII.33.

55. Ἀποκατάστασις πάντων: The restoration of all things.

56. This expression that decisions in time apply for all eternity is frequently found in Van Ruler's writings. For cross-references see his *Verzameld werk* 5C, 490, note 48.

V

The single person belongs in this in the fullness of his or her existence—for that reason, the resurrection of the flesh is the hinge on which everything turns.

But let us withdraw quickly from these desperate, fragmentary speculations about the integration of evil.[57] A problem awaits us that—from a Christian perspective—exhibits much greater clarity.

I mean the problem of the position of the individual person, not only in the historical process but also in the eschaton. That such a person stands within the whole of history as a whole of actions and stands there as active agent and that this is essential to her or his humanity are matters that we have already discussed.

But what is implied [regarding this] by the fact that no eschaton is possible without history and that history provides the ingredients for the eschaton? Can we content ourselves here with the idea that the single person is to be seen as manure on the field of the future?[58] People are there, they ought to do their duty and then they die. If necessary, one of them can be sacrificed. Then that person has been there but remains useful in helping to prepare the future, the ultimate ideal. [Should we say that?]

In the biblical future expectation, the biblical appreciation for the individual person plays its role. The person is not merely a means to an end but is also, as person, an end, in his or her selfhood a place where God comes to rest.[59] Therefore the individual cannot possibly be regarded as manure on the field of the future. The individual may also not be sacrificed for a higher ideal.

Still more important is the consideration that, from a biblical perspective, history and eschaton are not related to each other as temporary means and final goal. The eschaton is the pulling force, but as

---

57. *Theologisch werk II* inserts here: "This question perhaps goes beyond our capacity, perhaps even beyond our competence."

58. The German communist Eugen Leviné (1883-1919) was arrested and condemned to death after the fall of the Bavarian Radenrepubliek. Before his execution on 5 June 1919 he said that "he wishes to be nothing but manure on the field of history." See Ger Harmsen, "Een afscheid, maar niet van de dialectiek," in *Afscheid van de dialectiek? Rondom het afscheid van Ger Harmsen als hoogleraar* (Nijmegen, 1988), 79.

59. *Theologisch werk II* inserts here: "We are a dwelling of God in the Spirit." See Ephesians 2:22.

consummation and recapitulation: all things are added together, all things are gathered together. Thus history is the totality of the ingredients from which the eschaton is constituted. It is more than the run-up to the eschaton.

For that reason, the individual belongs there—in the eschaton. We can speak of an "eternalizing of the this-worldly life" [*Verewigung des diesseitigen Lebens*].[60] That does not imply, however, that the individual person will be there only in the conative memory of God, as a being that has been there just as that person was there in the conative counsel of God as a being that shall be there. The reality quality of created reality is too great to allow for that.[61]

In any case, the apostle Paul says emphatically: Then I shall be known as I have been known.[62] That also implies that now I am not quite there yet. At least, I *am known* to a greater extent than the extent to which I know.[63] But *then* I myself shall know in the same way that God now knows me—I shall know myself, God and all things in this way. To achieve that, I shall have to be there myself.

VI

But the social ideal is what it is all about.

Nevertheless, we should not be blinded by this position of the individual person in the eschaton. The individual may be what everything hinges on [draait om] but is not that which it is all about [gaat om]. The individual person is not the only or the essential thing. As a matter of fact, God is not that either.

---

60. Van Ruler's source is not clear. He may be referring to a passage in Karl Barth, e.g. his *KD, IV/3*, 363.

61. *Theologisch Werk II* inserts here: "That is why the eschaton shows to a far greater extent the quality of created reality than the eternal counsel of God does, however much the *res decreta* may be, in some or other way, a moment in this counsel."

62. See 1 Corinthians 13:12.

63. *Theologisch werk II* inserts here: "And knowledge, self-understanding, though it might not be the one and all of existence, does constitute an important moment in it in as much as in self-consciousness existence first fully encounters itself, 'has' itself and thus 'is' for the first time."

What it is all about in the biblical future expectation is the social ideal: the new earth on which finally righteousness will dwell.[64] The meaning [zin] of the historical process is that people should truly find their way with one another. That is realized in the eschaton through judgement, ruin [ondergang], salvation and glorification.

I shall have to arise from death, from the realm of death, from among the dead. I together with the fulness of my existence. That is the hinge on which all turns in the matter of the relationship between the biblical future expectation and the earthly perspective.

The fulness of existence also has to be taken completely seriously. We are not [doing that] when we say: human beings in the totality of their existence as body and soul. Naturally, that is of fundamental importance too. In view of creation, the incarnation and the indwelling, the body belongs to [existence] as essentially as the soul does. Even the word "flesh" as indication of that is acceptable and even indispensable. Therefore: the resurrection of the flesh![65]

But is time not an equally essential dimension of being human as the soul and the body are? I am, after all, also a piece of filled time?[66] This piece: from my birth to my death. It is filled with a series of acts and eventualities, all [being] events. All of this is brought to judgement. All of this is glorified. The whole of the life that I live here and now[67] returns. This life, that is what I am. This life arises from death. It is saved to eternal life. Only in this way does history contain the ingredients of the eschaton and is the eschaton the integration of history.

It is a community of people in breadth. It is also a community of people in length. The generations, all generations of the entire historical process, are reconciled with one another in the eschaton. Eternal bliss, according to Augustine, is saying "amen" and "hallelujah,"[68] that is, the

---

64. To describe the eschatological perspective on the kingdom of God more closely, Van Ruler uses, alternately, the "brotherhood of all people" or "the social ideal." For cross-references to literature in Dutch, see his *Verzameld werk 5C*, 447, note 57.

65. Van Ruler emphasized the resurrection of the flesh throughout his writings. For cross-references to literature in Dutch, see his *Verzameld werk 5C*, 957, note 121.

66. Van Ruler could have derived the term "filled time" from Karl Barth. See his *KD*, III/2, 648; *KD*, IV/2, 476. It is an expression that Van Ruler uses frequently. For cross-references to literature in Dutch, see *Verzameld werk 5C*, 891, note 5.

67. *Theologisch werk II* inserts here: "in the breadth of the community and the length of history."

68. It is not clear where Van Ruler derived this from. Possible sources in Augustine include his *Sermo* 236,3 or *Sermo* 362, 28.

pronouncing of the solidity of the historical reality and of the glory of God in it. It is a contemplation of and a listening to the historical process as a *pulcherrimum carmen*[69] passing right through all the dissonances of election and rejection, of guilt and atonement.

The eschaton is the full realization of the social ideal in the most ordinary and concrete but also in the deepest sense of the word. We should, in my opinion, not think of a communion with God or of a communion with one another in God that stands over against this communion with one another or, alternatively, that would transcend it. Outside of and above the social ideal there is nothing. In that the image of God beams out: in the society of human beings in whom the lines of the divine love and the divine justice [recht], of the righteousness and the mercy, of the divine joy have been etched.

It is to this end that Israel has been given [to us]. In Israel it was all about the seed, about the national community, about the Torah. Prophecy did not go beyond that; instead, it returned to exactly that time and again. The Messiah of Israel, Jesus the Christ, was also given with a view to the social ideal. He is the true king around whom the true community crystalizes out. The New Testament gospel is primarily a political matter. It posits[70] theocracy as a reality on earth, as *the* true content of all earthly perspectives.

At present we as Christians withdraw ourselves a bit—somewhat reserved. The king is also the high priest. He brings the sacrifice of atonement. Guilt is lodged too deeply in existence for us to rid ourselves of it with a flick of the wrist. We first have to let it be atoned for. We have to be incorporated into the Mediator. Before we can fully arrive at the social ideal, there is first the *unio mystica cum Christo*.[71]

Here we may even find a fundamental distinction between Israel and Christianity. In Israel theocracy is the axiomatic point of departure from which everything proceeds. In Christianity it is the vista towards which everything is directed. In this respect, Christianity is the mirror

---

69. *Theologisch werk II* inserts here: "an extremely beautiful song in which everything is intertwined, displays rythm and rhymes with [everything else]."
Van Ruler draws here on Reinhold Seeberg, *Lehrbuch der Dogmengeschichte. Zweiter Band: Die Dogmenbildung in der Alten Kirche* (Erlangen/Leipzig, 1923³), 475. See also Van Ruler's book *Waarom zou ik naar de kerk gaan?* (Nijkerk: Callenbach, 1970), 39 = *Verzameld werk 5A*, 387.

70. *Theologisch Werk II* inserts here: "—albeit in the most extreme concentration and in germ—"

71. *Unio mystica cum Christo*: Mystical union with Christ.

image of Israel: what is to the right in reality is to the left in the mirror image and vice versa. What stands at the beginning in Israel stands at the end in Christianity.

Christians withdraw themselves a bit within the church. They have become fully awake regarding the *condition humaine*. In the Mediator they see how fully terrible and abysmal guilt and atonement are. They stand with bated breath at the sight. They barely live anymore. They preserve themselves for the time being in the church.

But what is the church? It is the body that preaches the μυστήριον of the βασιλεία,[72] that is, of the world as the kingdom of God, that is, of the social ideal. It is the μυστήριον that has been erected, that has gained a firm footing in the μυστήριον of the atonement.

However, the church is not only the *preaching* body of Christ. It is also the body that has *knowledge* of the μυστήριον of the world as the kingdom of God. It confesses it. The confessional is as essential as the kerygmatic. For that reason, we should not too hastily pass over from the preaching in and of the church to enter the world. That is the disease from which Protestantism currently suffers. It is too kerygmatic, too little confessional.[73] Mary treasured up all [these] things and pondered them in her heart.[74]

Moreover, in the church there is the liturgical and the sacramental. It does not only preach and confess the μυστήριον. It also celebrates it. The liturgy is also a socio-drama in which the mystery of the world is acted out.[75]

---

72. Μυστήριον: Mystery; βασιλεία: Kingdom (of God).

73. *Theologisch Werk II* inserts here: "It knows about nothing but proclamation. That is ultimately about the destiny of the world. Then the temptation is great to take up tools immediately to go to work towards the realization of this destiny. Then, however, the things of the kingdom do not pass through the heart. They even pass over the heads. Moreover, people forget how much is necessary for the realizing of this destiny, namely, the Mediator and his work and our incorporation into Him. All of that is much too deep and too high, much too great, for us to leave it at calling it out and proclaiming it. We first have to let it get through to us completely. That requires time."

74. See Luke 2:19.

75. *Theologisch Werk II* inserts here: "There is a certain childlikeness about the church. Children play at the lives of grown people. They are not yet up to it themselves. They can grasp forward to it only in the form of play. The church is the play factor in the historical process, just as the eschaton is the seriousness factor in it. In this anticipation, they *have* the eschaton, but under the veil of the liturgy and the sacrament. About these—about the liturgy and the sacrament—we can never speak or think sufficiently 'realistically.' The church does indeed grasp forward to the eschaton. But it does so precisely as church, in its separate figuration [gestaltelijkheid], liturgically (heaven on

That then suddenly brings to the fore the κοινωνία.[76] The church is—in the reserve mentioned above—the realization of the social ideal. Nowhere else in the world is the communion so deep, going to the very roots, going even to the blood and to the guilt, as in the church. In that respect, it is not only the realization but also the paradigm of the social ideal: diaconally it beams forth communion over all areas of life.[77] Where else can we cling to the biblical future expectation but in the church? But also: where else is the truly earthly perspective than in the church, the community of the atonement of guilt?[78] Seen in this way, a minister is even more useful[79] than a politician and a demonstrator. The minister stands more deeply in the midst of life, stands more immersed in the depths of life. Therefore ministers also stand somewhat apart from ordinary life.[80]

VII

The gospel of love brings in its train the great hindrance and the equally great perseverance.

With this reference to the church and her reserve, we have already penetrated deeply into our next theme: the great hindrance that is brought by the gospel in the streamlining of the earthly perspective to the biblical future expectation.

---

earth) and sacramentally (*praesentia realis* [real presence]) and therefore in a deep hiddenness. Ecclesialism, liturgism and sacramentalism do not cancel the expectation of the eschaton. Instead, they preserve it in precisely the right way—in the way of reserve and modesty, of veiling and hiddenness."

76. Κοινωνία: Communion / fellowship.

77. *Theologisch werk II* inserts here: "It remains about the latter: about the social ideal in the ordinary, worldly, created life. But that remain an eschatological vista. In the present, we get no further than the church and Christianization. The church is, moreover, in an essential way a national church (in Israel it was all about the seed and the national community!). And Christianization—theocratically—penetrates right to the state. Therefore:"

78. *Theologisch werk II* inserts here: "Only there is the problematic of the social ideal taken up in all its profound seriousness."

79. *Theologisch werk II* inserts here: "precisely also with a view to the social ideal."

80. *Theologisch werk II* inserts here: "They deal—as central concern—with [the matter of] guilt and with the no less profound mystery of its atonement. But we have to deal with those if we are ever really to get to the social ideal as problem as reality."

BIBLICAL FUTURE EXPECTATIONS IN EARTHLY PERSPECTIVE 219

There is—from a Christian perspective—not only judgement and rejection of all the forms of earthly life. Nor is there only realization of the eschaton. History has to continue. That happens through the gospel of the cross and the resurrection. *That* is the gospel of love. But precisely love in the sense of the gospel is the great obstacle. In ἔρως[81] we pursue the perfect. In ἀγάπη[82] we turn to the lost. Ἀγάπη is a carrying and covering of *all*,[83] also of evil. In that there is undoubtedly atonement, namely, atonement for guilt. But things are also covered over in it. The entire problem that is the reality of the world is covered over up to the last days. The mantel of love is draped over it.[84] The carrying is not merely the carrying away of evil from Being [zijn]; it is also the carrying of being in evil up to the end. Christ loves the world in its lostness. Christians follow Him in this.

That is an unpleasant side to the love of the gospel. It is not the definitive solution to the riddle of the world.[85] That lies, rather, in the joy and the retribution.[86] But we do not get to that all that easily. Before that, we must love the world in its lostness and in that way keep our footing in it.

This maintaining is not only a hindrance. The positive side to it resides in the ὑπομονή, in remaining under the promise in the midst of the judgements. The gospel is not only the gospel of the cross. It is also the gospel of the resurrection. There is also an element of moving through and moving forward in it. The future is indeed kept open, throughout death and ruin [ondergang]. The new, that is, the renewed, form of life itself is already revealed in the crucified and risen Christ, through the work of the Holy Spirit—commencing with the apostolic kerygma and the apostolic paraenesis.[87]

---

81. Ἔρως: Erotic love.

82. Ἀγάπη: Love.

83. See 1 Corinthians 13:7.

84. *Theologisch werk II* replaced this sentence with the following: "Thus the purport of the whole is—that cannot be gainsaid—entirely positive. What is at stake is that the world should in all reality be saved. And to the very bone, at that. People become guilty. This [guilt] is atoned for. That further implies in a highly essential way that the things are not only atoned for and saved. They are also covered over."

85. *Theologisch werk II* inserts here: "Nor the definitive salvation of the reality of the world."

86. For cross-references to literature in Dutch regarding Van Ruler's views on retribution, see his *Verzameld Werk 5C*, 959, note 155.

87. *Theologisch werk II* inserts here: "and [continuing] in the life of sanctification. In imitation of the crucified and risen Lord, we lay hold of the reality of the life that lies

Yet this perseverance also has other sides to it. As the perseverance of the evangelical love, it also has the sides of patience and even resignation to it. We see[88] how deeply the world is sunk into lostness. That we accept. Time and again, we resign ourselves to it. In this way, we also love the world in its awfulness.[89]

In other words, we stand as Christians in the world in an exceptionally complicated way. [It includes] the bearing, the bearing away, the covering, the atoning, the covering over, the tolerating, the carrying on, the breaking *through*, the uncovering.

All these forms of life, these ways of existing, these figures [gestalten] of love, have to be realized by us simultaneously. The multiplicity of these forms of life to which the gospel drives us is more than [merely] a multiplicity. It is also a contradiction. That introduces, in an essential way, a brokenness and, in this sense, also a defectiveness, into Christian existence. To that is added that everything is subject to an eschatological proviso. All realization of salvation [heil] is by definition a realization in the initial stage.

Several things should guard us against the idea that the evangelical inspiration to act in the world should lead us per se and exclusively to pure progressiveness and pure radicalism. We would then, in my opinion, no longer stand in the world in the way of love. Then we replace the gospel by the last judgement. In the situation between the ascension and the parousia, that means that we land up in fanaticism. There are elements of radicalism in the gospel. But equally essential elements of resignation—to mention only two extremes. The essential [aspect] of the gospel stands between these. That is love.

---

lost in evil, also in our actions. In the mud of sin, we dredge harbors for ourselves where we can moor. All the mud cannot be dredged from the world just like that. But that does not mean that there is nothing to be done, that all we can do is to sink ever deeper into the mud. It is possible—both for the individual and for the the community—to construct habors *in* the world of mud."

Translator's note: The text before the insertion also follows the wording and punctuation of *Theologische werk II*. The handwritten text is enigmatic.

88. *Theologisch werk II* inserts here: "– beneath it all, through and precisely *through* the whole of the gospel of the resurrection and of the work of sanctification—ever more."

Translator's note: The precise meaning of this sentence is unclear.

89. *Theologisch Werk II* inserts here: "That too is a moment in the labor of the Mediator, in his work of atonement."

VIII

The earthly perspective—under the seal of Christianization—stands under the double sign of the crucifixion of Christ and the self-saving of humanity.

All of this also says, at least, that the gospel places us as Christians, fully active, fully in the world. There is the awe-inspiring mystery of Jesus, who is God and human being, and of his crucifixion and resurrection. That stands in between the equally awe-inspiring mysteries of creation and the eschaton. From the perspective of the mystery of Christ, we—with our eyes fixed on the mysteries of creation and the eschaton—have to live and act in the situation of lostness.

That is Christianization. If Jesus indeed has some meaning and if He indeed has some meaning for the world, if He means the salvation of the world, then we cannot, to my mind, escape from the word "Christianization."[90] Life is to be stamped and modeled from Him and from his completed work as points of departure. Christianization is the seal under which the earthly perspective comes to stand. World history revolves around the axis of the passage of the apostolic word through the peoples and the continents. That seems to be crazily presumptuous language that can arise only from a feverish brain. Would it appear so only in modern times? Was it ever any different? Were the apocalyptics such as Daniel, where these ideas have their origin, not already fantasists? In any case: in my opinion it has no sense to believe the gospel, to be church, to call oneself a Christian, if one is not to resort to such presumptuous language. In Christ, the μυστήριον of the kingdom and, along with that, of the world-historical process, has been given to us.

Naturally, not everything needs to be Christianized to the same extent. Matter as a whole does not have to be Christianized; even in the sacrament it is not transsubstantiated. Many of our dealings with matter, particularly technology, can get along without Christ and special revelation.[91] When it comes to science, things are perhaps already somewhat different, although we can speak of "Christian science"[92] only in a se-

---

90. *Theologisch werk II* inserts here: "In any case, we cannot escape from the matter [zaak] indicated by this word."

91. For Van Ruler's views on special revelation, see the cross-references to literature in Dutch in his *Verzameld werk 5C*, 959, note 168.

92. For Van Ruler's views on Christian science, see the cross-references to literature in Dutch regarding in his *Verzameld werk 5C*, 959, note 169.

verely restricted sense.[93] Art is in itself already and permanently in the eschaton.[94] It seems that the phase of Christianization can pass it over.

But as soon as *human beings*—they are sinners!—stand at the center, everything becomes different. Even the impulses of their blood have to be Christianized—in spiritual experiences.[95] They are wolves to their neighbors[96] unless they are immersed in the water bath of the love of Christ. Alongside the mystical and the ethical stand the social and the political. Should politics not be Christian, oriented to the righteousness and the mercy that have been realized in Christ?[97] Do we not, when we speak but a single political word from the perspective of the gospel (for instance, a pacifist word), point in the direction of theocracy and the corpus Christianum?[98]

I even gain the impression that there is much hyper-theocracy, that is, false theocracy, in the thought and speech of modern Christianity. For does life start *ab ovo*[99] with salvation [heil] in Christ? Are there not also the perspectives of creation and sin? Should a statesman not give these their due as well? Even if Christianization always starts with aggression towards heathendom from the cross and the Torah as points of departure, does it not always end in a synthesis with [heathendom]?[100] And is that not God's intention? Does the Holy Spirit not tie the ends together, the ends of salvation and creation?

---

93. *Theologisch werk II* inserts here: "that is, only in the sense that science is possible and meaningful only in a culture which is hedged around by Christian dogma."

94. For Van Ruler's views on art, see the cross-references to literature in Dutch in his *Verzameld werk 5C*, 960, note 171.

95. For Van Ruler's views on spiritual experience (Dutch: bevinding), see the extensive cluster of texts on "The experience of salvation [heil]" in Van Ruler's *Verzameld werk*, 497–808.

96. This is possibly a reference to Thomas Hobbes' saying *homo homini lupus* (humans are wolves to other humans).

97. *Theologisch werk II* inserts here: "and are thus not without more ado given as structure in created reality, as content of human reason or as product of the historical process."

98. *Theologisch werk II* inserts here: "After all, can we say that political speakers and their words are Christian and leave it at that? Should the political doers and their deeds not also become Christian? In other words, should the state itself not be ordered in a Christian way so that it may, in turn, order life in a Christian way?"

99. *Ab ovo*: From the very beginning.

100. For Van Ruler's views on a synthesis of revelation and heathendom, see the multiple cross-references to literature in Dutch regarding in his *Verzaled Werk 5C*, 960, note 180.

In other words, Christianization consists in an elastic warfare. Moreover, in many respects it takes place indirectly. The church with its preaching, dogma, liturgy and discipline acts as a perimeter fence[101] within which a theistic culture takes shape in all freedom—which also means all chaos. Alongside the indirectness of Christianization there is the prophetic: the church pronounces the truth, the truth concerning the ordinary things of earthly life, to the authorities and the people.[102] In my opinion, this prophetic [aspect] also leads to the coming to consciousness in Christianization. If human dignity is to be preserved in the matter [zaak], then we must ourselves know and will the truth of the things we do.[103] The state could acknowledge in the constitution that the Word of God is the truth. But perhaps that is asking too much of human dignity.[104]

Here too we have to keep it clearly before our eyes in what a complicated way the gospel places us in the world. The Christianization of life does not mean, without more ado, the improvement of the world. Obviously, it means that as well. At the very least the world-historical process is kept on course. And love is the only form of life in which people and their neighbors can endure it in this appalling world. But over against that stands the fact that Christianization also leads us fully into the battle between the Spirit and the flesh. Israel repeats itself. Just as Israel awoke from the slumber of heathendom, discovered guilt and became guilty, so too the peoples of the earth stumble over the law when they are Christianized and fall into guilt. Christianization is, among other things, this: that the cross is planted. That also implies that Christ is crucified anew.[105]

That is the one extreme aspect of Christianization: the crucifixion of Christ. The other aspect, formulated equally extremely, I call the

---

101. For Van Ruler's views on a church discipline, see the cross-references to literature in Dutch in his *Verzameld werk* 5C, 960, note 180.

102. *Theologisch werk II* inserts here: "That is even [the church's] ultimate and in that sense its most essential task. That is what it is there for. In this sense, in particular, it is there 'for the world.'"

103. *Theologisch werk II* inserts here: "The church does not go beyond the pronouncing of the truth. It leaves it at words. At most it penetrates reality—in an active way—to some extent in its church discipline. But for the rest it leaves it up to people to order life according to the proclaimed truth. Particularly in facing the state it retains the reserve of prophecy. If it is to advance from prophetic theocracy to realized theocracy, the authorities and the nation must themselves take up arms."

104. For Van Ruler's views on constitutional reform, see the cross-references to literature in Dutch in see his *Verzameld werk* 5C, 960, note 180.

105. For Van Ruler's views on Christ being crucified anew, see the cross-references to literature in Dutch in his *Verzameld werk* 5C, 960, note 189.

self-salvation of humanity. I am thinking of modern science and technology. They did not emerge in the world-historical process without the gospel. They could also not easily be passed on without this accompanying melody. Through them, human beings are integrated into the activity of the Creator and the Savior on a scale previously unheard of. They have—in the words of Teilhard de Chardin[106]—now taken further evolution into their own hands. They can now indeed move mountains, as Jesus said of faith.[107] The love that has compassion for the lost can now be realized on a scale previously unthought of. At least, nearly all suffering can be eliminated or ameliorated. Can injustice and violence also be brought under control in this way—cybernetically? Can we, by biochemical means, penetrate so deeply into all the inherited material that the will to evil is eliminated? Can we perhaps discover a serum for conversion? We shall have to wait and see. In any case: those who feed on the biblical future expectation, look entirely positively into what we are wont to call the earthly perspective. They see human beings as God's partners, counterparts, fellow workers.[108] The more these human beings master through science and technology, the better. To this there is something of sanctification and glorification and, in this sense, of salvation. Human beings are themselves active in it.

IX

The problem of the social ideal is too big to be solved except by passing through ruin [ondergang].

But we should not allow ourselves to be blinded by these possibilities of human self-salvation. The problem of earthly reality with its perspective,

---

106. Marie Joseph Pierre Teilhard de Chardin (1881–1955), Roman Catholic (Jesuit) priest, geologist and palaeontologist. He strove to integrate scientific insights with his faith. This led to conflict with Roman Catholic authorities. In his book *The Phenomenon of Man* (New York: Harper Colophon, 1975), Teilhard identified various evolutionary phases and regarded the phenomenon of man (the noosphere) as the center of the evolutionary process. For references to Teilhard in Van Ruler's oeuvre, see his *Verzameld werk 5C*, 914, note 39.

107. See Matthew 17:20.

108. Van Ruler often emphasizes the notion that humans are God's co-workers. For cross-references to literature in Dutch, see his *Verzameld werk 5C*, 915, note 51.

particularly the problem of the social ideal, is huge.[109] How do we get people—*all* people!—reborn right down to the very bottom? That, after all, is the one precondition for the realization of the social ideal! The other precondition is no less weighty. It resides in the question: How do we find the institutions, the structures, in which freedom *and* justice can be harmoniously realized?

The Christian faith has always taken this problem entirely seriously. It is the problem of the world, the matter of the social ideal. Authentic Christian faith has, when carefully considered, has never known any other problem, also not when it discussed, for instance, "the golden heavenly city".[110] Nothing on earth is as radically oriented to the world as the Christian faith with its dogmas of creation, the incarnation and the final judgement.

It is so radically oriented to it that it realizes that, if it were ever to come to the social ideal, it has to be through death, through ruin [ondergang]. There does not seem to be any other solution to the problem. All revolutions seem like child's play compared to the Christian insight. But the Christian faith has always maintained that the passing away of the world is a passing through for the world. It really passes *through* ruin [ondergang] and *beyond* it. This one and only reality that we have and are passes through it.

People are inclined to say that this problem and this solution are *so* huge that only God is capable of [handling it]. Who remains capable of saving himself or herself in death, in ruin [ondergang]? Apparently human beings are at most involved in it to the extent that they may unleash a nuclear war. We can hardly deny that this possibility is contained in the biblical perspective on the future for the earth. There is the man of iniquity. There is the antichrist. They are, as it were, moments in Christianization.

In this way, the tones of the Christian song do become highly sonorous,[111] not to say dark and somber. Who would not rather stop be-

109. To describe the eschatological perspective on the kingdom of God more closely, Van Ruler uses, alternately, the "brotherhood of all people" or "the social ideal." For cross-references to literature in Dutch, see his *Verzameld werk 5C*, 447, note 57.

110. This is an implicit referene to Hymn 126 in the *Psalmen en gezangen voor den Eeredienst der Nederlandsche Hervormde Kerk, in opdracht van de Algemeene Synode der Nederlandsche Hervormde Kerk opnieuw verzameld en bewerkt, aan de Nederlandsche Hervormde Kerk aangeboden door de Algemeene Synode in het jaar onzes Heeren 1938*, Amsterdam s.a. [1938].

111. Translator's note: Van Ruler writes "sonoor" (sonorous) but probably meant "solemneel" (solemn).

ing a Christian and become a citizen who stakes everything on the one card of science and technology, mixed with a stiff dose of social compassion plus, perhaps, a shot of revolution? These citizens are, however, no longer faithful to the earth. They hide their heads in the sand. They no longer wish to see the problems. In this respect, the Christian faith is more fundamental. It is dealing adequately with the problem that the world is.

Is it all only dark and somber in tone? It knows of the storm of the judgements that constantly rumbles through the firmament of history. But it experiences the judgements, the θλίψεις, as birth pangs.[112] History is a pregnant woman. She is in the pangs of birth. She gives birth to the eschaton. Therefore we stand, from a Christian perspective, completely positively also within all that is negative. Even in the ruin [ondergang] of the world, we take the world with us, right through the ruin [ondergang]. Even at the very last moment, we do not flee into another world. The biblical future expectation is the authentic earthly perspective and the so-called earthly perspective is fully incorporated in it.

---

112. See Romans 8:22.

All Things New?[1]
[1968]

IN ITS CREED CHRISTIANITY confesses the resurrection of the flesh. That is a rather crude expression that even seems to stand in direct contradiction to Paul's dictum that flesh and blood cannot inherit the kingdom of God (1 Corinthians 15:50). But Paul thought of flesh in the sense of a qualification of the sinful person. The church in the second century, on the other hand, thought of the flesh in the sense of created bodiliness.

Therefore it makes no sense to replace the word "flesh" in the Apostolic Creed by the word "body" or by the word "person" or by the word "from the dead". That could quite easily imply an element of spiritualizing. In the long run, we might again be left with nothing but the immortality of the soul. Whereas everything in the Christian faith depends on it that the entire person, also in the person's bodiliness, is to be saved.

That may be elucidated not only from the perspective of the individual person and the perfection of the salvation; we also have to think of the relationship between the person and the historical process. The eschaton is the summation of the historical process. Without such a summation, no history would even have been possible. But are individual persons simply manure on the field of the future?[2] Or are they themselves

---

1. The inventory number of the Dutch text, "Alle dingen nieuw?" is I,734. The original manuscript consisted of four hand-written pages which forms the basis of this edition. It was published previous in *Woord en Dienst*, 17/25 (23 December 1968), 349; also in *Blij zijn als kinderen: Een boek voor volwassenen* (Kampen, 1972), 147–149. It is included in Volume 5C of Van Ruler's *Verzameld Werk* (2023), 962–64. Deviations from the hand-written text in subsequent publications are indicated in footnotes where appropriate.

2. The German communist Eugen Leviné (1883–1919) was arrested and condemned to death after the fall of the Bavarian Radenrepubliek. Before his execution on 5 June 1919 he said that "he wishes to be nothing but manure on the field of history." See

present when this summation takes place? Christian faith calmly answers this question in the affirmative. Seen in this way, we can even say that everything really converges in the article about the resurrection of the flesh. Those who abandon this article cause the whole of the Christian faith to fall apart.[3]

The article is, however, far more unlikely than it would appear at first glance. Is it not completely unthinkable: bodily resurrection? Has the corpse not completely decomposed to dust and ashes? And yet the human being is not merely soul but also body. Have we got to the heart of the matter when we say this? Can we leave it at this reference to the human being as unity and totality of soul and body? Is that what the human being is? Or must we also say: No, the human being is, in addition, a piece of filled time,[4] this particular piece of time filled by the person's acts and fortunes!? Is time not an equally essential dimension of being human as the soul and the body?

If this is so, then the article about the resurrection of the flesh implies nothing less than that this temporal existence of mine returns (or however one wishes to call that) in the eschaton as saved. That has a much greater air of the fantastic about it than the idea that the decomposed body would arise from the grave. The total existence then arises from the past. But if there is salvation, as the gospel says [that there is], then we would have to say it after all. The Savior does not save only my soul and my body but my entire existence.

In other words, we take everything with us right through death, resurrection and judgement. We take all along with us into the eternal glory. From the prophetic perspective of the Bible, the animals, the plants and the things also share in the salvation in some or other way. At this point prophecy regularly becomes lyrical. In a type of spiritual drunkenness, it keeps speaking without precisely knowing what it is saying. Yet all joy would slip out of biblical faith at the last moment if we do not also keep speaking in this way. We must not even consider the idea that there

---

Ger Harmsen, "Een afscheid, maar niet van de dialectiek," in *Afscheid van de dialectiek? Rondom het afscheid van Ger Harmsen als hoogleraar* (Nijmegen, 1988), 79.

3. Van Ruler frequently states that the hope for the resurrection of the flesh is the article by which the Christian faith stands or fall. For cross-reference to Dutch literature, see his *Verzameld Werk 5C*, 964, note 6.

4. Van Ruler could have derived the term "filled time" from Karl Barth. See his *KD, III/2*, 648; *KD, IV/2*, 476. It is an expression that Van Ruler uses frequently. For cross-references to literature in Dutch, see *Verzameld werk 5C*, 891, note 5.

would be only human beings in the eschaton. Still worse would be the idea that only God would then be there.

In modern times, we have so much trouble with these things because we can no longer innocently assume that death is for human beings a punishment for sin and for creation a curse from God on account of human beings. Is death not natural? Does it not at least have a natural side? Is biological death, at least, not a reality that is given with biological life? In other words, is death purely punishment and curse? Did the leaves not fall from the trees in paradise?

It would seem that faith and natural science are at odds with each other in this matter. Theology has not found any solution to the problem thus far. It has merely made some concessions. However, to do so, it had to withdraw itself into the spiritual quite a bit. If one does not play along, one is left without an answer. One can but say that one does not know exactly how things fit together. Perhaps one can add that in the idea of the natural death[5] the tragic view of life, which is life-threatening, lies lurking. What a sunny thought [it is] that death is nothing but punishment and curse![6]

But even if we turn our thoughts from this complication, can we picture to ourselves anything of the eschaton? Can we in any way imagine it? We can parrot the words about it. That can fill us with an immeasurable.[7] The way in which we talk about the eschaton is decisive for the way in which we take our stand in life and the world. If we do not speak about it in a Christian way (resurrection of the flesh), we at least speak or whisper or sigh about it in another way. And we always necessarily speak in a mythological language.[8] It [the eschaton] is hardly really thinkable. We cannot picture it to ourselves at all.

In this regard, we should also consider that in the eschaton it is exclusively about the old (this piece of filled time! The historical process! The entire created reality!), but in the state of salvation. Does that "old" *become* redeemed from all guilt and sin and suffering only then? Or does it then merely become evident (that would be a momentous event as

---

5. In the printed versions, "the natural death" is replaced by "the naturalness of death", which makes more sense.

6. Editor's note: See Van Ruler's essay on "The Sunny Side of Sin" in *This Earthly Life Matters*, 211–13.

7. "Joy" is a core motif in Van Ruler's theology. For cross-references to literature in Dutch, see Van Ruler's *Verzameld werk 5C*, 869, note 65.

8. For Van Ruler's view on mythological language, see the cross-reference to literature in Dutch in his *Verzameld werk 5C*, 931, note 30.

well) that it has long been redeemed? In any case: all the tears—those that we have cried throughout our lives, throughout history—are wiped from our eyes.[9] [These] things are not merely old things. They are, in the eschaton, also new.[10]

It is not a matter of new things that come in the place of the old. It is really about nothing but the old things themselves. If there had been no history, no eschaton would have been possible.[11] But then the old things would no longer be old. They would be new. Therefore: all things new? Indeed: all things new![12]

There is one enormous anchoring point in all these considerations: the resurrection of Jesus, the risen Lord Himself! In Him we see something of this newness. At least, the apostles saw something of it. On the authority of their witness we can, through the Spirit, partake in it. That is how we are Christians. That we receive and celebrate in the church.

For that reason, we do not merely await the eschaton. To some extent we experience the newness of things now already. We live from the awe-inspiring mystery of Christ. In principle all things have already become new in that. That we do not merely preach and confess; we can also live it.

And [we do] that not only in the church. A newness of all things is also possible in our living together in culture, society and the state. But that too only from the mystery of Christ. Those who scorn the word and the matter of Christianization, may talk in as progressive and revolutionary a way as they please, but they are beating the air, they are striking right past the authentic, the only newness of all things.

---

9. See Revelations 21:4. Van Ruler often uses this turn of phrase.

10. The printed versions insert here: "Is that perhaps why it appears unthinkable and unimaginable to us?"

11. For cross-reference to literature in Dutch in this regard, see his *Verzameld werk* 5C, 964, note 17.

12. In the handwritten original Van Ruler placed a question mark at the end of this sentence. However, this was replaced with an exclamation mark in subsequent published versions of the text. The exclamation mark is therefore retained here.

Van Ruler's Eschatology and Ecotheology: An Afterword
Ernst M. Conradie

WHAT, THEN, SHOULD ONE make of Van Ruler's eschatology? Allow me to offer a few brief comments in this regard in the form of an afterword.

In 1980 Henk Geertsema published a doctoral dissertation on the philosophical background to Jürgen Moltmann's theology of history.[1] The title, *Van boven naar voren* ("From above to in front of") is significant and suggestive of a shift in eschatology (by the mid-20th century in Western theologies), away from the dialectical theology of Karl Barth towards the more dynamic, future-oriented theologies of Eberhard Jüngel, Johann Baptist Metz, Jürgen Moltmann and Wolfhart Pannenberg. Arnold van Ruler's eschatology may be understood as an early example of this shift but also as a critical response to how this shift was understood in the 1960s, amongst others by Moltmann. Van Ruler's early endorsement of Barth's theology and his later critique of Barth's Christocentric approach are well-known. Likewise, his influence on the early Moltmann and his later critique of Moltmann is amply annotated in this volume, especially in the somewhat reactionary essay on "Limits to Eschatologizing."

In simplified terms, Barth's (early) dialectical eschatology may be understood as the presence of a radically transcendent God, "senkrecht von oben", standing in dialectical tension with every moment in history—and not only at the end. Eschatology is not about the last things but about being in the elusive presence of the Eschatos. For Barth such presence is epitomized by the figure of Jesus Christ as the incarnation and self-disclosure of God. The incarnate, crucified and risen Christ is

---

1. See Henk G. Geertsema, *Van boven naar voren: Wijsgerige agtergronden en problemen van het theologische denken over geschiedenis bij Jürgen Moltmann* (Kampen: JH Kok, 1980).

the Eschatos par excellence albeit that each of these adjectives indicate the hiddenness of God's self-disclosure. Note that, especially for the later Barth, there is a shift to God's presence in this world. Eschatology is not about dreams for another, future world (the critique of Feuerbach and others).

Moltmann maintained this dialectical emphasis on God's transcendence but understood this in terms of the tension between the present and the future, between actuality and possibility. He emphasized the category of the radically new as God's promises that a different world is possible. For Moltmann's such a different world is necessary given the impact of social evil, although he also regards the new as a response to natural forms of suffering embedded in God's otherwise good creation (the threat of nothingness). The shift to God's presence in this world is maintained. Eschatology is about the impact of God's coming towards this world from a promised and anticipated future. The later Moltmann (after Van Ruler's death in 1970) developed these positions in more explicitly panentheist and trinitarian ways. The emphasis on God's coming that is reflected in the title of Moltmann's later eschatology (*The Coming of God*, 1996²) was pre-empted by Van Ruler already in the 1940s (he may well have influenced Moltmann in this regard). That God is coming towards us (including but not restricted to the parousia of Christ) is perhaps *the* key to Van Ruler's eschatology. He draws in this regard from the work of his teacher Gerardus van der Leeuw.[3]

One may therefore say that Van Ruler's eschatology occupies an uneasy middle position between that of Barth and Moltmann. This is possible through a radicalization of Herman Bavinck's theology of restoration: God's work of salvation is aimed at restoring God's work of creation given the impact of sin. Van Ruler radicalizes Bavinck's position by affirming that restoration (not repristination) also applies to God's work of consumption. What Van Ruler seeks is a thorough but elusive trinitarian theology with a focus on the economic Trinity. This implies that the whole of God's work needs to be held in tension: creation, ongoing creation, providence, election and covenant, salvation, church and

2. See Jürgen Moltmann, *The Coming of God: Christian Eschatology* (Minneapolis: Fortress, 1996).

3. See the quotation from Van der Leeuw in Van Ruler's essay on "The Kingdom of God and History" above: "The kingdom of God is nothing else but the entry of God into history. Therefore it has come, it is coming and it will come." The reference is to Gerardus van der Leeuw, "Het koninkrijk Gods en de geschiedenis," in *Het oecumenische gesprek der kerken* ('s-Gravenhage s.a. [1939]), 104, 109.

consummation. He resists any tendency to subsume all of this under one or the other category. This is why he rejects Barth's alleged Christomonism. This is why he identifies various limits to "eschatologizing" (perhaps a deliberately derisive term).

Note that Van Ruler affirms the same emphasis on this world and does so quite radically. This yields an emphasis on this earthly life, ordinary life, this age, this moment, this place. Especially in his earlier writings this brings Van Ruler to the twin themes of the fulfilment of God's law and the kingdom of God. One may say that the kingdom comes where and when God's good law is fulfilled. This is what the Messiah came to enable. This is the task of the Spirit. This is why the law is more eschatological than the gospel. The second table of the law expresses the social ideal of a just, equitable society. At times Van Ruler comes close to equating the kingdom of God with the social ideal or with humaneness, except that it would not help if only a future society benefits from that. Every moment in history matters. For him theocracy flourishes where and when God reigns (always indirectly), i.e. where God's law comes to flourish.

There is indeed something deeply secular in Van Ruler's theology. In this sense his theology clearly breathes the spirit of the post-World War II period, even in recogizing a theology of the death of God. Van Ruler refers to this shift to the world as the horizontal. It is all about this earth, this life, this present moment in history, this period, this place. However, he qualifies this with an equal emphasis on the vertical (albeit that this is underplayed in his essay on "Eschatologial Notices"): This life is to be lived in God's presence, before the face of God, according to God's will as expressed in God's law. The first table is necessary in order to make the second table possible. It is living in God's presence that enables one to find joy in this life. Without God's work of salvation, notably without coming to terms with the guilt of the past, well-being [heil] would not be possible.

This is where the distinction between the Dutch terms *draait* (hinges on) and *gaat* (what it is all about) is relevant. For Van Ruler even the Messiah is not an aim in itself. Everything hinges on the coming of the Messiah and the salvation accomplished by Christ, but this is necessary only in order to enable the kingdom of God to come. Likewise, the church is not an aim in itself; it is there for the sake of society. The Messiah came so that the kingdom may come.

There is a certain optimism about the current dispensation that permeates Van Ruler's theology. This allows him to welcome nuclear fission and space travel although he also warns of the dangers of self-destruction. He is able to take the cultural influence of Christianity for granted and regards that as beneficial. For Van Ruler the process of Christianization is not an aim in itself. The point is not to make things more Christian (see his early critique of Kuyper's notion of Christian culture[4]) but to allow society, culture and life to flourish.

However, such an emphasis on God's work of salvation cannot suffice given the lasting impact of evil in the world. Evil still needs to be excised from created reality. Although the Savior has come, the world, God's good and beautiful creation, is still not saved. There is a need that the tears that we now still weep (to use one of Van Ruler's favorite phrases) will be wiped from our eyes. According to Van Ruler, this requires attention to the eschata, not only the Eschatos.

Van Ruler does not understand the eschaton as life after death, or the termination point of history or the goal of history, even less as a different world beyond this one. Instead, he proposes the simple but perceptive formula: history + salvation = eschaton. History is understood here as proton (*creatio ex nihilo*), ongoing creativity (*creatio continuata*), to some extent also as evolution and as the whole of human history, each moment, all added together. Salvation is itself historical and is not a different history but touches upon the very same history. It is unpacked by Van Ruler christologically as atonement and pneumatologically as the appropriation of such salvation. While salvation is fully accomplished in Christ (atonement for guilt), it is already appropriated in history through the Spirit, but this remains necessarily incomplete (given the lasting impact of evil). Here Van Ruler shares Oscar Cullman's emphasis on salvation history and on the already of God's work of salvation.

For Van Ruler, history and eschaton are correlative concepts that mutually imply each other. Without history there is no eschaton and vice versa. History provides all the ingredients that will be there in the eschaton. Nothing else will be added. The eschaton is therefore the eschaton of history. However, the eschaton (God's coming towards us) is also what elicits history. It is the "pulling point" (trekpunt) of history. Van Ruler adds that only if there is an eschaton, is there history as a unity in

---

4. See Arnold A. van Ruler, *Kuypers idee eener christelijke cultuur* (Nijkerk: Callenbach, 1940).

a meaningful and irreversibly directed movement. This is why the very notion of history is of Israelite origin.

This raises the question whether there is any novum in the eschaton beyond history and salvation. Some may observe that Van Ruler is inconsistent on this point—which has much to do with his often implicit polemics.

On the one hand he resists any notion of *nova creatio*, i.e. that the eschaton would in any way replace the history of God's work of creation. He insists that *kaine ktisis* be translated as *recreatio*. Creation (as *creatura*) is being restored and renewed. God's work of re-creation uses the same building blocks that are there in God's work of creation. One may say that it is *creatio ex vetere*. The new earth is not another earth but this earth renewed. "The new is precisely the old, only radically renewed, completely liberated from all forms of corruption."[5] For Van Ruler this emphasis is necessary in order to cling unto God's sustained loyalty to the world (understood historically) that God so loved. This is Van Ruler's way of radically affirming the goodness of creation, of that which is temporal, material, bodily and earthly. This is why he rejects the immortality of the soul, affirms the unity of the human person, and holds on to the hope for the resurrection of the dead, or, more precisely, of the flesh. The resurrection of the dead does not imply a second opportunity to continue a life that was interrupted by death. It is one's whole life that "returns", that arises from the past, but then as saved. This should not be spiritualized in any form of gnosticism (which is something of a pet hate for Van Ruler, perhaps becauses he wrestles with that himself). With Bavinck, he resists any form of elevation as if creation is in some way deficient and needs to be elevated by grace. He acknowledges the possibility of natural suffering (e.g. mortality) but tends to underplay that given his critique of an emphasis on the tragic. He wants to affirm death as punishment for sin as a "sunny thought," but still wonders whether the leaves did not fall from the trees in paradise.[6] The eschaton is therefore not to be understood as elevation in response to natural suffering.

On the other hand, Van Ruler affirms that there is indeed an eschatological plus in relation to the proton but also in relation to history. He describes the eschaton with a series of intriguing categories that, one may say, is embedded in the "plus" sign in the formula creation + salvation

---

5. Quoted from Van Ruler's essay, "Biblical Future Expectations in Earthly Perspective" included in this volume.

6. See Van Ruler's essay entitled "All Things New?" as included in this volume.

= eschaton. This series of categories include *anakephalaiōsis* (recapitulation, bringing under one head, literally "summarizing"), *apokalupsis* (revelation, uncovering), *crisis* (judgement, verdict), *teleiōsis* (perfection), and *sunteleia* (closure, completion, consumption, culmination,).[7] Given his emphasis on the fulfilment of the law, he could have added εκπλήρωση. These categories cannot simply be equated with salvation. Consumption (literally: to sum up, bring together) implies that each event in history is added together and held together under one heading (*anakephalaiōsis*). For Van Ruler this is crucial in order to avoid the Marxian lure of a future utopia where previous epochs may be sacrificed for the sake of the classless society of a coming dispensation. While he affirms the social ideal, he resists the assumption that human lives can be "manure on the field of the future" (with several references to Eugen Leviné).

No moment in history is lost forever but is held in God's presence. How is this possible? How may one contemplate eternal life? Van Ruler allows such questions to be clothed in mystery, opting to leave that in God's hands, but he does resist the notion that we are merely remembered by God in a noetic way—as if God is a super-computer (again the danger of gnosticism). In any case, by itself that would be an image of hell as all the horrors of history would then become everlasting. The role of revelation and judgement is therefore crucial. Although Van Ruler does not always make this clear, it is at best related to the identity and character of the triune God—as a God of mercy and therefore of justice, for the victims of history but also for perpetrators. Van Ruler may also want to bring God's characteristic joy in creation into play: God's judgement is necessary to enable God's joy.

This leaves the question what the category of perfection (*teleiōsis*) entails. Given Van Ruler's emphasis on the fulfilment of the law, this is clearly included. One may add that creation will at least be made "fireproof" against the possibility of sin. Is there also room for an eschatological reconciliation? Van Ruler allows for the possibility of eternal perdition even if he wonders, at times and with reference to the *apokatastasis pantōn*, whether God's grace may not extend to the godless (beyond their deaths). Nevertheless, the eschaton is not only composed of human beings (or only of God). The whole of creation, the whole of history is being consummated. Will hell then remain eternally as a festering boil

---

7. See Van Ruler's essay entitled "Eschatological Notices" as included in this volume.

undermining a renewed world? Are some things to be excluded in the end? Van Ruler may well have been in two minds here. At best he leaves such questions open.

The question is then whether some form of healing that was not already accomplished in history is possible eschatologically? Only a healing of memories? Van Ruler is fond of saying that the tears will be wiped from our eyes. But what will justice to the victims of history entail? Only a day in court where they will be given their due? Or would there be some solace for those who were disabled, marginalized, assaulted, maimed, raped and murdered?

Some would say that more room should be allowed for an eschatological novum. Van Ruler is vulnerable to critique here but his polemic emphasis is clearly aimed at affirming the already of salvation (while not denying the dimension of the not yet) and on the continuity between history and eschaton (while not denying some discontinuity). At times Van Ruler seems to become absorbed in his polemics with other scholars who remain unnamed. It is also possible that he is engaged in an argument with himself, with his alter ego, noting that he was prone to depression.

Van Ruler is not shy of some speculation in imagining what the eschaton entails. This is evident from his essays on life beyond death. He repeatedly notes that we can only speak about that in images and kaleidoscopes. Theology entails reflection on such images, sorting them out. He knows the difference between promises and predictions. He acknowledges the power of such images but also the dangers that one can get carried away with such speculations. This is a slippery slope to escapism. The eschaton is not about the chronological end of time, another time or an endless extension of time. It is not about a final epoch in (human history) when a better future can be secured. It is also not just a qualitative experience of the present moment (the eternal now). He is nevertheless fond of the expression that the eschaton casts us back to focus on this life, this place, this present moment ("Zo werpt het eschaton ons in het heden terug"). This expression occurs numerous times in this volume alone. Perhaps "cast" (or thrown) is too strong a word but the point is nevertheless well taken. An orientation on the eschaton, to place one's hope in that, is not to escape from the current situation but to be refocused on the present. Van Ruler insists: the eschaton is about the present ("over dat heden gaat het in het eschaton"). This also accounts for his frequent references to "filled time" (a term borrowed from Barth), possibly also with a nod in the direction of Kierkegaard and the eternal now (as emphasized by Rudolf Bultmann and Paul Tillich).

Other scholars would relate that more clearly to the virtue of hope. Hope is a resistance movement against an unacceptable present. It helps us to see the difference between what reality is and what is should be and could be like. Van Ruler did not yet formulate it just like that. Nevertheless, his eschatology arguably paved the way for such insights to emerge.

Let me conclude with a threefold assessment:

There are some aspects in Van Ruler's eschatology that are clearly attractive within contemporary Christian ecotheology. This would include his avoidance of an escapist understanding of Christian hope and his eschatological affirmation of what is temporal, material, bodily and earthly. He insists that the *earth* is our dwelling, *that* is where we are at home, not in heaven. Heaven is regarded as an integral part of God's good creation, not as an eschatological category: It is "not a final goal in which everything will in the end come into its own or even to which it returns because it had come from it."[8] As Van Ruler argues, a Christian expectation of the future does not *include* an earthly perspective; it is about an expectation for this earthly life.

There are also some aspects in Van Ruler's eschatology that may challenge contemporary discourse in Christian ecotheology. Here his polemics against a form of replacement theology (the old shoes will be thrown away and replaced with new ones) and a theology of elevation (and perhaps theosis) instead of restoration comes into play. Van Ruler insists that any notion that creatures will be taken up into the very being of God is foreign to the Christian faith. For him, salvation means the opposite, namely that God pours out God's very being in and over God's creation.

Another aspect that may challenge contemporary views is Van Ruler's emphasis on linearity in history. For Van Ruler this has to do with God's election of Israel that created history. He claims that the very notion of history, of future expectation, and of the eschaton as the "pulling point" of history, is derived from Israel's understanding of a God who acts in history, to make history. This is quite different from any Indigenous notion of the eternal return of the same, but also of Egyptian ideology, Parsee religions or Greek philosophy and historiography. Such an emphasis on linearity, on the coming of God's reign, is not to be equated

---

8. See Van Ruler's essay, "I Believe in Eternal Life" as included in this volume.

with the modernist notion of quantified time although the latter assumes the former. It may well be regarded as an ecologically dangerous dimension of Van Ruler's theology, although the possibility of transforming the global economy from dependency on fossil fuels also assumes such linearity—as does the geological timescale and the "universe story" of cosmic, biological and cultural evolution (which Van Ruler affirms but also seems to shy away from).

Then there are aspects in Van Ruler's eschatology that may be deemed unattractive for contemporary discourse in Christian ecotheology. This would include his mid-20th century appreciation for the cultural influence of the *corpus Christianum* as the fruit of the gospel—which is nowadays popular in right-wing politics in Europe. This extends to an appreciation for the process of Christianizing a previously pagan Europe, and controversially even for establishing and maintaining colonies. Nevertheless, as the final section of his essay on "Eschatological Notices" indicates, Van Ruler's theology is clearly not Eurocentric. Asia and Africa, also Oceania, should not become (carbon) copies of Europe.

Another aspect of Van Ruler's theology in general is the heavy emphasis that he places on sin understood as guilt before God. Accordingly, he understands salvation christologically as atonement for such guilt (in Anselmian terms as satisfaction) and pneumatologically as appropriation of what Christ has done for us. By contrast, there is an overwhelming emphasis in contemporary ecotheology on sin as power or, alternatively, on the problem of natural evil. There is a widespread resistance against the categories of sin and salvation to allow, for example, for an emphasis on an evolutionary cosmology, kenosis or theosis. Alternatively, there is retrieval of the ecological wisdom embedded in Indigenous worldviews—where the resistance is then against imperialism, colonialism and extractive capitalism. Such resistance and the associated calls for justice do address Christian complicity in ecological destruction (e.g. climate change) and the guilt associated with that.

Van Ruler would insist that such guilt (perhaps in the form of climate debt) is the core problem that needs to be addressed. It may be possible to overcome ecological destruction but that will always remain temporary unless the alienation caused by guilt is overcome. He may well be on the right track in this regard. One may add the complicity of Christiandom in imperialism, white supremacy, slavery, colonialism, and industrialized capitalism. There is no way in which, for example, climate justice can be done without coming to terms with the legacy of the past, i.e. historic carbon emissions.

Van Ruler emphasizes the need for justice (God's reign) but does not denounce such injustices. Nevertheless, he may be right in that justice to the victims of such processes and to their descedants is well-nigh impossible. The only way forward may well be reconciliation with God. This requires coming to terms with guilt before God and the world. This problem can and in fact has been resolved. But where can evidence for that be found? One may have to say that it is the eschaton that needs to provide the conclusive evidence in this regard.

Index of Names

Aalders, Willem J., 3-4
Anselm of Canterbury, 58, 87, 107, 111, 165, 204, 239
Augustine of Hippo, 15, 53-55, 85, 111, 175, 189, 212
Barth, Karl, 2, 4, 8-9, 57, 64, 74-75, 84, 139, 157, 187, 210-11, 214-15, 228, 231-33, 237
Bavinck, Herman, vii, 10, 47, 56, 63, 85, 117-18, 130, 140-41, 193, 232, 235
Berkelbach van der Sprenkel, S.F.H.J., 72
Berkhof, Hendrikus, vii, 11
Berkhoff, A.M., 11
Bloch, Ernst, 18, 174
Bornhausen, Karl Eduard, 75
Bultmann, Rudolf, 170, 238
Chantepie de la Saussaye, Daniël, 35
Coccejus, Johannes, 84
Cullmann, Oscar, 78, 234
Dijk, Klaas, 11
Doorne, Koos van, 17, 18
Geertsema, Henk, 231
Gogarten, Friedrich, 74-75
Graafland, C. 7
Graham, William Franklin (Billy), 132
Gunning, Johannes Hermanus, 50-51, 86, 146
Hajtema, Theodorus L., 4
Harnack, Adolf von, 78, 89
Heer, Johannes de, 11, 12
Hegel, Georg Wilhelm Friedrich, 4, 86, 87, 75, 193

Heim, Karl, 84
Hepp, Valentijn, 11
Hoedemaker, Philippus Jacobus, 4, 9, 72, 78, 92
Hoekendijk, J.C., 76
Huizinga, Johan, 72-74, 86
IJsseling, Paulus Cornelis, 50, 51, 53
Kant, Immanuel, 160
Keulen, Dirk van, ix, 18, 20, 30
Kierkegaard, Sören, 4, 62, 75, 130, 238
Kohlbrugge, Hermann Friedrich, 57, 89, 90, 103
Kraemer, Hendrik, 76
Kuyper, Abraham, vii, 4, 44, 84, 85, 158, 234
Laplace, Pierre-Simon, 22
Leeuw, Geerhardus van der, 35, 71, 77, 81, 82, 86, 132, 232
Leviné, Eugen, 19, 213, 227, 236
Lodenstein, Jodocus van, 193
Marcion, 41, 42, 89, 181
Melsen, Andreas Gerardus Maria van, 165, 171
Miskotte, Kornelis, vii, 82
Moltmann, Jürgen, 18, 128, 178, 179, 186, 203, 231-32
Niebuhr, Reinhold, 2, 111, 112, 171
Nietzsche, Friedrich, 21
Noordmans, Oepke, vii, 85
Otto, Rudolf, 77, 81, 86
Pannenberg, Wolfhart, 231
Pascal, Blaise, 62, 159
Puchinger, George, 2, 3
Rad, Gerard von, 39, 77

Reinhold, Otto, 23
Ruusbroec, Jan, xi, 157
Scheeben, Matthias Joseph, 181
Schilder, Klaas, 9, 52
Schmidt, Karl Ludwig, 34, 37–42, 47, 77
Schweitzer, Albert, 77
Seeberg, Reinhold, 216
Skydsgaard, Kristen Ejner, 42, 47
Sneller, Zeger Willem, 85
Sölle, Dorothee, 188, 208
Spengler, Oswald, 55, 169
Sprey, Karel, 79, 80
Stauffer, Ethelbert, 83
Teilhard de Chardin, Marie Joseph Pierre, 162, 185, 224
Tillich, Paul, 238
Troeltsch, Ernst, 3, 4, 8, 73–75, 80, 86, 170
Valk, M.H.A. van der, 11
van Ruler-Hamelink, Joanna Adriana, xi, 114, 199
Veldkamp, Herman, 11, 12
Verbrugh, A.J., 9
Voetius, Gisbertus, 72
Waterink, Jan, 11
Westhuizen, M.J. van der, 11

www.ingramcontent.com/pod-product-compliance
Lightning Source LLC
Chambersburg PA
CBHW070245230426
43664CB00014B/2408